NO GOING BACK TO MOLDOVA

No Going Back to Moldova

MOLDOVA

ANNA ROBERTSON

MAINSTREAM
PUBLISHING

First published in 1987 by
MAINSTREAM PUBLISHING COMPANY (EDINBURGH) LTD.
7 Albany Street
Edinburgh EH1 3UG

British Library Cataloguing in Publication Data
    Robertson, Anna
    No going back to Moldova
    1. Czechoslovakia——Social life and customs
    I. Title
    943.7'03'0924   DB2188

    ISBN 1 85158 085 9

Typeset by Pulse Origination, Edinburgh.
Printed in Great Britain by Billing & Sons, Worcester.

To the memory of my sister
who shared these days with me.

1

SOME PLACES HAVE a magic of their own. Such a place is Uj-Moldova, a small town in the Banat, now in Romania and lost forever behind the Iron Curtain.

My family on my father's side first came to the Banat, then the most southern part of Hungary, in the Austro-Hungarian Empire, in the eighteenth century. They came as pioneers from Germany, following the call of the Empress Maria Theresia, to start a new life in a devastated land. The Turks, who had occupied the Banat for two hundred years, and had penetrated into Europe as far as Vienna, had been driven back to this, their last stronghold. When they were finally defeated they left behind only burnt villages and a deserted countryside.

Settlers were urgently needed, not only to revive and cultivate the land, but also to act as a bulwark against the Turks. The Empress, the daughter of Marie-Antoinette of France, sent her agents to Germany, where they found willing settlers for the new country. At the order of the Empress these settlers had to be young, mostly farmers, and preferably vine-growers. They had to be married with at least two children and, if possible, should ply a trade in case of a bad harvest. They would be given some land, a grant towards the cost of public buildings such as churches, presbyteries and mills and also towards necessary equipment such as butter churns, vinepresses and tools. In addition, they were promised freedom from taxes for three years and given permission to quarry limestone, copper, silver and iron.

Germany, the land they had left behind, had been repeatedly invaded by the French; it had been subjected to constant wars between its own princes — those who suffered most had, of course, been the peasants and small farmers. All the land belonged to dukes and princes, who cared little for the welfare of their tenants; the peasants were poor and many were still serfs. The opportunity to work, however hard, in a new country, was one they could not resist. They left Germany in their thousands, and came to the Banat in three large and two small waves. So great was this migration that it was called the *Grosse Schwabenzug* (Great Swabian Trail). The settlers drove to Ulm or Passau and, from there, sailed in the square boats called 'Danube boxes' down the Danube, through Austria, to their destination in the southernmost part of Hungary. It may be that from one of those emigrations came the legend of the Pied Piper. Many villages and towns in Germany were left without children, who had literally gone over the mountains and disappeared for ever.

Life was very hard in the early days. Much of the land was still marsh and many died of the so-called marsh fever; others suffered for years through Turkish raids, when houses were burned down and livestock taken. The first settlers were decimated by the plague.

The Stiller family settled in the then newly founded town of Uj-Moldova, situated on the south side of the Carpathian Mountains, near where the Danube squeezes spectacularly through the huge rocks known as the 'Iron Gate', below Orsova. Serbia, now part of Yugoslavia, was on the other side of the river and Transylvania to the north-west.

They must have arrived with the second wave of the *Grosse Schwabenzug*. There is an entry in the church register which tells of a son being born to Kaspar and Elizabeth Stiller on 7 August 1760, who, in turn, married Katherine Gartner on 8 September 1781. Shortly afterwards came a new attack by the Turks.

It is interesting that every generation in my family, as far as we know, lost everything they owned, at least once in their lifetime, right down to myself. It was not always the Turks who were responsible. My great-grandfather lost all his possessions in the Hungarian Revolution in 1848. He applied for compensation to the military authorities, but also wrote a letter to the Emperor Franz Josef in person, listing all that had been taken by the soldiers: his house had been burned down, the vineyards ruined and the livestock taken. We still have a copy of that letter, very, very humbly written. Apparently he did get some compensation — enough to start the process of rebuilding.

My grandmother also remembered the 1848 Revolution. She told my sister and I as children how, on her knees, she had begged the soldiers not to shoot her father, when she was only eight years old. We were told many stories like these when we spent our holidays with her in Uj-Moldova. When our own hard times hit us, later in life, we needed only to remember what our ancestors had gone through and then the hardship and losses were easier to bear, and we could cheerfully start all over again.

My grandfather, Ferdinand Stiller, brought his bride, Anna Bauer, from Werscez, a village not far from Uj-Moldova. Her ancestors had

Moldova from the air

9

also originally come to the Banat from Germany with the Swabian emigration. It was a custom amongst the Banater Germans to arrange a dance for all the marriageable girls of one village, or small town, and to invite the young men from another village or town. This was called the *Brautschau* (Viewing of the Bride). My grandmother had refused to attend — she was not going to be on exhibition! However, when my grandfather heard about the girl who would not go to such a party, he went to her house, decided that she was the one for him, and married her.

My father was born on 4 September 1879 in Uj-Moldova, the sixth child of my grandparents. The record of his christening gave his names in Latin — as was the custom in Hungary — as Eugenius Maximilianus Aloisius Stiller, but he was known as Jeno, the Hungarian for Eugene. After leaving grammar school, he was sent to a seminary to train as a priest. Most families loved to have one son in the Church and he had been highly recommended by his teacher. However, his elder brother, Lajos (Ludwig), who was already working in Budapest, knowing my father's temperament better, insisted on his coming to Budapest and giving up the study for the priesthood to become an engineer instead. My father had not been too keen on the priesthood anyhow. However, by this time his Latin was so good that he could converse in it as well as in any other language. Most people in the Banat could speak Hungarian, German, Serbian, Romanian and some, like my father, also Bulgarian, so Latin was an extra bonus!

I remember a train journey, many years later, when my father conversed with a French priest in Latin, to the great amazement of my sister and myself. Occasionally, too, my father would gently reprimand us by quoting a Latin proverb, such as, 'If you had kept silent, one would have thought you a philosopher.' I still remember the saying in Latin but I could never spell it. There were many similar proverbs he used and they certainly made a lasting impression!

In Budapest my Uncle Lajos introduced him to the Listl family, whose eldest daughter Ilona was a great friend of her namesake, Ilona, my uncle's wife. Ilona Listl was called Big Ilona and my aunt Little Ilona, so as not to mix them up. They were often invited to the Listl family's home and my father became a great friend of Big Ilona. The friendship was interrupted when my father left to do his military service with the Honveds (the Hungarian Regiments). On his return from the army my father found a job in a machine factory. Big Ilona, meantime, had become engaged to a certain Baron Bezisc and my uncle, aunt and father were all invited to the wedding. It was on that occasion that my mother, the youngest Listl daughter, Aranka, made her debut into society and my father for the first time took notice of her. Before that she had been just a schoolgirl, who had been far too busy with her own affairs to take any notice of her mother's or sister's guests.

It was love at first sight. Six months later they were married, on 5 March 1904. She was seventeen years old and my father was twenty-four. The Listl family was not too pleased, because Aranka was the youngest child and they had hoped for a brilliant marriage — a rich baron perhaps, rather than a young clerk. Therefore the relationship was cool, and never improved. We have very few photographs of my mother; her best feature was her hair, chestnut brown, extremely long and thick. On one photograph she wears it plaited and wound round and round her head like a high crown. She had brown, slightly slanting eyes, which my sister was to inherit.

My mother's family was quite different to that of my father. One side, to which my grandmother, born Amelia Wagner, belonged, had also come to the area with the *Grosse Schwabenzug*, but they had then married Hungarian or Yugoslavian, that is Serbian, partners. The ancestors of my mother's father, Anton Listl, were not pioneers at all. They had all been born in Hungary and could count amongst them Hungarians, Croats and Germans. He himself was, and always felt, a Hungarian.

During their first years of marriage my grandparents had lived in Semlin, a small town which is now part of Belgrade, the capital of Serbia. It was there that my mother, Aranka Listl, was born on 8 January 1887. It was shortly after this that the family moved to Budapest. There my mother and her sisters and brothers had been left in the care of a nanny while my grandparents led their extremely busy social life. Grandmother's invitations were widely sought after: she not only had good connections with important people, but was also known to encourage and help young artists. Of course, she also had a marvellous cook! She was a first-class hostess and managed to make her *salon* the centre of the bourgeoisie society in Budapest. She had a taste for luxury and a certain kind of showing-off, as for instance when, whilst living in Semlin-Belgrade, she would drive four-in-hand to the theatre in Budapest, or just for shopping. Time did not matter to her. When she lived in Budapest she would do the same journey the other way round, four-in-hand from Budapest to Semlin to visit friends.

My grandfather bought and sold houses and land and at the same

11

time, as he was keen on horse racing, he bought, sold and trained racehorses. His wider family connections with the landed aristocracy proved profitable for his business and provided him with friends who shared his passion for racing and nightlife. Many of them would come to stay at his house, when Grandmother gave her famous parties. It was in this atmosphere of pleasure and luxury that my mother had grown up with her three brothers and one sister, spoilt with expensive toys and an outward show of happiness, but experiencing no real family warmth, which she would find only later with my father's mother.

At four o'clock in the morning on Saturday 22 November 1905 I was born. 'Saturday's child works hard for a living' — that was to prove true for me, but only much later in life. I was told that I was a very good baby. As soon as I was able I spent most of my time quietly sucking my big toe, an early exercise for yoga later in life! I inherited my father's blue eyes and fair hair and was christened Anna Berta, but was called Nushy, the Hungarian abbreviation of Anushka. Not quite thirteen months later, on 6 December, a Sunday morning, at four o'clock, my sister was born. She was a real Sunday child, but it certainly did not show while she was a baby. She quickly made herself known through a lot of loud and continuous crying, especially at night. Lilly was not a beautiful baby. She was long and thin, had brown eyes and a mass of dark brown hair.

My parents had hoped for a son; a second daughter was a slight disappointment, because my father had to think of the dowry, which all girls could expect at their marriage. However, she had chosen a very special day for her arrival. While the midwife, or rather the 'wise woman', was still busy with her, cannon shots were heard and, soon afterwards, all the bells of Budapest began to ring. Everywhere throughout Austria and Hungary the day was celebrated with colourful processions, bands, folk-dancing and all kinds of festivities. This was to happen every year on my sister's birthday and it took years to convince her that it was not in honour of her, but to celebrate the ascension to the throne in 1848 of the Emperor Franz Josef, who had then been just eighteen years old. This was the same emperor whose soldiers my grandmother had begged to spare her father and to whom my grandfather had written a personal letter. He remained our emperor throughout our schooldays and only died during the First World War, in 1916.

Lilly soon became, through her continuous crying, the tyrant of the family. My father suffered most: he worked in an engineering factory

Grandmother

where they started at six o'clock and came home late. One night, when my mother had tried everything she could think of to soothe the crying baby, my father became quite desperate, through lack of sleep. My sister was, like all babies at that time, wrapped in swaddling clothes, that is laid diagonally on a large pillow, the sides of which were folded over and tied down with a long swaddling band. This rather convenient bundle was grabbed by my father and held under a running tap. Shocked and blubbering, my sister stopped her unnecessary crying immediately and from then onwards did so whenever my father appeared. At last he had some peace and quiet when he came home!

This early experience was to leave my sister with a holy respect for my father, which remained with her all through her childhood, in spite of her great love for him. She adored him but was always anxious not to annoy him in any way, although he was the kindest and most patient father anyone could wish for.

After five and a half years of marriage my mother died, at the age of only twenty-two. She had suffered from tuberculosis of the lungs and, later, of the brain, which made her completely confused towards the end. During the last few months of her life she stayed, with us two children, with our Grandmother Stiller in Uj-Moldova. My father, who was by then a representative of the Vacuum Oil Company, was based in Linz on the Danube; he had to be away from home most of the time — and was also away when my mother died. My mother was taken back to Rakocz Palota, a small spa near Budapest, to our home, and buried there. Unfortunately, her own mother could not get over the fact that her daughter had got on better with her mother-in-law than she did with her and she blamed my father for it. In a fit of jealousy she destroyed most of the photographs of my mother and took away many small items which would remind us of her. My father never forgave her for this.

Both my sister and I remember the funeral, although without really understanding at that time what was going on. We were both dressed all in black: we even had black lacy underwear. My sister remembers clinging to Uncle Lajos' neck and nearly choking him, while he held her in his arms. She remembers a dark box, which puzzled her, especially when she had to throw a little posy, which somebody had put into her hand, on top of the box.

I also remember that box, as I held my father's hand amidst so many people of whom I could mostly see only their legs. I watched the box gliding down a deep hole with fascination. I never noticed the ropes, of course, and I awaited with trepidation the bang when the box would finally reach the bottom of the hole. I was immensely surprised when nothing happened and there was only silence and the sound of suppressed crying. My father threw some earth into the hole with a little shovel, then I had to do the same and also throw down my little posy. My father lifted me up and let me look into the hole. There I could see the box with our little posies on top of it.

I have another memory of my mother — only one: of a lady sitting in the garden at Grandmother Stiller's house. I had been told to call her in for the evening meal. I only remember a pale, sad face, and a quiet voice saying something to me. After Mama's funeral we were taken back to our Grandmother Stiller's in Uj-Moldova, where Uncle Lajos and Aunt Ilona were staying with their family for the holidays. My father gave up his flat in Budapest. He boxed the few valuable things, jewellery, some small furniture, clothes and linen and brought them to Moldova for storing, so that we would have something to remember Mama by. It would get lost after the First World War, but that is another story.

The Danube squeezing through the Iron Gates

2

AT THE START of the next school term, Aunt Ilona and Uncle Lajos prepared to return with their children to Jaegerndorf in Silesia, and offered to take us with them. My father agreed. We spoke better Hungarian than German at that time and he thought that it would be a good opportunity to make us speak German and also for us to be well looked after. He would also have a better chance to visit us there more often.

My aunt was a very impressive personality, blessed with a good deal of charm. She had numerous interests and led a very busy social life. She had three children of her own: two girls, three and five years older than me, and one boy, still a baby.

At Jaegerndorf, we were sent every morning to the kindergarten at the convent school. A nursemaid took us there, and collected us again at lunchtime and in the afternoon. She was very good to us and was usually waiting for us when we came out of the convent. Only once was she late — very late. It was the beginning of December, bitterly cold, and there was deep snow on the ground. When we came out of the convent we looked for the familiar wooden sledge with the high back, always so easy to recognise, but it was nowhere to be seen. That sledge was like a comfortable chair; it was wide enough for both of us to sit comfortably next to each other, stuffed into a fur sack to keep us warm.

At first, several other children waited with us to keep us company and have a go later at pushing our sledge. They loved to do this and there was usually a fight for the privilege. However, after some time they went home and there we remained, the two of us, like forgotten, frozen parcels.

There was a stone cross at the corner of the park, opposite the convent, and we sat down on its cold, marble steps. How long we sat there I have forgotten, but we were extremely cold, had stiff fingers and finally started to cry in misery. That picture of us sitting there is still fresh in my mind. At last, a young lady who took painting lessons in the convent came out, recognised us and took us home.

Towards the end of the year my uncle, who also worked for the Vacuum Oil Company, was transferred to Graz in Styria, Austria, whereas Papa came to Jaegerndorf. He wanted to see us regularly, and Graz was rather far away, so he had to look for some other place for us to stay. Finally, he was advised to try to get us into a convent boarding school, although we were still too young to start school properly. The sisters, he was told, would have no interests of their own and would be the right people to care for us. Papa decided to take this advice.

On 7 January, the Feast of the Sacred Heart, my father rang the bell of the convent in Gross-Herrlitz in Austrian Silesia. One at each side, my sister and I were clinging to his hands — two little girls, four and three years old. The nun who opened the door led us into the visiting room and asked my father to wait, as the other nuns would soon be returning from church.

In a short while the Reverend Mother arrived. Papa asked for the two of us to be accepted as boarders, explaining that our mother had died and we had no relatives living nearby. Reverend Mother explained, in turn, that no children under school age were accepted at the convent, in fact, not until the age of fourteen, as this was more like a finishing school, with the emphasis being on domestic science. She said she was very sorry . . . but then she remembered that this was the feast day of the 'Sacred Heart', and that of the convent itself. It appeared that there existed a custom whereby any stranger arriving at the door on that day had to be treated as if he was Christ himself, and his wishes had to be fulfilled, as far as was humanly possible.

Reverend Mother then suggested that she would keep us for the time being; she would write to the Mother Superior and to the Bishop for permission to accept us as boarders. She pointed out, however, that although we were only small children, the fees would be the same and we would need to bring the same quantities of personal linen, underwear, sheets, towels etc, as the other boarders — one dozen of each item. Furthermore, there would have to be an additional charge for a young girl from the village to look after us and take us for walks, while the other boarders were having their lessons.

We also had to have at least two dozen handkerchiefs and socks, and half a dozen dresses and aprons, to give us ample change. These would have to be replaced as soon as we grew out of them; they would not be wasted as they would be given to the poor. From then on Papa called us his 'dear little ones'!

Gross-Herrlitz was a small village, about one hour's carriage drive from the nearest railway station, at Skrochowitz, between Jaegerndorf and Troppau. In the middle of the village, on a small hill, stood the old church, overlooking all the other buildings, with the convent on one side of the churchyard and the presbytery on the other side. These three buildings were reached by a drive and then a broad flight of steps led up to the main entrance of the church.

At the entrance to the village was the castle belonging to Count Bellegarde, with a large park and lake and surrounded by a high wall, over which could still be seen many old trees. The lake was later given to the public for canoeing. The Bellegarde's ancestors had fled to here from the French Revolution; now they owned Gross-Herrlitz, several of the surrounding villages and most of the woods. The Count was the patron of the village and also of the church and the convent. Being a pious man, he took a special interest in the latter.

Over the years I was to get to know every inch of the convent. It was a large, long house, and built into the hill so that it started with two storeys and finished on the top of the hill with only one. The main entrance was situated in the middle of the house and was reached from the drive. The first room you entered was a large hall, open at the front and with three steps leading to it from the drive. This hall had a glass roof and was used by the pupils during breaktime in bad weather.

On the ground floor was a refectory, a huge kitchen, also used for cookery lessons, the store rooms and cellars, a laundry with a bath in it, an ironing room and various old boxrooms for storing things like suitcases. On the right-hand side of the first floor was the sewing and needlework room. This also contained a piano, on which pupils did their practice after school if the music room was occupied. Next to this were several classrooms. On the left-hand side were two larger classrooms, a small office, another, small, classroom for private lessons, a music room which also served as a room for visitors, and then a corridor leading to the door of the private rooms belonging to the nuns.

On another side of the building was a long glass-covered veranda — lined with seats along both sides. In summer this veranda was used by the nuns during their leisure time. However, whenever there was a thunderstorm at night, the boarders who were frightened could go down there and walk up and down with the nuns, saying the rosary. A life-size cross with Christ displaying his pierced heart provided added assurance of security! I was always one of those who went down to the veranda, not because I was frightened, but because I loved thunderstorms and the lightning could be seen much more clearly from there.

On the second floor were all the dormitories; those on the right side were for the boarders and those on the left side were for Reverend Mother, the nuns and novices, and for occasional visitors. There was also a small sickroom. Finally, near the stairs, was an extremely large room with a long table running right through the middle. It was here that all the boarders would sit and study from five to six p.m. on weekdays, write their letters home on Sundays or merely enjoy their leisure. It had a balcony overlooking the whole village and providing a lovely view far into the countryside beyond. The French window leading onto this remained locked, except on special occasions.

Under the roof of the convent was a loft, extending across the whole building. It was divided into two parts: in one were many numbered wardrobes in which each boarder kept her linen and clothes. In the middle was a table used for folding garments and in the second part of the loft were several partitions for drying the washing, storing large trunks and spare furniture. Best of all, there were various kinds of things needed for playing theatre. A specially built, huge wardrobe contained numerous theatre costumes, collected over many years. They smelt excitingly of camphor and mothballs.

Within the convent was also a small chapel in which we held our daily morning and evening prayers and asked forgiveness from God whenever we had done something wrong. After each reprimand by a nun, and after each punishment, whether it was standing or kneeling in a corner, or having to do some work again, we had to go to the chapel and tell God all about it. Sometimes I thought He must get fed up with hearing about so many little sins!

19

There were no flush toilets at that time, only the old-fashioned kind — cubicles with large, flat seats reaching from wall to wall, and a hole in the middle, covered with a wooden lid when not in use. There were about ten such cubicles in a building which was situated at the end of a cobbled yard, surrounded by bushes and divided from the henhouse and pigsties by a fence.

Right at the back of here was a cesspit, only noticeable by a large iron cover in the ground. There was a large open space between the fence and the actual garden, where there were several benches, a summer house and a sandpit for the smaller village schoolchildren to play in. A few trees provided shadow on very hot summer days.

A rock garden along the churchyard wall led from the gate entrance along the drive to the playground for the schoolchildren and further up the hill to the flower and vegetable gardens. Box-tree hedges surrounded the gardens. Apart from the flowers, which were grown to decorate the chapel and the church, there were the usual vegetables, as well as strawberries, blackcurrants and redcurrants, loganberries, gooseberries, apple, plum and pear trees and even a mulberry tree with red and white fruit. The surrounding walls at the back of the convent were used to grow grapes and peaches, but I only ever remember the grapes being small and sour.

At the end of the gardens, framed by lilac trees, was a life-size statue of the Virgin Mary and to the right of it, hidden by more bushes, was a big beehouse with one wall missing. Inside were huge boxes for the bees, instead of the usual beehives, as my grandmother had them. Not far from the beehouse was a small iron door in the wall, which opened to a lane, in turn leading out of the village into the fields, meadows and finally to a large and quite deep pond. For us, several years later, this door, which we never used, would lead to the 'world' which, according to the nuns, was full of temptation and sin.

The convent accommodated twenty-five boarders; most of them were the daughters of farmers. They were taught domestic science or, rather, everything that a good housewife ought to know. There was, in addition, the normal provision of a primary school for children from the surrounding countryside and the village, as well as a small kindergarten. The convent also offered the opportunity to have private tuition in French, piano and shorthand. All this was accomplished by only twelve people: they consisted of ten nuns, a lay teacher for the primary school and a girl from the village who took care of the heavier domestic work. These were joined , on our arrival, by another girl from the village, who came daily for a few hours to look after my sister and myself and who took us sometimes for walks.

We must have been very confused at first. I was told later that we were always getting lost in the various rooms and landings, even in the gardens. I only remember that my sister was always running after me, calling out 'Nushy, Nushy, wait for me!' I felt entirely responsible for her. It was she and I against all those grown-ups!

We did not have too much difficulty with the German language. Children tend to pick up any language if it is spoken by the people around them. We missed, though, the familiar faces of Grandmother, Uncle Lajos and Aunt Ilona and our cousins. Fraulein Schnurch, the primary teacher, told us in later years that they all got rather tired of our continual asking where Auntie or Uncle or Grandmother, and of course Papa, was, although we had already become used to our father's long absences. Now he came to visit us every fortnight, for a whole afternoon, and later he was able to come every weekend.

The Bishop, meantime, had confirmed that we could stay on as the youngest ever boarders, because of the 'Sacred Heart' feast day. Now we were called the 'Sacred Heart children'. This had its advantages and disadvantages.

When the Bishop came to visit the convent he gave us each a rosary brought back from Jerusalem and a prayer book bound in white leather. I don't think we really knew what it was all about but we had to say 'Thank you' very nicely. On all the Bishop's visits we sat next to him; Lilly before long would sit on his knee. She was a real charmer and everybody adored her. The Bishop let us share the special delicacies prepared for him — and we thoroughly enjoyed being in the limelight.

However, it was different when we were naughty — then we heard: 'How could you, a Sacred Heart child, ever do such a naughty thing?' and every slight misdemeanour seemed a crime. It was usually I who got into trouble even though I tried hard to please, whereas Lilly just smiled at everybody and could do no wrong. She was a naturally affectionate child and the nuns all spoiled her.

I regarded myself as Lilly's protector, although she did not need one. If she fell and hurt herself it was to me that she would come and I would try to console her. We loved each other fiercely — two little mites stranded in a crowd of strange grown-ups and Papa only coming every fortnight, when he again belonged to us, and we to him.

However, as children do, we eventually settled down and became used to our new life. We soon learned to speak only German and forgot Hungarian, as Papa also spoke to us in German. At first, when he visited us, he always brought some little toy as a present, but after a while he stopped bringing presents because he wanted us to look forward to his visits for himself and not for the presents. And we did look forward to his visits.

He made quite sure that we learned good behaviour and good manners. I still remember how he taught me to blow my nose — he couldn't bear a snivelling child. 'Open your handkerchief like that,' he showed me. 'Hold your nose with it like that and blow. Blow hard. Now fold the handkerchief again so and so, then put it in your pocket.' It was perfect — but not at all ladylike. He had taught me to blow my nose like a man, and I never forgot it, unfortunately!

Father Franzl, the Catholic priest who visited the convent regularly, was also very fond of children. Now he had two little girls there to spoil. He always called for us, lifted us high up in the air and even let us ride on his shoulders. We loved him dearly — and also his cook! She made special cakes whenever we visited the presbytery or she would send us some with the priest.

3

OUR FIRST YEAR at the convent being over, we were to spend the summer holidays with my Banater grandmother. Although we lived first in Budapest and then in the Austrian part of Silesia, we were to spend nearly all our childhood holidays — except during the war years — at Grandmother's. To us, Uj-Moldova was, and would remain, our home also, providing as it did the only sense of continuity in our lives. Nevertheless, as the Banat was part of the Balkans, there was a great difference between where we normally lived and Moldova, especially that part of the town where the Romanian, Bohemian and Serbian peasants lived. Their quarters seemed very primitive to us, their customs quaint and life much more colourful, especially at market time. It was an exciting place to be!

The journey was very long and we had to travel for two days and nights. Sister Firmina, who acted as the boarders' 'mother', had told us to be good girls and not give any trouble to our dear Uncle Herrmann, Papa's youngest brother, who still lived with Grandmother and who would take us from Vienna to Uj-Moldova. Papa would take us as far as Vienna.

'As soon as it gets dark,' Sister Firmina had said, 'take off your dress and lie down and go to sleep.' Thus it happened that after passing through a long tunnel we emerged only for my astonished uncle to find us lying half-undressed with tightly closed eyes, on the bench pretending to sleep. We thought we had been very good, but unfortunately Uncle Herrmann was not of the same opinion!

Earlier in the journey, on the way to Vienna with Papa, Lilly insisted on crossing herself furiously. 'What is the matter with you?' asked my incomprehending father. She was too busy crossing herself to answer and only when he physically stopped her hand did she tell him that she had to make the sign of the cross for all those tall crosses flying past the window. How could she know that they were telephone poles? We were so used, when walking in a crocodile on our daily walks from the convent, to making the sign of the cross whenever we saw something tall on the side of the road, whether it was a cross or a *marterl* (wayside shrine), without really looking!

At last the journey came to an end, and we reached Grandmother's. By my grandparents' time the family had again become quite well off. The house at Uj-Moldova was a comfortable one: it was only a single-storey house, but had a porch at the back, running across its full extent. In the yard were a pear tree and a walnut tree and an old-fashioned well

Grandmother's house, the front

with bucket and chain. Under the house were the wine cellars, and standing next to it a vinepress and brandy distillery.

A small workroom, which also served as a shop, equipped with a hatter's wheel, was to be found at the front of the house; next to this was the salon and behind both was a huge kitchen. While my Grandfather was still alive felt hats had been made and sold there, and sent to neighbouring markets. By the time that we knew it, only the display cabinet remained in the erstwhile shop. In that cabinet on one shelf was a big oval dish piled high with Grandmother's speciality, *apfelpitta*, a delicious apple pastry. That was a sure sign that Grandmother had looked forward to our arrival with love and care. 'Words of welcome don't count much,' she used to say. 'Prove it with baking something special.'

Grandmother had lost her husband when she was only forty years old. He died as the result of a fall from his horse and the pneumonia which followed. He left her with five children: four boys and one girl. My father and his brother were the two youngest boys, then aged six and four respectively.

There were three vineyards for her to look after, a lime kiln, bees, hens and pigs, as well as the children; the pigeons looked after themselves. It was more than enough to do for one woman. Of course, she had help, but the responsibility and the organising of work fell on her alone.

Grandmother was a remarkable woman. Although small and in her youth very slight, she had a great fund of energy. She knew what she wanted. She was just, full of good ideas and always helpful in a motherly way, not only to her own family but to all who worked for her and to their families also.

She was greatly respected in the area. When I was about twenty-two years old I travelled on my own to Moldova and the last part of the journey was on a local train. Somebody asked me where I was going; when I said 'Moldova', the lady who had asked wanted to know to whom. When I mentioned that I was going to my Grandmother, Frau Stiller, everybody in the compartment joined in the conversation — and they all had something pleasant to say about her. They also remembered my father and uncle. I felt terribly proud to have such a highly thought of and respected grandmother.

She had a cheerful nature, a good sense of humour and iron health. Even when she was over eighty years old she still managed a daily visit to her vineyards, and supervised the vine harvest. She was called upon

25

whenever there was a birth or a family crisis and her advice was usually taken. Many of her wise sayings were to be a guideline to me in later life.

She not only made sure that her children had a good education but also provided a dowry for her daughter, and for the sons a generous personal outfit at their marriages; shirts and towels, and, for each one, twelve pairs of hand-knitted socks in thin wool with a pattern on the side with his initials knitted in. Each son was also given the old, treasured family recipes, especially those for the traditional Christmas baking — which we are still using today.

It was the custom in those days for the youngest son to inherit the property when the other children already had their own jobs and were well provided for. Unfortunately, my father's youngest brother went missing in the First World War before he could get married. We never heard from him again.

When Grandmother died, the property was therefore divided between all her remaining children, but my father gave his share to my sister and myself. By that time, however, the Banat belonged to Romania and we lived then in Czechoslovakia and had become Czechoslovakians. A new law passed by the Romanian government forbade any foreigner to hold property in any part of Romania. Everything, the vineyards and the house, which had been in the family for nearly two hundred years, and had been rebuilt so many times, had then to be sold. We were all very sorry: our last links had been severed.

I remember that Grandmother was very proud of her vineyards, especially those on the hill, which was called the *Huterberg*, because of the family's hatmaking (*hut* was the word for hat). This hill was about two kilometres outside the village. Up to her death at the age of eighty-four, Grandmother would walk daily throughout the season, from April to the middle of October, to see that all the work was properly done and to watch the growing and ripening of the grapes.

Slightly below the hilltop stood a stone hut, divided into two rooms. One was used as a kind of combined kitchen, living and sleeping room for the vineyard guard, from spring to autumn. The other room was kept for members and friends of the family. The guard was a necessity, not so much as protection against human intruders, but against dogs. Once they have tasted ripening grapes, dogs can wreak havoc in the vineyard. The guard carried a gun and any stray dog was frightened away with a shot.

Both rooms in the hut were quite comfortably furnished with a sofa,

Grandmother's house, the back

cooking utensils, and bedding in a drawer under the sofa. The family room had, in addition, a small bookcase with a few books. The roof of the hut was almost flat and from both there and from the top of the hill one had the most glorious view: the Danube flowing between its rocky banks, the 'Babagaia' rock in the middle of the river and the 'Casan' (the rocks on both sides) leading to the Iron Gate.

'Babagaia' means 'old woman' in Turkish and there is a story people tell that, while the Turks were there, one man had put one of his querulous wives on the rock to starve; it made us shudder whenever we looked at the rock and thought about her. We liked our food, and to be left to starve seemed the most cruel deed imaginable.

The 'Casan' was that part of the Danube where the river squeezes between the high rocks on both sides and, with the additional

27

whirlpools it made, it was quite dangerous for shipping, at least in those days. Now it is all changed.

The view from the hill was exceptionally beautiful at sunset, when the land and the rocks were glowing crimson and the red light would spread over the many, many vineyards, meadows and fields on one side, and on the other side across the river, to the ruins of the ancient Turkish castle, Golabascz, built into the rocks, and to the reflections in the water with all its eddies and whirls.

Grandmother told us many old legends and stories during this and later visits, some true ones from when she was young, and others about the war years of 1870-1871. There was famine in the land at that time and some people were reduced to catching rats to keep alive. But when she became tired of storytelling and we did not want to go to sleep, she had a special story, the end of which we have never been told.

'There was once a shepherd,' she would start, 'who wanted to take his sheep to another meadow which could only be reached over a very narrow bridge. There were several hundred sheep and they had to go one by one.' She would then continue: 'Now you will have to wait until they have all crossed the bridge,' and we would quite happily go to sleep. The sheep might still be going over that bridge as far as I know! Whenever we asked for the end of the story she would give a number and count a few more sheep, and we had to be satisfied. A hundred or a million meant the same to us in those days.

The summer passed quickly at Moldova. Hot days in the garden — where I discovered a salamander sunning himself on the hot stones of a low wall. He was a living wonder. I didn't dare touch him, he was so strange and wonderful. I also remember watching a bumble bee disappearing into a flower. I stood fascinated. I called Lilly to show her what I had discovered. Those first impressions are never forgotten.

Preparations were being made for the vintage, which took place at the beginning of October, while the weather was still dry and very warm. First the big vinepress was uncovered, checked and thoroughly cleaned again. Then the big casks in the cellar were turned over so that the opening was easily accessible. We were allowed to get inside these. I remember that both of us could stand up and, once, holding hands, we tried a little dance. Then the cask began to roll and we ceased to enjoy our game and quickly crawled out.

Our cousin Oscar, who studied medicine, was home for the holidays that year. One day he had come to visit Grandmother and was waiting for Uncle Herrmann. He sat by the table outside the kitchen, reading a paper and, with his back to the cellar, he was rocking to and fro with his chair. The cellar entrance was near the kitchen window with wooden steps leading down to it. It was said that it actually was the end of a copper mine. Normally the cellar was closed by two heavy doors. Unnoticed by Oscar, a servant had gone down to the cellar and left the doors open.

Suddenly there was a tremendous crash and Oscar and chair were both down in the cellar. Lilly, who had just come out of the kitchen, caught a glimpse of his legs waving in the air and then disappearing. She went to the entrance of the cellar to investigate, but it looked dark down there, only right at the back could she see a faint light, the servant's candle. Eventually, to her great relief, Oscar tried to get up, moaning and groaning but little the worse for his fall, except for some bad bruises. Lilly, however, got such a shock that for a long time afterwards she refused to go near the cellar doors.

Oscar was the son of Papa's eldest sister, who also lived in Moldova. They owned the only hardware store in town and lived not too far from Grandmother. We partly admired him and partly disliked him, because we had heard that he was so keen on his medical studies that he had dissected dead cats and mice even before he went to university. Although we found this a terrible thought, I had the sneaky feeling that I would also have liked to have a look at the insides of those dead animals!

He was studying to become a doctor in Vienna. Oscar's political sympathies lay with the Austrians rather than the Hungarians, which is why he had not chosen to go to university in Budapest. The Austro-Hungarian Empire was composed of a multitude of different nationalities, of which the Austrians and Hungarians were only the main ones. This resulted in constant political tensions, though my sister and I were still too young to understand these. Everyone felt a greater allegiance to one national group rather than the others. For my father, this was the Hungarians.

At last the vintage day had come. It started very early in the morning between four and five o'clock. A group of women grape-pickers climbed into the already waiting cart, on which were piled a great vat with a wide opening on top and butts for the women to carry on their backs when collecting the grapes.

Lilly and I, still asleep, were each put inside a butt, which two women then put on their backs and off they went with the rest of the women, all of them singing and joking. I remember, probably when waking up and looking over the top of the butt, the rhythmic movement of being carried and seeing only the high banks on both sides of the sunken road which led up to the vineyards.

In the vineyard each woman took one row, for which she was to be responsible. She cut the grapes with a small, very sharp knife, and threw them gently over her shoulder into the butt on her back. When that butt was full she would empty it into the vat on the waiting cart, and as soon as that too was full, the cart started on its way back home, where another one was already waiting.

All day they went to and fro. At the house the grapes were emptied into a very large vat, or enormous tub, almost the size of a small room, but only one and a half feet high, which stood in the middle of the yard, not far from the vinepress. Most of the grapes were by then already half crushed; the rest were crushed later by two women with their bare feet.

We had been provided, for our day at the vineyard, with little knives with which to cut our own grapes. We knew that one should never try to pull them off by hand. We wore only shorts, and the knife and a little beaker for drinking the grape juice were tied to the belt. When we returned from the vineyard and had finished our lunch and had a rest, we tried a little game. Standing at the side of the tub, we tried to catch some undamaged grapes with our beaker. Lilly reached out too far and fell in. She was soon pulled out, not hurt, but dripping with grape juice and her whole body plastered with crushed grapes. Grandmother assured her that they would not have poured her into the vinepress, as she would certainly have spoilt the wine!

As soon as the big tub was almost full the two girls would crush the remaining grapes with their feet and then the pulp would be poured into the vinepress. The liquid coming out, called Most, tasted delicious and we caught it with our beakers until we could drink no more.

There were many people involved in the vintage, mostly women and girls. Grandmother also had many girls working permanently in her household. Some mothers brought their thirteen- and fourteen-year-old daughters there, in order to learn the domestic skills. This would improve their chances of making a 'good' marriage.

The Romanian peasant girls and young women were usually very beautiful and moved gracefully. They wore the traditional custume: a white, coarsely woven linen gown. This was worn very loose, with the top held together by a cord and serving also as a shopping bag.

Sometimes they would keep their lunchtime tomatoes in their cleavage and if they were very ripe, the juice would colour the front of the gown bloody red, which looked quite horrific. A tight, handwoven belt, brightly patterned, held the gown in at the waist and colourful, handwoven and traditionally patterned aprons covered the front and the back, from the waist down.

Before the vintage, Grandmother's personal maid would go to the vineyard early each morning to bring choice grapes, still with the bloom on them, in time for breakfast. She wore only a long sheepskin coat, with the leather side inside for coolness, and nothing else underneath. I remember once when she placed the butt down in front of Grandmother, the coat opened and there she stood as the Lord had made her.

Neither Grandmother nor anybody else remarked on this, but for Lilly and I this was what we imagined Eve in Paradise must have looked like. There were, of course, no mirrors in the convent, at least not where we were, and we had never seen a naked person before, nor a picture — not even each other. It seemed quite natural that Lenka should look like that. We, our family, the nuns in the convent and anybody else we knew, certainly did not look like that, only the Romanians!

During the morning break, the servants and workers would have a glass of peach brandy. One day, Grandmother pointed to Lenka, who had been sawing wood with one of the men and was now resting and enjoying her drink. She offered a glass of peach brandy to the man and Grandmother said: 'Look, child, how gracefully Lenka offers that glass — that is how a queen would do it. Remember that when you are older and learn in the convent to move gracefully.' This might have been said to me some years later, but I have never forgotten it. Thinking back, I must admit that I have seldom seen such graceful movements as Lenka's — and she had no training, or even schooling.

During the summer months the peaches had ripened and then the pears. Now came the almonds and the walnuts. We had many almond trees in the vineyards and Grandmother preferred to use ground almond flour to wheat flour for her baking. We ate lots of nuts for our tea while sitting on the step of the porch. Even to this day I cannot think of anything better than fresh baked bread, grapes and new nuts.

It must have been in wintertime, when we were staying with Grandmother before being sent to the convent, that I remember her baking bread. Lilly and I lay on top of the tall oven, out of the way. The top was big enough to allow room for both of us, plus a dog and the cat. As it was quite high we were able to look down and watch Grandmother bake the bread. The loaves of dough were put into flat, large baskets and these were placed on a board, about four or five of them, and then the board was pushed into the oven. The board was wide and long enough for a grown-up person to lie on it.

The oven had been heated beforehand with a wood fire; then the fire had been taken out or burnt down and only the hot ash was now left. It was easy for us to understand the story of Hansel and Gretel, when Gretel pretends that she does not know how to climb on the board and into the oven and the witch shows her, by sitting herself on the board, before Gretel quickly pushes her in. No child in Silesia, with their small cast-iron stoves, could ever really imagine it, but for us it was real.

But back to the harvest. All through the summer and autumn peaches and pears were being dried. They were either cut into halves or left whole, laid in shallow trays and put on top of the wall which divided the yard from the garden. The walls were just high enough to deter the dog from jumping over them, and the cat preferred the hot bricks to the trays. The fruit dried in the sun, before being stored in the loft. The fallen and damaged peaches, even the only slightly damaged ones, had been collected in a wooden butt and were then distilled into brandy. Peach brandy sounded delicious to me and when I was older I tasted it, but was appalled that anybody should drink it!

Grandmother also grew maize, known locally as *kukurutz*. The cobs were first left to dry on the floor of one part of the loft. In winter, once we were back at school, the corn was rubbed off the cob. Everybody helped with this and it was usually done in the evenings when neighbours and friends also came to help. We understood that it turned into quite a party. Stories were told and one or another would sing an old ballad. The corn was then stored in a big heap on the loft floor. To us it seemed like a small mountain and we liked to bury ourselves in it.

The corn was used to feed the hens, geese and ducks. It was not just scattered on the ground at feeding time, but placed in flat, oval, wooden containers — and I was sure that the hens, geese and ducks were trained to pick their food so tidily from those dishes! At about the end of October one or two geese were chosen for the privilege of being held on Grandmother's or Lenka's lap and fed some specially baked lozenges. These geese were not forcibly fed to the extent of French geese for their enlarged livers, but just enough to make them nice and fat for Christmas.

The hut on top of the hill vineyard

In another part of the loft strings were tied across the ceiling, on which were hung a certain kind of grape, long, pointed ones with a thick skin. These were called 'goat tits', and they lasted at least until Christmas and even longer.

4

USUALLY WHEN WE returned to the convent from our prolonged summer holidays, the winter weather had already started. This first year was no exception. We now went for long walks; it was too cold to play in the garden with Emma, the young girl from the village who had been engaged to look after us. We could run round and keep warm, but it was different for her.

Emma was very friendly with the maid of the Liedauer family. Herr Liedauer was steward of the Bellegarde Estate and his two daughters were about the same age as Lilly and I. They became our first personal friends. Their mother invited us often to their house and we were allowed to play with their toys and even ride on their three-wheeler. To us, they seemed to lead an enchanted life; they had a mother and father all to themselves; there were only a few rooms where they lived and only Mama or Papa to know what one was doing, instead of so many Sisters — who also were not as prettily dressed as Frau Liedauer. Up until that time we had taken Grandmother's home, Uncle Lajos and his family and our whole life style just as a matter of fact, without realising that it was a normal thing for children to have both parents, and to live with them.

Meantime, life continued in a certain routine in the convent. Every Sunday we went to church, dressed in our best clothes and, as a special treat, we were allowed to leave our hair unplaited, like the little comtesses. The first row of pews, lined in blue velvet, was reserved for the Count, his wife and their eight daughters. Emma called them the 'organ pipes'. The second row was for the Count's staff, and then the convent boarders had their pews. The rest of the church was filled by the villagers. Reverend Mother and the other nuns had several niches on the side of the church walls. They could see us but we could not see them. Sister Kasiana, who taught us music, played the organ, high up at the back of the church. During the school term the boarders would sing in the choir, which was trained by Fraulein Schnurch, the primary school teacher.

Every Saturday was bath night at the convent, which took place in the washhouse in a large bath. While Sister Firmina was supervising the other boarders, Sister Renate, who was normally in charge of the kitchen, bathed Lilly and I. She insisted that we each put on a long, loose nightdress, then she washed us beneath the garment with a soapy sponge, so that we had no chance to have a good look at our bodies. Of course, we were each bathed separately, so as not to see each other being undressed. In fact, we were so impressed with the severity of the sin that such a look would be that we never dared. Lilly was a very active child, who could not keep still, so she was bathed after me, because Sister Renate was always quite exhausted when she had finished. She never became cross with Lilly, however, because she was so funny and charming that nobody was ever cross with her. She was not a beautiful child, as I was told later, but she had the most enchanting smile and her slightly slanting eyes seemed to be constantly twinkling with mischief.

Now I should describe some of the comforts of the convent. First, there were the dormitories, each holding about twelve beds. The beds were always placed in pairs, but with a high board between them to prevent the girls seeing each other undress, or talking to each other. Naturally, there had to be complete silence in the room!

In one corner was the cell for the nun, enclosed by white curtains. The other boarders wondered what was behind; sometimes, some girls near the cell could see spidery shadows moving behind the cell curtains, if they were not already asleep when Sister came to bed. We knew exactly what lay behind those curtains, because when we were very young, if one of us had not been too well or crying, Sister would take her into her cell. We knew, for instance, that she wore a long white gown at night and had a funny-looking cap over her short hair which, of course, we never saw during the day. Although nobody had said anything to us, we never told the other girls what we had seen.

Our beds had real straw sacks. There was a slit in the middle where you could put your hand in and shake up the straw. When we were older we were supposed to do this every day. On a small table next to the bed was a wash bowl and a jug full of water, which in winter was quite often frozen in the morning. I don't think we minded, because it was such fun to break the ice.

At night we wore a long chemise, and over that a so-called propriety skirt. This was made of thick cotton: it was perfectly straight and reached only to the knees, but it could not slip upwards. On top we wore a cotton bed-jacket, with long sleeves and embroidered collars and cuffs. We were supposed to lie on our backs and place our hands on top of the coverlet. If we wanted to be especially good we folded our hands as in prayer, before Sister came to say 'Good night'.

There was no electric light — or any ceiling light — in the dormitories. Sister would bring an oil lamp, which she stood on a small table while we undressed, before taking it, extinguished, away to her cell.

In winter the big tiled stove in another corner of the room, opposite Sister's cell, would be lit. This reached almost to the ceiling. On very cold nights, once we had seen that Sister's light had gone out, we all crept, as silently as possible, with our coverlets to the stove to warm them on the tiles. If Sister heard the patter of bare feet on the uncarpeted floor, she never let on!

For Lilly and I the board between the two beds played an important part in our lives. As far back as I can remember we pushed our little hands through the small opening between the board and the straw sack and this gave us a great feeling of reassurance. There was another meaning to that quiet hand-pressing. We had heard, some time ago, how a farmer's wife had died and had woken up again just before the funeral as they were about to nail down the coffin lid. We had also heard that only a cut in the sole of the foot would be painful enough to awaken someone, if apparently dead.

We were horribly afraid to think that one of us might die in the night and be buried alive, so we had promised each other to cut the sole of one foot of the other one, whoever might look dead. The touch of our hands each night reassured us both that we remembered that promise. Then we could go happily to sleep, knowing that a loving sister was there to cut the sole of one foot if it ever became necessary.

It might seem strange that at such a tender age we were already quite familiar with death, but it was all around us in our prayers. As our mother was dead, which we were reminded of often enough, Sister Firmina had composed a special evening prayer for us, addressed to the Virgin Mary, who should be our mother now. It went, roughly translated, something like this:

Good night you darling Mother mine,
Your child is now going to rest,
Oh, give her your blessing, dear Mother mine;
And if your child should not wake up again,
And this night be her death night,
Please open wide your arms,
And lead your child into its Father's house.

We loved this prayer and, with the promise we had made to each other, there was now nothing to worry about.

I, however, worried about another prayer which we were also supposed to say every evening. This was for the souls in Purgatory where, according to Sister, our mother was. We prayed something like this:

Dear Jesus, be so kind,
And let your precious blood flow into Purgatory,
Where the poor souls do penance.
Oh, they suffer such great pain,
Please be merciful to them. Amen.

I worried a lot about this prayer. How long would our mother be in Purgatory? Everybody said that she had died very young and we had now been such a long time in the convent; surely her sins should have been forgiven by now! Furthermore, it was mostly children who were naughty, or very bad grown-ups. Mama could not have committed so many sins!

One day I asked Sister how long people, or rather souls, usually stayed in Purgatory. Sister replied: 'Oh, until the end of the world.' I was flabbergasted: we had always been told that God was our Father in Heaven; surely He could not be so cruel. I told Sister that I preferred my real father to God and then it was her turn to be horrified. I was a wicked child and must never say such a thing again. So in my next prayer I asked God to make an exception with my mother — and I stopped worrying.

As winter progressed, Lilly found it more and more difficult to spend the time between five o'clock and supper time, at six o'clock, quietly playing while the older girls did their homework. I was quite happy to spend this time looking at books, quietly asking one or other of the girls what the words meant, as I had already started reading, although I was not yet old enough to attend school. A child had at that time to be six years old before the beginning of the autumn term.

Lilly was so lively that she could not sit still, even on Sister Firmina's lap, so, quite often, when she was becoming too restless and disturbing everybody, she was put, as a punishment, in the corner behind the tiled stove. That did not help much as she tried successfully to play *kuckuck* (cuckoo), which proved even more disturbing to those pupils who had to do their homework.

Sometimes, she managed to escape and wandered off into the nun's quarters, where she was always welcome. One day, something dreadful happened while she sat wriggling on Reverend Mother's knee. Reverend Mother suddenly fainted and Lilly slipped from her knee to the floor. It was a terrible shock to her. Apparently Reverend Mother had, through some sudden movement of Lilly's, banged her elbow hard against the edge of the table. Of course, she quickly recovered, only to find Lilly kneeling in front of the statue of the Holy Virgin, crossing herself and praying loudly to God to save Reverend Mother, while her face kept turning round to see if she was getting better. We were told this story many years later.

Lilly was such a cheerful child, but she had to be loved, and she tried to charm everybody. She had to be the centre of attention — only then would she be happy. I tried hard to be like her, but I could not show or express my feelings as she could. Only once did I try to imitate her and climb on Reverend Mother's knee. I was immediately rebuked: 'You great big girl, you don't want to sit on my knee. You are no longer a baby!' Yet I was only thirteen months older. I never tried again.

That winter was full of dramatic little incidents. One early evening I remember that Emma took us to the toilets outside. It was a cold, stormy night and it was pitch dark. Emma carried a lantern so that we could see our way. We were shivering with cold and the lantern cast ghostly shadows on the ground. Before the three of us had reached our destination there was a sudden noise in the bushes, an open door creaked and then banged shut. With the cry 'the Devil comes!' the superstitious Emma turned back, stumbled, and then fell. The glass of the lantern shattered, the flame died, but the storm continued to howl, nearly tearing our clothes from our bodies. We tried desperately to

The convent boarders (the two little girls in front are my sister and I)

grasp hold of Emma, but in vain.

We stumbled back in the darkness towards the entrance hall. Lilly fell over the foot-scraper with its sharp edges, and we crawled up the steps into the hall, where we both tumbled onto the icy floor tiles. Screaming blue murder, we soon had the whole convent congregating round us to see what all this noise meant. We both had cuts and bruises; Lilly's lip needed stitches and a doctor was called. For years after this Lilly remained frightened to go out in the dark. Emma didn't come any more!

Another time, it might have been towards spring, when it was still daylight at study-time, I went alone to the toilets. As I was walking along I looked up at the sky. It was again stormy and, to my horror, I noticed that the clouds were moving. I had never noticed that before: as far as I knew the clouds were there for the angels to sit upon and play, or to water the earth with rain. What a tragedy! What could be done to help them?

I ran to the study room where everybody was quietly reading or doing some homework. I burst through the door, screaming and shouting, but could not make myself understood. I pointed upwards and, amid sobs, gasped something about angels falling and the sky falling down. All that could be understood was that there was a lot of falling going on.

They all rushed outside with me, down into the yard, where I pointed excitedly to the sky. They shook their heads and could not see the danger the angels were in. I must have been hysterical by then, but when at last everybody understood what I meant, I was in disgrace. How could I play such a silly prank? Of course, everybody knew that the clouds *always* move. I had *not* known, and my world had collapsed!

Not long before, at Christmas, we had received many toys, amongst them new dolls. They had real hair and they had two cords under their dress, one with a blue bead, the other with a pink bead. If you pulled either of these, the doll would say 'Mamma' or 'Papa', though, naturally, you had to use a bit of imagination as well. I decided to cut up the body of Lilly's doll to find out where the talking came from. Again I was in disgrace, especially as I had chosen to cut up Lilly's doll. Why not my own? They should have understood that. From then on, special dolls and the best toys were put in a glass case and only taken out when Papa came on a visit, and the school nursery finally inherited almost new toys.

Later in the spring another dreadful incident happened, but this time it was a very smelly one. We were both playing outside, actually in that part of the garden where we were not meant to be, the cobbled yard between hen-house and pigsties. Somebody had left the cesspit cover off. We were playing ball. Lilly's ball fell in. It bobbed up and down on top of the dark liquid. Lilly knelt down and tried to retrieve it; she over-reached herself, and fell in. Luckily she held onto the edge of the cesspit and I immediately grasped hold of her other hand and, kneeling and sitting on my heels, I held her up as we both screamed for help. Within minutes, one of the nuns arrived and pulled Lilly out. As soon as she had firm ground under her feet again, she fell round my neck, pressing me close and kissing me, repeating over and over again, 'My darling Nushy'. Now Sister had to roll *both* of us in paper, and we were carried as the most objectionable parcels to the washhouse. For days afterwards everybody seemed to avoid us!

One day, Papa came, with his sister, Aunt Marie from Moldova, to visit us. We were given permission to travel back with him to Troppau, about half-an-hour's train journey from Skrochowitz, which we reached by landau. Papa wanted my aunt's help in taking us both for complete new outfits and then to the photographer.

We came out of the shop in new white dresses, with white ribbons in our hair, everything new underneath, white shoes, and a huge parcel for Papa — we looked just perfect for the photographer. We walked hand in hand in front of Papa and Aunt Marie. It had been raining and we both fell into a puddle. There had been no 'crocodile' in front of us to make us avoid the puddle!

The photographer and my aunt did the best they could. They wiped us down, but the white dresses still looked definitely dirty. However, the photographer positioned us facing slightly sideways, but opposite to each other and holding hands, as if we were just starting to do a little dance, in the hope that the shadows might hide the dirty garments. We had, of course, been crying at the sight of Papa's scowling face, and the smile the photographer urged us to put on was rather watery.

I have another memory of these early years. Shortly before I started school, there was great excitement in the village. As far as we could understand, and the woman who helped in the kitchen confirmed this, the end of the world was near. In fact it was destined to happen on a certain day. Some dreadful huge thing would come down from Heaven, clash with the Earth and destroy it and everybody in it as well. The nuns did not believe this story, but a neighbouring farmer sold his farm and went with his wife to Vienna 'to live at last', as he said. We heard all this from the woman in the kitchen and we decided we would look out for it and try not to miss it.

Nothing eventually happened on the day it should have happened, so we decided that we would stay awake all night. As soon as everything was quiet in the dormitory and Sister had retired to her cell, I crept round the board dividing our two beds and sat down on Lilly's bed. We held hands, counted our fingers, pinched each other, anything just to keep awake.

From time to time I crept to the window, but could only see the starry sky, which looked perfectly peaceful. I could not see the moon, so that had probably already been destroyed. However, nothing happened and towards the morning it grew chilly, so I crept into Lilly's bed. Then we fell asleep and the next thing we knew was, not the end of the world, but certainly a rude awakening!

Sister Firmina stood in front of us and pulled the coverlet back. There we were in each other's arms. Shocking! 'Get up at once,' she said, 'and see Reverend Mother after breakfast.' Reverend Mother was very cross. 'Silly talk about the end of the world,' she said. 'You know you should not get into each other's bed and you ought to be severely punished. However, go to the chapel and say five Hail Marys and never do it again.' We went to the chapel but we would have preferred the end of the world!

Years later, I realised that it must have been Halley's Comet which everybody was expecting. I had not yet entered school, which I did in September 1911. It could well have been in 1910 when the comet really was seen.

5

WHEN AT LAST I started school, Lilly was left without a playmate, but not for long. Another little girl, called Maritschel, arrived to join us. She was Lilly's age and was admitted because there were already two little girls in the convent. She was the daughter of a Roman Catholic priest (again the woman in the kitchen supplied this information) but that made no difference to us. The nuns were to take care of her, as her mother had died, and she would stay there until her education was finished.

As she grew older Maritschel would help occasionally in the kitchen, but meantime she played with Lilly, and with me after school hours. We shared our toys with her, were all naughty together and were punished together. Afterwards we always had to go to the chapel and say a little prayer and ask God's forgiveness. Maritschel and Lilly were sent to the chapel very often and as there was no supervision for those visits, I suspect there must have been a lot of giggling instead of prayer, but as God seemed to us like our own father, He certainly would have forgiven them.

One Sunday all three of us did not want to go to church, so we hid in the feather bed, unbuttoning the coverlet, crawling in between the feather bed and the cover and then buttoning it up from the inside. It was rather difficult, but all three of us managed. We lay quite still, each in her own bed. As we lay, stretched out, we thought nobody would realise that we were there. It took a long time before we were found out as nobody thought of looking for us in the dormitory.

This time the punishment was meant to be severe; we were locked inside the huge wardrobe in the loft, where all the theatre costumes hung. Far from being upset, we found it rather exciting, although the air smelt strongly of mothballs. We had a lovely time, playing among the garments, pulling them down, opening the box of hats and wigs, and we got it all into a dreadful mess. The punishment had turned into fun. Nevertheless, when we heard Sister coming to let us out, we all started to cry bitterly and, as we emerged, we looked so utterly miserable that Sister Firmina took pity on us and gave us each a biscuit.

Sister Kasiana was responsible for the flowers in the church and the convent chapel and we were sometimes allowed to accompany her to carry some flowers and throw the dead ones away. As a reward she would let us taste her speciality: some marzipan mice. Lilly and I did not like the thought of eating mice, even if they were chocolate, but Maritschel wolfed hers down and ate ours as well.

Another time Sister Kasiana let us go with her to the beehouse. Maritschel ran away when a bee looked like descending on her. A little while later two bees stung Lilly and she was quite ill afterwards. None of the bees stung me, so Sister Kasiana let me go again and from then on I was allowed to help her. No bee has ever stung me, although I proudly showed the other children how bees could sit in my lips and on my hair when I helped Sister with the centrifugal machine for extracting the honey; I also loved to carry the full honeycombs to the machine, when my hands were covered with bees who did not harm me at all. As a reward I got a full honeycombe — a little one, of course.

Later when Sister Kasiana realised that she had a fearless assistant, I was sometimes taken from lessons to help her. The other children envied me for that, although they would not have liked to go near the bees themselves, but I loved every minute in the beehouse.

In spite of having Maritschel to keep my sister company, Lilly would quite often suddenly realise that I was not there and become afraid that she might have lost me. Then she would run into the classroom where I was, just to make sure that I was still there. Naturally, the lesson was interrupted — not that the children minded — but Sister would call her a little nuisance, calm her down and take her back out. Half the lesson time was wasted by then, but the others loved that kind of interruption and Lilly became very popular!

I too was often a nuisance in the classroom, but for a different reason. I could read quite well and quickly became impatient with the slow readers; reading was done aloud by each child in turn, right through the class. I showed my boredom and impatience by making clicking noises with my tongue, which annoyed everybody. With Papa's permission, I was therefore taken out of the class for part of the time, for extra lessons — piano playing, French and shorthand. Papa had to pay for these, of course. I loved those lessons, especially the piano playing. French helped me later in school, and shorthand I found really fascinating. To this day I continue to use many of the signs and abbreviations I learnt at such a young age. It was Gabelsberger shorthand and it made it easy for me in later years to learn the Gabelsberg International amendments.

The next autumn term Lilly and Maritschel also started school and could now join me and the others at the big tables in the refectory. Up until then they had to remain at the small, low table. Now they were big girls like me.

The refectory had two long tables running right along the walls, with wooden benches on each side. There was just enough space left in the middle of the room for the servers. At the far end of the room one of the nuns would stand during the meal, reading aloud from *The Lives of the Saints*, taking one for each day. We happily ate our meal in silence while listening to the most dreadful and sometimes disgusting tortures.

Most of us did not aspire to be saints, but I had once declared that I had better become a saint, as there was no St Nushy in the calendar to enable me to celebrate my nameday — and namedays were more celebrated in Austria than birthdays. Luckily for me, I was told that I already had a saint and a nameday — 26 July for St Anna — and I learned that one St Anna was the mother of the Virgin Mary, therefore the grandmother of Jesus, and a second one had lived some time in the Middle Ages and had been a humble servant.

But back to the refectory. Lilly disliked fat meat very much, whereas I loved it. We did not sit together, but luckily we did sit on the same bench, which was against the wall. Lilly was able to send me her fat meat on a spoon along the bench behind the back of the other girls, and I pushed a spoon with stewed fruit or pudding towards her. The other girls, of course, helped pass the spoons along. No wonder Sister Firmina complained about the dirty frocks! If I did not have enough stewed fruit or pudding to 'pay' for meat I had to tell a story on our walks. I loved telling stories and we kept a strict account about who owed a story and who owed fat meat.

The months passed quickly and busily now that I was a proper schoolgirl. Day-to-day happenings have blurred together in my memory, as winter gave way to summer and then returned again. The winter term at the convent heralded a season of feast days — always welcome in the life of a child.

At the beginning of November was St Martin's day. Special cakes were baked for this and, in the evening, so we were told, St Martin rode on his white horse through the village and through the houses. We never saw him, because we were not allowed out of the day room. It was a mystery to me why this saint, who had given half his coat to a beggar in his lifetime, should, now that he was dead, ride through the streets and houses. Did he want to collect coats for the beggars in heaven? I never quite understood.

On 5 December it was the eve of St Nicolas Day. This saint had been a bishop in his lifetime, and had loved children. He always used to have apples and sweets in his pocket for them, wherever he went. The legend says that when he died an apple tree grew out of his grave. St Nicolas watched from Heaven as the children collected the apples. The Lord, in his kindness, saw that it made St Nicolas sad, and allowed him to go back to Earth on the eve of his birthday, 6 December, and give apples, nuts and sweets to the children. At the same time he would collect their lists of Christmas wishes. When back in Heaven, St Nicolas would give those lists to the little angels, who then made themselves busy getting the presents ready for Christmas for the Christchild to take down to earth on 25 December, his own birthday. That is what we children were told — and we firmly believed it.

As soon as it got dark we all assembled in the biggest classroom, children and staff. The desks had been set against the walls so that there was a wide open space in the middle of the room. We had not long to wait. St Nicolas soon entered, dressed as a bishop in golden cope and mitre, carrying a crozier in his hand. He was accompanied by Krampus, a mixture of devil and servant, who was dressed all in black, with a red tongue hanging out of his mouth and a long black tail with a red tassel. He carried an enormous birch, which he swung menacingly.

St Nicolas called each of us to him in turn, asked if we had been good, and accepted our list of wishes for Christmas. Of course, we all said that we had been good, otherwise St Nicolas would have instructed Krampus to use the birch on us. We were each given a bag of apples, nuts and sweets and then walked back to our place, while Krampus threatened us with his birch. When we had all spoken to St Nicolas we sang a song, then he gave us his blessing and disappeared.

Within seconds, Krampus came back, and chased us through the room with his birch. No harm was done, we screamed and ran, yet thoroughly enjoyed it, until Reverend Mother ordered Krampus to go, and he, too, left. Reverend Mother had power even over the Devil!

At the end of the Christmas term a play was produced by the boarders, and one year I was given a part. The play was the adapted story of the thieving magpie. I was to play the orphan who had to work very hard in a rich family. When a brooch went missing from the house I was accused of having stolen it. I was arrested and brought before a judge, who sentenced me to have my hand cut off.

The Count and his family had been invited for the performance, as well as the parents of the boarders and of the village schoolchildren. I was so excited that the story had become real for me. When the time came for me to put my hand on the block for the executioner to cut it off, I pulled it back, screaming: 'I'm not having my hand cut off', and I ran to the edge of the stage, leaving the executioner, and the prompter, in total confusion.

However, at this moment the Virgin Mary, who stood on a pedestal in the corner, stepped down and motioned to the executioner to drop his axe. A magpie flew, or rather was pushed on a stick, towards her; she took the brooch from the magpie's beak and handed it to the judge. I came quickly back and all was well. There was great applause, especially from Papa and Lilly. I was teased about my refusal to let my hand be cut off for a long time afterwards.

At the summer term concert, just before the holidays, Lilly and I performed a little dialogue, 'The Apple and the Pear'. We were dressed up with a cardboard cut-out of an apple and a pear pinned to the front of our dresses. Lilly was the pear and I was the apple; one had just fallen off the tree and the other had voluntarily climbed down. It was extremely funny and we remembered it for many years. If one of us was in a grumpy mood the other one would start reciting her part and then we both repeated the whole thing alternately and finished with laughter — an innocent pleasure for two old ladies! Unfortunately we were to live very far apart, but that is another story.

One year we started our summer holiday late, on 4 September, which was Papa's birthday. For some reason neither Papa nor Uncle Herrman had been able to take us to Uj-Moldova before that date. We had been able to get our holiday prolonged so as to enable us to stay for the vintage in October. Luckily, we could easily make up for the lost lessons as we were boarders; we would just get a bit more homework to do when we came back.

It was arranged that one of the nuns would accompany us to Skrochowitz in the landau, as usual, where Papa would collect us and would take the next train with us to Vienna. Sister Firmina had taught us a birthday poem, which we were to recite to Papa. Unfortunately, Sister had to go back to the convent immediately, and left us alone in the waiting room at the station. The station-master had promised to keep an eye on us.

Papa's train was late. When Papa eventually rushed in, we jumped up, I produced a bunch of flowers which I had hidden behind my back, and I started at the top of my voice: 'Dear Papa, for your birthday we wish you . . .'

I could not go on. Papa grabbed the flowers, threw them into the nearest wastepaper basket, took our suitcase in one hand, Lilly by the other, and dragged us out of the waiting room. We rushed past the other, astonished, people waiting there and into a train which was already standing on the platform. Lilly and I were by then both howling loudly, and everybody was staring at our little group.

We managed to find an empty compartment and once Papa had closed the door, he began to explain. His own train had been so late that if we had not quickly caught the Vienna train which had already arrived, we would have had to wait until the evening for the next one and would have missed Uncle Herrmann in Vienna. On hearing this we calmed down and felt quite happy again, especially when Papa assured us that he had been pleased about the flowers, and that the station-master would be pleased too. As the flowers were in the wastepaper basket, nobody could tread on them, so they would not be spoiled. Then he asked us to say the birthday poem for him.

We stood up and recited it. I began with one line, then Lilly said the next and so on, alternately. It was quite a long poem, with promises that we would always be good, to please our dear Papa, and thanking God for such a good father and wishing him happiness and a long, long life. Papa embraced us and called us his 'dear children'. All's well that ends well!

Mama and Papa on their wedding day

Our holiday at Grandmother's soon passed, as always: carefree and running free in the vineyards. That year, we saw how slaked lime was made. There was a pit under the yard, more like a high-ceilinged cave with a big wooden cover, like a door. Inside were steps leading down into what looked like a pond of thick cream. Once every year, I believe, loads of chalk stones arrived, pipes were laid from the pump outside the kitchen to the heap of chalk stones and then the pump was worked by one of the workmen.

There was a noise as if a fire was burning, steam rose up and the stone heap slowly changed into what looked like very thick, white cream, which, when cooled, could be cut with a trowel. How it was transported into the pit I cannot remember, because we watched through a window and were not allowed to go near. I imagine that it flowed, while still very hot, into the lime pit, because for days afterwards there was a white path from where the chalkstone heap had been to the limepit cover.

Grandmother sold the slaked lime to the Romanian and Bohemian peasants. They built their houses themselves with the help of neighbours — just a few rooms — and then they whitewashed them inside and outside. They bought the slaked lime in buckets and then diluted it with water. I remember seeing Grandmother selling some to a customer. It was quite a procedure.

The cover of the pit was raised and a board was laid across the opening. One person went down a few steps and filled the bucket with slaked lime, which was then pulled up on a rope by another person, standing on the board. Lilly and I were told never to go near the pit if the top was ever off, and never, never to touch it, or we would be terribly burned.

At the end of September the logs for the winter arrived. Only wood was burned in the tiled stoves, so plenty was needed. These logs were piled into a high wall outside one of the big outhouses. I climbed up on the logs, as they were laid down, higher and higher. Nobody seemed to notice me; only once all the logs had been loaded and reached right up to the roof, did I realise that I was not able to climb down again. The logs were piled flush with the house wall and I did not dare attempt to come down the way I had come up. The men had left before they realised my predicament, the woman servants did not want to climb up and Grandmother could not.

There was no ladder high enough to reach me. I had to wait until Uncle Herrmann, who was out hunting, came back. He fetched a long ladder from a neighbour and soon got me down. I had had to wait so long and had been so miserable, that Grandmother was sure I would not do it again. Lilly, of course, was most upset. Whenever I got into trouble she suffered with me in sympathy.

6

OUR RETURN TO the convent that year was to be for the last time, but not the last time ever. However, that lay in the future. Papa often brought us toys when he came to visit us and bought us new clothes. We knew that everything we had was bought by him. He even paid for everything the nuns gave us in the convent. And he always bought the best.

We often wondered, when the other girls went home for a weekend or for holidays, and said that they were going 'home', what such a home would be like, just being with a mother and father. Why could we not have a mother as well? So we started to pray to God that he should tell Papa to buy us a new Mama. God and Papa together could certainly do it.

Our prayers were answered. One Sunday, Papa came to us and asked: 'What would the two of you think if I brought you a new Mama?' (We were nearly seven and eight years old by then.) 'I know a very nice lady, who would like to be your new Mama.'

We became very excited: 'Yes, please, Papa, bring her next time.' Papa promised that he would.

There was great excitement in the school, even among the Sisters. Lilly and I walked about in a dream.

When the Sunday on which they were to visit arrived, we went onto the balcony immediately after church. Sister said that we would have quite a while to wait, but she opened the balcony door nevertheless so that we could look out and see the landau coming along the road. The other boarders also took a keen interest in our new visitor and joined us later. We felt immensely important. After all, not everybody could boast of a father who could buy a new Mama.

We were not to be disappointed. The lady who came with Papa was lovely. She was slightly smaller than Papa, very slim, her dark blonde hair piled high and swept up in front. She had a lovely smile and a soft, very kind voice. Lilly remembered that she wore a silk blouse with greenish dark-blue stripes, the feel of which she found unexpectedly soft, contrary to the starchy embraces of the nuns. I was never very observant — I only looked at her face. She seemed so kind and we fell in love with her right away.

When she told us that she lived with her married sister who had six children, we were really delighted. That meant we would not only have a new Mama, but also another aunt and uncle and six more cousins, who, best of all, would live in the same town as Papa, and not far away, in Graz. We wanted to know the names of every one of them.

After Papa and the new Mama had left, we had to tell everybody about our new relations — and we invented even more cousins with every beautiful name we could think of. We would also be invited to the wedding, which nobody in the convent had been able to do at the wedding of their mothers. From then on we prayed every evening: 'Dear God, please protect our dear Papa and our new Mama and please God, let the wedding be soon.'

The wedding took place on 8 May 1913 in the parish church in Jaegerndorf. It was an exceptionally cold morning for May, when at six o'clock in the morning we were warmly packed into fur footbags, which reached right up to the armpits, and set off from the convent in a landau for Jaegerndorf.

We arrived about three hours later at our new aunt's house, and were received in the hall by a lady in a red housegown. Before she could welcome us, Lilly burst out: 'We want to see our new Mama, who is a lady in a greenish dark-blue striped blouse.' The lady laughed and said: 'I am your new Mama and I shall soon get dressed as a bride and you will be my little bridesmaids and will see me again in church.' She gave us each a kiss and an embrace and Lilly realised that it was really her.

We were then introduced to our new cousins: one, Mimi, was almost as old as Mama; then came Otto and Hannic, still going to grammar school; then Christl, who was Lilly's age, and Liesel, who was two years younger and finally a little toddler, Fritzl. Then Fritzl's nanny helped us into our bridesmaids' dresses and off we went to church.

The wedding mass took place at eleven o'clock. I remember Mama wore a creamy lace gown with a long train which Christl, Liesel, Lilly and I carried. We felt immensely important as we walked slowly up to the altar.

Afterwards was the reception in a huge dining room at the house of our new aunt and uncle. There were so many people there; it seemed like one of the Bishop's visiting days in the convent. We sat at a little table with our two small cousins and Fritzl's nanny, who held him on her lap. Everybody had had a good look at us, as if we were something special. Long speeches were made and, best of all, there was delicious food to eat.

There was no wedding cake but, instead, a big castle built of ice cream, chocolate and sugar, which stood in front of the bride, and a pair of ice-cream slippers for her husband, our Papa. Husbands in that part of the world were often called jokingly, *Pantoffelhelden* (slipper heroes), and instead of being 'under the wife's thumb' they were said to be 'under the wife's slipper'.

The castle looked so beautiful that it seemed a pity to cut into it. When we got our portion it came as a big surprise. We had never eaten ice-cream before and this was very cold. We tried to warm it on the little gas stove which stood near our table, which was also something we had not seen before. The cousins all laughed at us and Nanny shook her head. The ice-cream melted and we drank it out of the dish, to the great amusement of those who sat near our table.

Towards the end of the meal we were called to the bride to say our congratulations. This time the Reverend Mother had composed a poem. Translated it ran something like this, as I have never forgotten it:

> With the sweet name of Mother do we call you today and our hearts will joyfully join with you in a bond of love. We offer you the true love of a child and ask for your mother-love and mother-kindness. We come to you and beg you to accept us as your children, that we may be your joy and you our joy.

We recited it line-by-line alternately, and finished together: 'Live long, oh dear Mother, take us to your heart, so that we never again will be left alone without a mother's love.'

Papa and my second Mama

Mama was beautiful in her creamy white dress and she seemed very moved, wiping a tear away when she embraced us both and calling us her 'dear children'. Everybody applauded but we could not understand why so many had tears in their eyes.

There were more tears and embraces when we left in the late afternoon. Well wrapped up and again put into the fur bags, we were then placed into a horse-driven sledge. Sister sat opposite us, wrapped in her cloak and with a blanket on her knees. Although it was May, it had snowed all afternoon and there was quite a thick layer of snow on the ground. It was a lovely journey back to the convent, the bells of the

55

horses tinkling, and the powdery snow thrown up by the horses' hooves.

We had such a lot to tell the nuns and the other boarders, yet we had to wait until the next day as we were both half-asleep on arrival. It had been a wonderful day, but rather tiring with so many new impressions and experiences. Even the happiest day finishes with tiredness and sleep.

Our new mother, Hedwig (Hedl) Sehors, came from a Jaegerndorfer family. Her parents had died, through some kind of epidemic, when she was twelve years old. Her eldest sister, our new Aunt Marie, had married the owner of the first steam-powered flour mill in Jaegerndorf, and he was our new Uncle Franz. They had taken Mama into their home and brought her up. She had money of her own from her parents, and her brother-in-law looked after it. There were also two brothers who were already grown up. One owned a bakery in Jaegerndorf and the other had a job in Germany.

Our new Mama was the first girl in Jaegerndorf to go to Vienna to a training college for nursery teachers; she then did a two-year *Haushaltungskurs*, a kind of domestic science course. She also had been trained in singing, played the piano very well, had taken painting lessons in the convent at Jaegerndorf and was what in those days was called 'a very accomplished lady'. She was five years younger than my father and had met him just as she had finished her courses in Vienna. They then found out that she was the lady who had rescued Lilly and I when we sat some four years ago, frozen and miserable on the steps on the cross outside the convent. She had taken painting lessons in the convent and so knew us by sight.

Papa and Mama went to Uj-Moldova for their honeymoon. They stayed in Budapest and then went by boat on the Danube, which in itself was a delightful journey, as we ourselves were to experience several years later. Papa showed her the historical places round his home, but on one of those trips they nearly lost their lives.

There was an island in the Danube, Ada Kaleh, dating back to the Turkish times. When most of the Turks withdrew, those living in Ada Kaleh stayed behind. It could only be reached by a small flat boat and, on the way back to the mainland, my parents' boat got caught between two passenger ships and the high waves nearly pushed it into a whirlpool, of which there were many in that part of the Danube.

The Danube has been regulated since the Second World War and Ada Kaleh has been completely submerged. Travelling is now much safer, although there are now other difficulties with customs and various permits needed to land in Romania. However, luckily for my parents on that trip long ago, nothing worse happened than that they got thoroughly wet. My parents did not know then that many years would pass before my father would see the Banat and his mother and sister again, and for Mama it was the only time. She would never come again. It is just as well we can't see into the future.

Lilly and I stayed in the convent at Gross-Herrlitz until the end of the summer term. We felt somehow sorry to leave the convent, especially to part from Maritschel; on the other hand we were looking forward to a new and exciting life, although we were understandably apprehensive about the unknown future.

Each nun gave us a small picture of a saint to put into our prayer book. We left most of our larger toys behind, such as dolls' prams and pushchairs, a doll's house and some big dolls.

Many years later, when I left with my little daughter for England, when she was just six years old, we had to leave nearly all her toys behind and the single little suitcase with a few boxed toys was stolen in the train at the Dutch frontier. There were no new ones waiting for her as there were for us. But that is another story.

Papa donated a holy water basin to the church. Then we said a tearful goodbye, never thinking that we would one day come back again as boarders.

Our new home was in a villa, a large flat on the ground floor with high rooms leading into each other. It had a big garden with two lawns, trees and shrubs. In one corner was a table with garden chairs and a sun umbrella. There were also several benches under the trees and, of course, flower beds. It was a lovely place to play 'hide and seek'. It was as big as the nuns' garden at the convent and was all for us! The owner of the house, an old lady who lived on the first floor, never came into the garden. She loved children and often invited us to her flat to play board games with her and to spoil us with delicious cakes.

There was also, however, a caretaker, a rather forbidding-looking, elderly woman, who lived in the basement. She disliked children and was always ready to criticise whatever we did. She had a dachshund with whom we would have loved to play, but he too disliked children and growled whenever one of us tried to stroke him.

At the back of the house, before reaching the big garden, there was a fair-sized yard, covered with smooth concrete, on which we could trace out the lines for a game of 'hop-scotch'. The caretaker could see us playing from her window and she never stopped shaking her head and scowling whenever she saw us playing that 'hopping game' as she called it. However, we were far too happy to mind.

For the first time in our lives we had a well-furnished room of our own. The beds were placed behind each other along one wall; there was no dividing board and we could speak to each other before going to sleep. This was for always, not just for holidays. It was bliss.

The first few weeks in our new home must have been rather trying for my parents, especially Mama, as Papa was mostly away during the week. We were so unsure of everything; we did not know what we were allowed to do and what not. However, quite soon we felt at home. Yet occasionally we behaved quite extraordinarily stupidly, unlike any children Mama had known before.

One Sunday, our parents took us for a 'Sunday walk', like all the parents in town; the children walked in front, the parents behind. I was busy telling Lilly a story, which I did not owe her this time, but gave voluntarily, when suddenly I felt Papa's hand on my shoulder and he hissed into my ear: 'Where on earth do you think you are going?'

He seemed to be out of breath. We looked round and there we saw Mama left far behind. We had been rushing forward, following some strangers; we were so used to walking in a crocodile, to have somebody in front of us, like a dark shadow, and not looking where they would lead us. Papa was extremely angry, but Mama calmed him down, when she finally caught up with us. Papa must have thought he had a pair of idiots as children.

The holidays passed far too quickly. It was the first time that we had not gone to Uj-Moldova, but our new life, the new surroundings, the new cousins, were so interesting that we did not mind. Everything was new and strange, because now it belonged to us, it was part of our life, and not just a holiday in Moldova which would invariably end after a few weeks. We had a home like all the other children we knew, and we would now have it for ever and ever.

School started again in the middle of September and we were sent to the convent school in Jaegerndorf, the same one where we had attended the kindergarten, years and years ago. Now we went to the primary department. We had quite a long way to go to school — about half-an-hour's walk. For the first few weeks our maid, Lydia, took us there and collected us again, then we went on our own.

It was on one of those homeward walks that I first realised that I had an unusual name. It was quite a normal name for Hungary, but rather strange for Austria. I had always been called Nushy, the abbreviation for Anushka, and nobody had ever found it funny before.

Our route led us through a park, past the boys' school. One day, Lilly was dawdling on the way and when she realised that I had walked on ahead, she came running after me, shouting as usual: 'Nushy, Nushy, wait for me!' A group of boys coming out of school took up the refrain and ran after me, calling, 'Nush, Nush, come here little pig, come here!' I was in tears by the time I reached home. Mama then explained to me that in Silesia little pigs were called in with 'Nush, Nush!' Now I was really heartbroken; I did not want to go to school ever again.

Then Mama suggested that, as we were now in Silesia and not Hungary, I should be called 'Nussy', which would sound quite refined and, indeed, would sound more like Tussy, the abbreviation for Tusnelda. Soon the name Nushy would be forgotten and no longer would rude boys call after me. However, although I was quite pleased with my new name, for years to come, in fact through all my life, I had to explain how I got that name.

On 2 November, 'All Souls' Day', we went with other schoolchildren to the cemetery after school, to light candles on the neglected graves. Some graves had a monument, sometimes an angel or a weeping woman leaning on a stone pillar; others had the photograph of the buried person. The monuments were all of grey, white or pinkish marble. The graves themselves were planted with flowers during spring and summer, but now at the beginning of winter, with snow already on the ground, there were pot plants instead.

Nearly all the graves had lighted candles in glass containers and people were still arriving to light the candles. We had our pockets full of candles and there were little tin pots on the neglected graves into which we could put the candles. The man who was responsible for the cemetery had those provided for this special day.

As we went out, we looked back. The graves, decorated with flowers and burning candles in glass bowls, the flickering flames of the candles on tin saucers, the carved monuments and the snow on the ground gave the place in the early dusk a hallowed atmosphere. We hurried back through the now dark streets, lit only by a few gas lamps, back to our warm room at home.

Then came 'Nikolo' or St Nicolas Eve. He came to our day school but not to our home. However, during the evening the front door mysteriously opened and then shut with a bang. When we rushed out to see what the noise was; there were nuts and apples on the floor, as if hastily thrown in. As we grew older, the nuts and apples would be replaced by a plateful of Christmas baking, which we found in our room when going to bed, but that was many years later.

Christmas Eve is the real Christmas on the continent. The Christchild brings the presents to each house. A week beforehand one room, even if it is only the parents' bedroom, was reserved for the angels, who needed to get the Christmas tree ready. We didn't dare peep inside because a dreadful tale had been told to us about a curious boy who peeped into the reserved room and saw his presents, only to find that they were all gone by Christmas Eve.

Sometimes we found 'silver hair' or 'angels hair', or even a Christmas tree decoration, and that was proof enough that some angels were doing their work. The house was filled with magic. Of course, we had to be especially good during these pre-Christmas days, because we never knew whether an angel was in the house or not, even if we had our doubts.

The morning of Christmas Eve was extremely busy. The Christmas loaf and nuts and raisins, as well as poppyseed and nut-strudel were being baked. Somebody had to go to the market to buy a carp for the traditional evening meal. The fish was bought alive, taken home in a water-filled bucket and then released into the bath. Lilly and I watched it happily swimming around, but we never thought about the inevitable end of it; that happened in the kitchen, which was out-of-bounds for us.

At lunchtime we had cocoa and our first taste of the Christmas loaf, or sometimes soup with noodles. The day was full of repressed excitement and anticipated pleasures.

In spite of our excitement, the table was laid and we had to have the traditional evening meal before the *Bescherung* (the giving and receiving of presents). We had wine soup with croutons, then carp fried in egg and breadcrumbs with potato salad, and afterwards the traditional *weihnachtsbaekerei*, and a kind of punch.

Towards the end of the meal, a little silvery bell tinkled, the double doors of the dining room opened as if by magic and there was the Christmas tree with lighted candles on every branch, reaching from floor to ceiling. The presents lay underneath it. We sang the carol, 'Silent Night', and everybody, Lydia included, joined in. Then Lilly and I played our party pieces on the grand piano.

We wished Papa, Mama and Lydia a Happy Christmas, and only

then could we at last open our presents: dolls and books and, I remember well, a box with all kinds of animals to fill up a zoo or Noah's ark. For Lydia there was a set of sheets and duvet covers for her dowry.

As a special treat we were allowed to go with Papa and Mama to midnight mass in a horse-drawn sledge. Lilly fell asleep on the way back, but I remember that starlit sky and a feeling of peace and, deep down in my heart, I wondered whether the Christchild had already gone back to Heaven or whether he was still somewhere in another part of the country.

The first family Christmas is so well remembered because it was the only one when we went with Mama and Papa to midnight mass, and feeling only happiness. The year after that, life would have changed very dramatically.

When we arrived home there were delicious smoked sausages, which Grandmother had sent. They were served hot in a terrine and I remember the rich juice into which we dipped our bread. Then there was a *banater stollen*, also sent by Grandmother. This is a gingerbread filled with dried peaches and pears and baked like bread in a bread oven or at the baker's.

On Christmas Day itself we had to go to nine o'clock mass, where the convent schoolchildren sang in the choir, while Papa and Mama went to high mass at eleven o'clock. Going home from church we passed the house of Mama's eldest brother and his wife. They had no children and always tried to spoil us with presents, which Papa did not like. Nobody should give presents to his children but he himself. It might also have been because we were not really Mama's children and therefore not the real nieces of our new uncle and aunt.

However, Aunt Bertha saw us as we passed the house and invited us in to receive our Christmas surprise. It was a large wooden box, full of various board games — chess, draughts, Nine Men's Morris, etc. She gave us lemonade and cakes and then we left for home. Papa was angry that we were so late and, worse still, that we had accepted the present. He declared that the box of games must be returned, but it never came to that.

On the second Christmas Day, St Stephen's Day, Uncle Franz died of a heart attack. How glad we were not to have hurt him by returning his present! At the funeral we got to know Mama's second brother, Uncle Max and his beautiful wife. They had come over from Germany. They had a little girl, Annemarie, about two years old. They stayed with us over New Year, much to our enjoyment. We played with Annemarie as with a live doll. It was really wonderful to have so many relations living so near.

On Sylvester, that is New Year's Eve, we were again allowed to stay up late. We melted some lead in an iron spoon. When we emptied this into cold water it reformed quickly, into various shapes. From these we were supposed to be able to tell what next year would bring. Mine looked mostly like spiders and Lilly's bits and pieces looked like bells and coins.

In later years we peeled apples and threw the peel, if it was still in one piece, over our shoulder. If the peel fell in the shape of a letter, that would be the first letter of a future husband's name. However, in 1913 we were not yet interested in husbands.

We ate all kinds of nuts and, as there was a little party with aunts and uncles and cousins, we played *Vielliebchen.* If one nut had two kernels, then they had to be shared with a partner. An unbroken walnut could also be used. Then the one who wished the partner a 'Good Morning, Vielliebchen' (most beloved) early the following morning, would receive a present.

I watched the clock and at the stroke of twelve I rushed to Aunt Hedl, with whom I had shared my nut and wished her a 'Good Morning, Vielliebchen'. I had won and could choose a present. I chose a book. Lilly got a box of chocolates as consolation prize, which she shared with me; I offered her my book to read, but she declined.

On New Year's Day we had suckling pig. It was roasted at the baker's and served with a lemon in his snout. I did not much like the look of it but it was supposed to be very lucky and our fortune would grow as quickly as piglets grow. We did not really believe in this, but it was the custom for New Year's Day.

Spring was soon with us. Lilly and I loved to watch the birds in our new garden and on our walks. I envied them their flying — if only I could fly — and Lilly agreed with me. We had never heard of an aeroplane and never seen one, of course. One night I had a dream. I was swinging between the two bed ends, higher and higher, and then I let go and flew right out of the window. It was a glorious feeling and I nearly cried with disappointment when I woke up to find that it was only a dream.

However, I thought that I now knew what to do to be able to fly. I had to tell Lilly the good news. We decided that she should try it first, because if I did fly first, I might fly away and not be able to tell her what to do. Lilly had to swing between the bed ends, as I had done in my dream and then, when she was high enough, I would say 'let go' and she could fly out of the window and I would follow her.

I quietly opened the window and showed Lilly how to hold on to the bed ends and then swing between them. Higher and higher she went. When her legs were almost horizontal I whispered: 'Now let go,' and she did, and fell so hard on the floor that she bit her tongue almost right through. Blood spurted out of her mouth and she screamed.

Papa and Mama rushed from the next room. There was Lilly, her mouth full of blood, and blood dripping onto the floor. She wanted to explain but as she pointed to me and could not speak properly, they thought that somehow I was to blame. They were horrified. What a dreadful child, who could treat her little sister so cruelly, and in the middle of the night.

I was too shocked myself to explain what had happened and was ordered to kneel in the corner while the doctor was called. He put some stitches into Lilly's tongue and then, at last, I was allowed to explain the whole story and was released from the corner.

When Aunt Marie, Mama's sister, heard about this episode she said that none of her children had ever thought out such stupid games; it must be because we were born in Budapest and were half Hungarian that we acted like that. There must be some traces of Attilla the Hun in us! But Mama laughed. 'They have just more imagination,' she said, and she was right.

Our first year at home was full of new impressions; new customs and new behaviour had to be learned. Even the saints' feasts and the seasonal celebrations were different from those at the convent.

On the Thursday before Easter (Maundy Thursday) we had spinach, the first green vegetable of spring, with *pofesen* (French-fried toast); and the day was thus called 'Green Thursday'. All morning, the bells rang in the town, until about noon, when they stopped, not to ring again until Saturday evening for the resurrection. We had been told in school that the bells would all go to Rome to be blessed by the Pope. We searched the sky for their return, knowing quite well that bells could not fly, but it was fun to tease the younger children, especially our little cousin Fritzl.

On Good Friday we went to the church of the Minorite monks to visit the tomb of Christ and say special prayers. This tomb was constructed like a cave, in a side chapel, and inside lay the body of Christ, wrapped in white sheets. The wrought-iron gates of the chapel were closed and two soldiers stood on guard each side of it. Austria was very much a Roman Catholic country and the Emperor a devout Catholic.

After the first feeling of awe and dutifully saying our prayers, we returned again and again to the chapel, though not, as I must confess, out of piety, but to join the other children from the convent school in trying to make the soldiers at least smile. We never succeeded.

In the parish church was a huge crucifix lying on the floor in the middle of the aisle in front of the altar. People came there, knelt down and kissed the stone body of Christ. Nowadays it would be regarded as very unhygienic, but we never caught any germs from that act of worship or devotion.

On Easter Sunday we rose before sunrise and walked with Mama and Papa up through a wood to the top of a hill at one side of the town. There were really two hills, on one of which stood a church which had a miracle-working picture of the Madonna. Pilgrims came there throughout the summer to be healed. The porch of the church was filled with crutches and arms and legs made of plaster, donated by people who had already been healed.

The other hill housed the ruins of a castle which had once belonged to the Robber Barons, hundreds of years ago. There was supposed to be an underground tunnel leading to the highway which was used by the Robber Barons, after they had seen the merchants on the highway, to rush to ambush them and snatch all their goods away.

We went up the first hill to the church, to see the sun rise. We were told that if we were pure and virtuous we would see the Easter Lamb jumping in the sun, when it rose. Nobody ever seemed to see it, but Lilly was sure that she had.

Then we went home via the other hill, through the ruined castle, and arrived home with an enormous appetite. Normally we just had croissants for breakfast, but on Easter Sunday we had ham, hard-boiled eggs, the plaited Easter bread full of raisins and nuts and, the highlight of the day, we were allowed to drink a small glass of egg flip.

On Easter Sunday we had kid for dinner because lamb was unobtainable; it was fried in convenient-sized portions in egg and breadcrumbs and with it we had the first salads of the year. All this was to express the new awakening of the earth and the new hope for mankind.

On Easter Monday we were sent into the garden to find our Easter eggs, which an obliging Easter hare was supposed to have laid, especially for us, coloured them and must have cooked them as well!

We did not question this, but thoroughly enjoyed finding the eggs. It was better to believe these fairytale happenings; even though we already had doubts in our hearts we did not want to admit it. When we could find no more eggs we counted those we had found and shared them between us.

Later on in the year, the feast of Corpus Christi was again different from that in the convent. There we had walked in a procession just round the church, whereas here there were altars erected all through the town with a carpet in front of each. After high mass all the schoolchildren, followed by the grown-ups, marched in the procession.

One priest held high the monstrance under a golden canopy carried by the other priests, and they were accompanied on both sides by young girls dressed in white. We all carried candles and sometimes, if it was a hot day, they bent in the sun. With everyone singing hymns, the procession wound its way through the streets. By each altar it stopped, and small cannons were fired by the soldiers. Lilly, predictably, was terrified by these shots and in the years to come she dreaded Corpus Christi because of these terrible noises. After hours of marching and singing at each altar in the town, we finally went home, tired, but feeling very holy.

Now we began to look forward to the summer holidays at Grandmother's in Uj-Moldova, especially as we had not been the year before. However, we did not get there, not until several years later.

65

7

ON 28 JUNE 1914 the heir to the throne, Erzherzog Franz Ferdinand and his morganatic wife, Sophy, were assassinated in Sarajevo. Four weeks later, Sunday 26 July, was my namesday. For a special treat we all went into the mountains. It was a glorious day and I remember vividly the rowan trees which lined the road on our way down the mountain. They were laden with red berries glowing in the sun. Whenever I see rowan trees even now, I think of that day.

There was great excitement in the train on our journey back. War had broken out; the guard had mentioned that mobilisation was imminent and Papa was anxious to get home. He thought he would catch the evening train to Budapest to rejoin his regiment, as the Hungarians were the first to mobilise in order to get to Serbia

As it happened, Papa was late for his regiment, although he had left that same night. The trains had been delayed and it was a long journey. However, it was lucky for him, because his regiment was one of the first to attack Belgrade and was completely wiped out.

We did not notice much of the war in the beginning, except that Mama often had red eyes from weeping. From the first day on, Mama decided that the three of us should say very special prayers for Papa every day, until he came home again for good. These were quite long: the full rosary and then a made-up prayer of our own, asking God to send his angels to protect our dear father wherever he went.

Usually we said these prayers some time in the afternoon, as we might be too tired before going to bed. However, they seemed to us so long that, when Mama went out, we would tell her on her return that we had already said them. She would praise us, but then we felt guilty and could not go to sleep. If something happened to Papa it would be our fault. So we knelt down in bed and said them quietly, with a few extra Hail Marys as penance for the lie we had told earlier in the day. Only then could we go to sleep. God must have heard us, because Papa did come home finally without ever having been wounded, although he had been on the front.

When Britain entered the war, the English teacher at the grammar school committed suicide. The whole town was at her funeral: nobody seemed to understand why she had been so frightened. Later, Britain came more and more to be regarded as the worst enemy, Serbia had been the reason for the war, France was a neighbour of Germany and there had always been trouble on the French frontier, but why did Britain come in?

We started to wear small badges with 'Gott strafe England' ('God punish England') printed on them. Even in the convent the pupils started to say this when entering the classroom, instead of saying 'Praised be Jesus Christ' and the nuns would answer with 'Gott strafe es' ('God punish it'), instead of the usual 'In all eternity, Amen'. It was years later, many years after that war, that Britain again became a country and a nation to be greatly admired by us.

On one occasion Lilly and I played at soldiers with some branches we had found in the garden. Lilly's branches had thorns and she hurt my ear so much that it bled profusely. I had to go to the doctor with Mama, and Lilly had to kneel on dried peas in the corner of the hall as a punishment.

Dried peas are very painful to kneel on. You could sit on your heels to relieve the pressure, but Lilly was determined that Mama should see the impressions the peas made on the soft flesh of her knees, and feel sorry. When I came back from the doctor's and it was clear that no real harm had been done, Mama did feel sorry for her, and played games with her all evening to make up for her punishment.

Aunt Bertha, the widow of Uncle Franz, now came quite often to visit Mama and she turned out to be a tell-tale. She had been left the bakery, the house they had lived in and a lot of money. Unfortunately, when she was a young girl, she had had an accident and had hurt her leg very badly; she refused, out of modesty, to let a doctor (male) see her leg. The wound had turned gangrenous and her leg had to be amputated. She was therefore unable to keep the bakery; she sold it and the large house, took a flat and became quite a recluse. Now she seemed to take a great interest in what we were doing, especially what Lilly was doing, and reported everything back to Mama.

Jaegerndorf was a smallish town with about sixty factories, all neatly hidden away, mostly cloth manufacturers. It lies between hills on the river Opa, which runs partly through the town and then around it. In those days it formed part of the border between Austria and Germany — Prussia to be more precise. We did not like the Prussians, though we did not know why this was so.

There was a current little joke about a policeman stopping a boy from fishing in that part of the river. 'But I only catch the Austrian fish,' explained the boy. 'How do you know which are the Austrian fish?' enquired the policeman. 'Because the Prussian fish can't be caught — they always have their mouths wide open,' replied the boy!

Where the Opa ran through the town it had high, built-up banks. In winter, when it was frosty, it was delightful to slide down those sloping banks, sitting on a school bag. Of course, there was a danger that you could slide straight into the river, whose surface was only slightly frozen, if you were not careful.

Although we were supposed to come straight home from school, Lilly had many friends who always tempted her to take different routes. One time they went sliding down the river bank. It was great fun, especially as they could show off to the people watching from the bridge. Some of the observers merely watched, but others shouted a warning, of which the children took no notice.

Lilly came home late one day, and was very surprised that Mama did not wait for some of her well-prepared excuses, but told her where she had been. She was extremely cross, mainly because she had been playing such a dangerous game. Lilly could not understand how Mama could possibly know, until she heard from Lydia, the maid, that Aunt Bertha had been to see Mama.

Another time, one of her friends had asked her to come to the mortuary in the cemetery. What she had been told had aroused her curiosity, but as soon as they opened the door they got a terrific shock, especially Lilly, with her nervous disposition. On the bier lay a crippled figure with an enormous head, staring open eyes and a toothless open mouth. She ran outside in panic, fell down (she was always falling down), and became almost hysterical. Her friend took her to her home and her mother calmed Lilly down. Then she gave them both a piece of bread with a lovely sausage on it, which was a real treat in those days. Later Lilly found out that it was horsemeat, but it had tasted very good.

By the time she got home, Mama again knew that she had been to the mortuary. Again Aunt Bertha had seen her, as she was visiting her husband's grave. Lilly was made to stand in the corner of the dining-room, but she started to scream and scream until everybody in the house came to ask what was the matter, what was that stepmother doing to the poor child. So Lilly was released again, but had to promise that from now on she would always come straight home.

However, she did not keep that promise. On her next adventure her friends took her to a house where, behind bars, the Russian prisoners were kept. They seemed quite happy, called to them in a funny language and made faces to make them laugh. They put their hands and arms through the bars and lifted them up and then let them slowly down again. The children thought it was a lovely game.

Unfortunately, Aunt Bertha, who used to wander round all day just to watch what Lilly was doing, saw her yet again and reported to Mama. She said that she was too ashamed to make herself known to Lilly and the others; she could not believe that a niece of hers would join in such a vulgar game — and with the enemies as well.

Lilly insisted that the so-called enemies had been very nice indeed. Mama was cross and kept on saying: 'I wish Papa were here, I don't know what to do with you.' Lilly only said, cheekily, 'Kiss and be good again.' Lilly knew how to use her charm.

I seemed to be luckier in avoiding trouble. I had in fact been to the mortuary twice, but what I saw was a body in a white gown, lying there so peaceful and smiling, as if he knew something nice but did not want to tell it. Both times it had been the same.

However, I could not quite escape being reported to Mama by Aunt Bertha. We had started to knit for the soldiers: wrist-warmers. I could do it on four needles, and was so keen once I had mastered that art that I knitted on my way to school and on the way home again. I always took a short-cut through the parish church, going in through the east door, kneeling down in the middle of the aisle and crossing myself before the High Altar and then walking out through the west door.

When knitting on the way to school, I kept the ball of wool in my pocket. Sometimes it would fall out and roll behind me, to the annoyance of other people. However, when I explained that it was for the soldiers, somebody always picked the ball of wool up and put it back into my pockets, saying what a good girl I was.

It so happened that the wool fell out of my pocket when I walked through the church and rolled under the pews and I had to go down on all fours to retrieve it. I was so busy knitting and then looking for the ball of wool, that I forgot to kneel down and cross myself before the High Altar, and who should see me? Aunt Bertha, of course.

I wasn't so lucky in making friends as Lilly, even if they did tempt her into trouble. I once made friends with a girl whose parents had come from Germany. She was a Protestant, but I did not know that. I took that girl through the church one day and told her to kneel and cross herself. That was to be the end of the friendship. The next day she told me that her mother had forbidden her to be friends with me because I was a Roman Catholic and taking her through the church had proved I wanted to make her a Catholic. We were both very sorry, and still smiled at each other but daren't go home together. In those days children mostly obeyed their parents, especially if they could so easily be found out.

There was another girl I admired very much. She was both beautiful and clever. However, she told me that she was Jewish, and her father would not let her play with me because I did not go to the synagogue. I was quite willing to go there with her, but she was horrified.

'Oh no, strangers are allowed in.' I was very puzzled. Of course, she did not come to our church, but she could have come if she had wished and, anyhow, I was no stranger to her. Yet her father, although a Jew, sent his girl to a convent school. I certainly was unlucky in choosing my friends.

In the spring of 1915 I became ill. Tuberculosis was diagnosed. The doctor said that I needed milk and good food, both of which were getting scarce. It was a hard blow to Papa as my mother had died of TB. I did not know what my illness was, I just felt very, very tired, had a dry cough and very often a slight temperature.

It was decided that we should all go to the country where milk and butter could still be obtained, and some meat above the rations. We were taken from school early in May and Lilly was especially delighted. I didn't care. Mama rented rooms on a farm, in Erbersdorf, a small village, also in Silesia. It was surrounded by pine forests and the farm was at the edge of the forest.

Our rooms were in a small house, next to the main farmhouse. It had been built for the retirement of the farmer, but was meantime occupied by his daughter, whose husband, a cobbler, was in the war; she let rooms and cooked delicious meals. Her name was Frau Brotkorb, which we found very funny, as it meant literally 'breadbasket'.

She had a son, Rudi, who was Lilly's age, but was not much good as a playmate. He thought we were snobs and stupid as well, because we did not understand a lot of his expressions. When we tried to play hop-scotch, he used a word for jumping backwards which was new to us. When I repeated it in front of Mama I was in trouble. She told me never, never to use such an expression and when I told Rudi, he said something much worse, but which I had heard before, then turned his back on us and stalked off.

Across the road from the farm was the forest. There, into a small clearing, I was taken every morning, placed in a deckchair, and wrapped in blankets when it was cool. I had to stay there until evening, only going back to the house for the main meals.

Starting at six o'clock in the morning, I had to drink a mug of goat's milk every four hours. I hated that milk and if I thought nobody was coming, I would pour it over the roots of the little tree next to my chair. Lilly saw me doing this once. She promised not to tell anybody, but implored me to drink the hateful stuff, because she wanted to see me well again.

The little farm cat came regularly to lie on a sunny spot nearby and I tried to make friends with her, but unsuccessfully. She jumped on my chair but as soon as I touched her she was off again. Once I got hold of her and tried to hold her down by force, telling her how much I would love her, but the little beast scratched my arms and hands.

Lilly missed my company but soon found other occupations. She watched Mrs Brotkorb making butter, milking the cows, and baking bread in the big farm kitchen. They still made it with real flour there, whereas in the town we only had bread made with maize flour, which made it very crumbly. Lilly always brought me a slice of the fresh bread with real butter on it and it reminded me of Grandmother.

She went with Mrs Brotkorb to the woods and watched the woodcutters who, after having cut down several trees, peeled the bark off and made the naked wood look like ivory. There were ant-hills to watch too, especially after giving them just a tiny poke with a finger. Lilly wished she could have taken an ant-hill to me, because it was so interesting, she said, but that was impossible. I was incredibly bored in my deckchair, although I did get out of it whenever I felt sure nobody

71

would come. But that was always only for a short while, and there were no ant-hills round my chair.

Some days, Lilly went with some other children to swim, or rather paddle, in a very shallow river. There was a weir there, and you could sit right under it, hidden by a water curtain. They would throw little stones across the water to see who could make them jump the most; often it was the boys who could do it best.

How I envied them their freedom. Meantime I was still in my deckchair. But one day Mama went to Jaegerndorf and was away for the whole afternoon. As soon as Mama had left, I got out of my chair, borrowed Lilly's hoop and ran with it through the village. Never had freedom tasted so good. Lilly called after me but I was deaf to her pleadings. Never mind what would happen in the evening when Mama came home, I would meantime savour my freedom to the full!

I ran about all afternoon, sat under the weir (you really could sit there without getting wet) and only went back to the deckchair when it was time for the evening meal. Mrs Brotkorb hadn't seen me, and called me in for the evening meal as usual. Lilly expected me to die any moment, but nothing of the sort happened.

Mama never found out and it seemed that from that day on I really got better. I certainly felt more lively. By the time the school holidays were over and we moved back to town at the beginning of September, the doctor declared me cured.

Actually, I had never quite known what was the matter with me, but when we were in Jaegerndorf again and I was walking with Mama we met our old house-doctor. He was very old and had treated Mama when she was a child and the young doctors had all been away at war. I heard the doctor say to Mama with a look at me: 'She has recovered well. I never thought I would see her like this again.' Only years later did I learn that it had been TB.

Everybody said that my recovery was due to the rest in the pine woods and the goat's milk. I knew better: it was that lovely afternoon of freedom and running about with the hoop which had cured me.

Before long Papa came home on leave for a few days, bringing with him beans and dried prunes from Serbia. We ate the prunes like sweets and always carried some in our pockets. I have forgotten what we did during his leave but I clearly remember the sadness I felt when he went away again.

School had started by now and we spent many afternoons with the teacher, a novice, in the woods, collecting blackberries, blackberry leaves and strawberry leaves to be used as tea. Russian tea was now almost unobtainable; children didn't drink real coffee, it was also too expensive, and the barley coffee which we drank also seemed to have disappeared, as barley was used instead of rice or flour.

On one of these expeditions I found a hedgehog, and took it home in the little rucksack we carried for the leaf collecting. I had always longed for a pet of my own. I knew Mama would not welcome the hedgehog, so I did not tell her. I put it (or him or her) in the wardrobe and left the door very slightly ajar. I fed it with milk and bits from my plate, which I hid in my fist before leaving the table. We always had a cup of milk before going to bed and that was now for the hedgehog.

As soon as we went to bed I let it out to run around. Hedgehogs' feet make a funny sound on a parquet floor and suddenly Mama, whose bedroom was next door, came in to find out the reason for such a funny noise. Inevitably the hedgehog was despatched into the garden and, to our great amazement, the wardrobe, the rugs and all our clothes were fumigated because, as Mama said, hedgehogs were full of fleas. We hadn't seen any, so how did she know? However, I had to promise her never to bring a hedgehog into the house again.

I didn't bring a hedgehog, but I found a snake instead. Luckily it was a harmless grass-snake; I carried it home in a rucksack and again I put it into the wardrobe, this time on a shelf with my underwear. I did not let it out at night, but put it on the bottom of the wardrobe, where I put a dish of milk. I felt so happy with my new pet. It was warm and when I could hold it, it would wind itself round my arm.

My happiness did not last for long. Lydia was putting some clean underwear into the wardrobe, when she nearly had a heart attack as the snake suddenly slithered out. She screamed as if it were a cobra — and yet another of my pets had to leave.

Winter returned, and we began to knit again for the soldiers. This time it was socks, mittens, ear-warmers, breast- and stomach-warmers. We knitted and knitted, yet after the war we learned that none of the returning soldiers had ever worn any of our knitting. My father and uncle laughed. 'Newspaper or brown paper is much more effective than socks, and who would have darned them, anyhow?' they said. 'And as for all those special warmers, we were too busy keeping alive to bother with them.'

Now every time we went to the woods we collected small branches of wood, as wood and coal were getting scarce. Food was scarce, too, and very expensive. So-called 'war kitchens' were opened for the poor people. We had to go to school without the usual sandwiches for our breaktime.

One girl, who sat next to me at school, always had sandwiches with slices of horsemeat sausage. Her family got their bread from the black market, which we couldn't do, as Mama explained, because Aunt Marie and Uncle Franz had a flour mill and they might get into trouble if it was known that we had extra bread. Their flour went straight to the army. The authorities were very strict, watching out for black market dealers and there was a government supervisor in the mill. As for horsemeat, Mama refused to buy it!

However, we did go to the country, as everybody else did, to do what was called the *hamstern*, where bed linen or table linen was exchanged for eggs, butter and milk. The farmers always wanted linen for their daughters' dowries, as that had also become very rare.

One day, a life-size wooden figure of a soldier was erected in the square at Jaegerndorf and everybody was urged to buy a nail, preferably paying for it in gold, and then drive it into the wooden soldier. Finally, the whole figure was covered with nails and a plaque underneath stated: 'Gold I gave for Iron'. There were posters all over the town asking for war loans. Unfortunately, Aunt Bertha was advised by her trustees to invest all her money in these war loans. At the end of the war she was left destitute and had to rely on help from all her relatives.

More and more announcements appeared on the church door listing soldiers fallen in the war. Many went missing, amongst them our Uncle Herrmann. Then we heard that he was a prisoner-of-war with the Russians and the last news we had was that he was in hospital with a leg wound. None of this news was reliable, however, because it was not official. Nothing was then ever heard of him again.

In November of that year Mama became very ill, with pneumonia and pleurisy. She did not seem to recover totally and remained extremely weak and listless.

Christmas was somewhat sad. We stayed at Aunt Marie's house with many other aunts and cousins, but all the men were away in the war. Only Otto, our cousin, was still at home, because he was only sixteen. Somebody played the piano most of the time, and two or three people would join in a singsong, but there was no real Christmas spirit. Again and again the talk turned back to the war and how much longer it would last.

After Christmas, as Mama still did not seem to be getting better, the

Uncle Herrmann, who hunted bears

doctor suggested that she should go to a sanatorium in the mountains, where the food would probably be better and where she would have plenty of fresh air and rest. Unfortunately, with regard to the food, it was a great disappointment. Dried herrings were the staple diet and Mama didn't even like them when they were fresh.

Whilst Mama was away, Lydia was to look after us and report regularly at the end of each week to Aunt Marie, to give an account of her expenses. Aunt Marie was to write out the menu for our meals for a whole week in advance.

Lydia had a boyfriend in a gendarme uniform, who frequently came to our flat. Perhaps one day she had been too busy looking after him, because somehow the rubber hose leading to the gas stove got burned. She was terribly upset and moaned about the expense of replacing it.

As we were fond of Lydia, we agreed that she should pay for it out of the household money, and we would not tell Aunt Marie. She could give us semolina pudding every day of the week, instead of meat and vegetables, which were on the menu. The money thus saved would certainly pay for the hose.

Sometime later, Lilly came home from school when Lydia was scrubbing the kitchen floor on her hands and knees. Her posture was so inviting that Lilly took a flying leap onto her back and asked her to ride with her round the kitchen. Lydia was naturally shocked and angry and ordered her in no uncertain terms to get off her back.

Lilly refused and Lydia grabbed her umbrella, which stood in the corner of the kitchen and tried to hit Lilly with it. It broke. Lydia was now really upset. She said that it was her best umbrella, and a very special one — until again we both begged her to buy a new one and pay for it from our meat money. Semolina was once more on the menu for the week. This was bigger punishment for me than for Lilly. I begged her not to cause any more expenses for Lydia, because I did miss my meat portions, even if they were very small.

I also got into trouble, not with Lydia, but at school. One day, in the embroidery lesson, Sister's scissors could not be found. Several children, and I amongst them, had often been told by Sister that she always had her tools to hand, never mislaid them, and if it should happen, she would always find them quickly enough, and we should endeavour to do the same. That attitude had annoyed me. Now her scissors were missing. The whole classroom was nearly turned upside down; still no scissors.

Then I went quietly to the tiled stove in the corner of the room, opened the little ash door and took out the missing scissors, I admitted that I had put them there, just to prove that even Sister did not always find everything. I cannot now understand how I had the cheek to do such a thing, and admit it calmly. Of course, Aunt Marie was informed of my dastardly behaviour. I had to appear before her and she muttered something about our early upbringing and again mentioned our being born in Budapest. 'I don't envy my poor sister, your Mama, and your dear Papa,' she finished her tirade.

Then it was Lilly's turn, yet again, to get into more trouble. One day in school she was sent out into the corridor for some misdemeanour. It was cold and she amused herself by jumping in and out of an opening in the wall. When the bell rang for playtime, the teacher did not see her and, after playtime, had probably forgotten all about her.

I was sent with a message to another teacher and saw Lilly, rather cold and miserable. I told her if the teacher had forgotten her, then she should certainly not stand any longer in the draughty corridor, but go straight home. I opened the entrance door for her and she slipped out, without being noticed.

Unfortunately, when Lilly arrived home, Lydia was out; so she rang the bell at the flat belonging to the lady who owned the house. She welcomed Lilly and, not realising that Lilly had run home from school without permission, asked her to stay with her until Lydia came back. They played cards together and Lilly was enjoying herself so much that when Frau Richter asked her to see if Lydia had returned, Lilly said that Lydia would not be back until later and would know where to find her.

Only when it became dark did Frau Richter insist that Lilly should go down and see if Lydia was back. Meantime they had missed her at school. I had been sent home to confirm that she actually had gone home. When Lydia, who had been back for a while, and I discovered that Lilly had not returned there, and still did not come when school was finished, we both became worried. Lydia first telephoned some of Lilly's friends and then informed Aunt Marie, who in turn informed the police.

It was only then that Lilly, quite happily, rang the door bell of our flat and was confronted by Aunt Marie and a policeman. Poor Lilly, she finished the evening kneeling in a corner on dry peas, and with no Mama there to feel sorry for her afterwards!

Back at school, her friends thought her a heroine. Never had anyone run home before, after being sent out to stand in the corridor. Of course, she did not tell anybody that I had told her to do so. We always stuck together, she and I.

Lilly's visit to Frau Richter reminds me of our first and subsequent visits to her flat. Her cook used to bake lovely little cakes, and Frau Richter would offer a plateful to us. Lilly took one after another until there were none left. I thought she was terribly greedy, felt ashamed for her, and complained to Mama.

Lilly excused herself by pointing out that Frau Richter had offered them to her again and again. Mama, in turn, pointed out that this was done out of politeness, and nobody expected that a visitor should eat them all up. So, the next time that she offered the plate of little cakes, Lilly asked: 'Do you really mean it, or are you only asking me out of politeness?' I kicked Lilly under the table. Frau Richter laughed, but before she could answer, to my horror, Lilly continued: 'Nussy has just kicked me under the table, she does not want me to ask you, but you will tell me the truth, won't you?' I could have died with embarrassment but, of course, I denied having kicked her. When Frau Richter had recovered from laughing, she assured Lilly that she really did mean it, and Lilly finished all the cakes.

I looked at her as if I could kill her, which is what I did feel like doing and, to make matters worse, she told Frau Richter that Mama and I had said that nobody was expected to take more than a few cakes. All the while she was munching away and did not even leave one for me!

That evening Mama told Lilly that if she did not mind her manners and did what she was told when being a visitor, she would no longer be allowed to visit Frau Richter. That cured her. A few cakes were better than none!

We children were now taking a great interest in the progress of the war, mainly for selfish reasons. We were sent home from school whenever there was a victory. We would be told about it in the morning. We were also told how many prisoners had been taken. I remember well when, for example, Lemberg fell; we raced home through the streets, shouting 'Lemberg' or whatever had 'fallen' and 'ten thousand' or whatever number 'prisoners taken'. By the time we reached home, the numbers of prisoners had increased hundredfolds. Nobody minded our shouting in the streets; in fact people stopped what they were doing or looked out of the windows and rejoiced with us. The rest of the day was a holiday. Unfortunately, as time went on, the victories and the holidays became fewer and fewer.

Then the refugees arrived — hundreds of them. We got twelve girls in our class, to start with. They looked like tramps or gypsies when they arrived, although we soon found out that some came from very wealthy families, but had lost everything they possessed. One thing that they had acquired, however, in abundance, was lice — lots of lice — and sooner or later we all had lice.

Lydia combed our hair regularly with a fine toothcomb, but one day she found lice on my head. Aunt Marie told her to rub my hair and scalp thoroughly with paraffin, then bind a towel round my head and leave it overnight. This Lydia duly did. I moaned and cried all night that it hurt, but Lydia was adamant. 'It is the lice that bite you before they die,' she said, 'and the towel must not be taken off.'

When at last morning came and the towel was removed, the sight was incredible. The skin on my scalp nearly came off and great yellow blisters were on my neck, where the paraffin had dribbled down. I was terribly burned. The lice were dead but the doctor had to be called.

I had to stay at home with a bandaged head. When it had healed and I finally returned to school, I got into trouble because I spent my time rubbing the dead skin off my scalp onto the desk, to the gruesome interest of those sitting behind, next to and in front of me. Of course, it was more interesting to watch me covering my desk with bits of dead skin, than to listen to the teacher, who became very annoyed indeed with me and lectured the class about disgusting behaviour. I found her reaction very unfair: I had suffered so much pain that I might as well get some amusement out of it.

8

AT LAST MAMA came back from the sanatorium. She was still very thin but apparently well. We were delighted to have her home and made good resolutions not to give her any trouble.

Not long afterwards Papa arrived home on leave and announced that we would all go with him to Szabac in Serbia. It had been taken by the Hungarian army a while back and was now occupied by the Austro-Hungarian troops. Some of the officers had obtained permission to bring their families as there was still plenty of food there. Papa, being a quartermaster, was also given permission.

At last everything was arranged, we were given leave from school and we were 'off to the war', as we called it.

The journey took three-and-a-half days and three nights. We took a train which, although mainly transporting soldiers, was allowed to carry civilians as well, but only those who travelled with soldiers. There were only third-class compartments, with hard benches, and many freight wagons, all overcrowded. Nobody got out on the first day, but we had to wait at various stations for those returning from leave to climb aboard, although there was barely standing room left.

We watched their relatives crowding in front of the windows taking leave of their menfolk. I remember there was a lot of crying and weeping and much shouting of good wishes and prayers, and a lot of noise and smoke from the engine.

In Szabac in occupied Serbia during the summer of 1917

We tried to read the names of the stations as we passed through each one, so as to write them into a notebook to show in school later on, but when darkness fell there was very little light at the stations and only a tiny lamp for the whole carriage.

When we travelled through Hungary there was no light at all at night, except from the stars in the sky. There was a full moon later on in the

81

journey and we could look over the Puszta, the Plain of Hungary, as far as the horizon. We spotted some of those typical Hungarian *ziehbrunnen*, like ghostly shadows, stretching one arm high up towards Heaven. They consisted of a high pole with a cross bar on top; on one side was fixed a bucket, on the other side a stone. It worked like a see-saw, when one side goes up the other side comes down. A chain was attached to the bucket, which was let down into a primitive well, with the weight of the stone on the other end drawing it up again once it was full. In the moonlight they looked to us like a see-saw for giants, and full of mystery.

Some old peasants sat on the floor around us, smoking pipes, spitting and coughing; they looked terribly dirty during the day, but in the moonlight they resembled Tyrolean woodcarvings of old men. The nauseating smell of cheap tobacco, garlic, cheese and sweat permeated the air, yet when one of the woman offered us a piece of white Hungarian bread we were delighted and Mama allowed us to eat it.

Lilly and I were tired and sleepy. Papa was standing next to Mama, so that we could have a bit more room. Lilly put her head on Mama's shoulder and tried to sleep, but she was restless. I could not sleep, in spite of being so tired, so I watched the monotonous landscape through the window. 'We are going where the war is or has been,' I thought. 'What will it be like?' I had heard people say that war is always painful and dreadful.

Suddenly I felt a burning sensation on my arm. I did not utter a sound. 'I must be brave,' I thought. Then I heard Papa's voice: 'I am so sorry. Why didn't you tell me, you silly girl, that I was burning you.' He had inadvertently rested his cigarette for a few seconds on my arm as he had tried to make Lilly more comfortable. When I told him that I thought it was part of the war, he sighed. He hadn't realised that even his elder daughter could be so remarkably stupid.

The train travelled on and on, stopping and moving again, sometimes slowly, sometimes fast, and we thought we would never be able to get out of it. From time to time Mama gave us maize bread with honey-butter and, of course, we chewed prunes. Now and then we drank some water from Papa's field-bottle.

At last the train reached the last station on the wrong side of the River Save. We had to cross a broad stretch of the river in a small rowing-boat, without any light, and we were told that we must keep very quiet. We found it deliciously romantic and dangerous, which it probably was not.

That river crossing made a great impression on me. The starry sky, the moonlight and the glittering river, with the monotonous sound of the oars dipping into the water still live in my mind to this day. Once on the other side we were at last in Szabac in Serbia — in enemy territory. I don't know where we slept for the rest of the night; we were too tired to take any notice of our surroundings.

The following morning, Papa took us to the rooms he had rented for us. The lady of the house welcomed us with a traditional, very sweet, confiture; we were given a spoonful of this and a glass of water — the traditional welcome gesture. To me that seemed extremely agreeable of her, especially as we were more or less her previous enemies.

We were given two very large rooms in a house which had not been damaged during the recent siege. The living-room was probably meant to be the summer room, because the floor was made of stone and there were no windows to the south, only a large door, left open all day and leading into a small garden. That was also the main entrance for us. There were two more doors on each side, one leading into a large bedroom and the other, opposite, into the private quarters of the lady who rented us the rooms. Both those doors were of glass but had curtains.

The single large bedroom was to accommodate all of us. Lilly and I had our beds along one wall and my parents' bed was against the other wall. Two chests of drawers, a wardrobe and a wash-stand with a bowl and jug stood in the middle of the room, thereby dividing it into two. This room also was cool on hot summer days and had a large window facing the east.

Papa was allowed to sleep at home with his family and also took his meals mostly with us. This was probably also for security reasons, for us that is. After all, we were living in enemy country — and there was a guard at the main entrance, which constantly reminded us of this.

Each mealtime we obtained our food from the Officers' Mess. Sometimes a soldier would bring the meal in mess tins in a carrier, and later Lilly and I were allowed to go to collect it. The Officers' Mess was not far away from where we stayed and we enjoyed the walk. We were allowed to go barefoot, because it was so hot and we had only wooden scandals which were painful to walk in. Leather shoes had long ago disappeared. The road was dusty and we loved to wriggle our toes in the hot dust.

There was a large prison camp nearby, which we had to pass. We felt sorry for the men being so far away from home. They looked bored and sometimes we risked a small, friendly wave, but made sure nobody saw it. However, these prisoners were not so lonely as those we had seen before in Jaegerndorf, as groups of Serbian girls often stood by the fence surrounding the camp and there was then a lot of laughter.

We watched the workmen on the road, having their midday rest and eating polenta, a stiff porridge made of maize flour. With this they ate onions, and tomatoes as big as a fist, and sometimes garlic bulbs as if they were nuts.

There was no supply of drinking water in the house and we had to fetch it from the pump in the main square. There were many wells in the town, but most of them had been damaged or polluted during the fighting, so everybody was advised to use water only from this pump. At the back of the house was a *ziehbrunnen*, like those we had seen on the Hungarian Plain, but the water was only fit for washing.

Lilly and I took turns to fetch water in a big china jug. It was an enjoyable task. The main square was a meeting place for old and young in the late afternoon. Unfortunately, the ground round the pump itself was paved, and you had to put the jug down on the ground in order to leave both hands free for pumping, moving the big *schwengel* or pump handle up and down. I don't know how it happened but we broke many jugs between us. The first belonged to our landlady and, of course, once it was broken she insisted that it had been one of her most treasured possessions and Papa had to pay a lot for it. It was worse when we went together for water, because, although one of us then held the jug, we talked and laughed and giggled and . . . crash! There was another jug broken.

There was a park nearby, where the rainwater was collected into huge containers which stood near the entrance gates. Lilly and I had never seen such huge spiders as those which stalked over the surface of the water. We spent many hours in that park, collecting the small coloured stones which abounded there. Similar stones could be found on the banks of the Save. The river was extremely wide here with flat banks, and to us it seemed like the sea, which of course we had never seen. When we eventually came to leave Szabac we wanted to take a whole drawerful of these lovely stones home with us and were heartbroken when Papa categorically declared that he was not carrying stones in the already heavy luggage. However, we managed to drop quite a few of them in, at night when the suitcases were already packed, and slipped them between our clothes. That, however, was some time later.

The house we lived in had only four windows towards the street, but it stretched far into the cobbled yard. All along the walls were flower beds, mostly with those bright red flowers which the young local girls wore behind their ears. At the back of the yard was the *ziehbrunnen*.

We often played there using the *ziehbrunnen* as a see-saw, but we had to be careful not to be seen as it was regarded as a dangerous game. I could confirm that; it was not so much dangerous, as painful. The landlady had a son about our age, Miksha, who often played with us. One day Lilly and he had pulled the bucket down into the well, to haul me up on the other side. As soon as I was high up in the air, somebody came. Lilly and Miksha let go of the bucket and I came down with the stone, landing right on top of a bed of nettles. As I was only wearing a tee-shirt and little shorts, it was a rather stinging experience!

Further to the back of the cobbled yard stretched a huge neglected garden, which had a summer house with a broken window; a bench was inside with lots of cushions, an ideal place for many happy hours 'playing house'.

The whole complex was surrounded by a high wall, which was damaged on one side. Through that opening we could get out. There was a long winding road along which we walked one afternoon. On one side were planted sunflowers, as far as the eye could see, and on the other side were poppies, also apparently planted, as they were growing in even rows. The sunflowers grew tall, with big heads, and we noticed that nearly all had their flowering faces turned towards the sun. The poppies were comparatively small, but they made such a vast expanse of brilliant red colour they were something to remember always.

When we returned home we told Mama and Papa about the sunflowers. Papa said that they always turned their faces to the sun and we could see in the evening that their faces would be turned to the east ready to welcome the sun the following day. They took us out later in the evening — and it was true! However, there were a few whose faces were not turned. 'Those are the blind ones,' said Papa. After that we often went for an evening walk to visit the 'blind sunflowers', as we called them.

Papa also told us that when he was a boy they believed that if one day the sunflowers forgot to turn their heads to the east, the sun would not rise and the world would be in darkness. There were lots of sunflowers near Uj-Moldova also, but not such huge fields of them like in Szabac. Many people here, especially the young men, would eat sunflower seeds; that I found rather disgusting, because they went about spitting out the skins onto the ground.

One day we visited the Greek Orthodox church. The beautiful cupula had been badly damaged during the fighting and was just a yawning opening. Broken fragments of it were still lying on the floor, which was covered with a colourful mosaic. There were neither pews, benches nor chairs in the church. Most of the painted-glass windows were also damaged, as were some beautiful ikons, though they were still hanging on the walls. In spite of all that destruction several women were to be seen, dressed all in black, kneeling on the stones. It wasn't a bit like a church to me, and yet I could sense an awesome atmosphere, which remained imprinted in my memory.

Nearly every week in Szabac a market was held not far from our house, in the main square. We marvelled at the large tomatoes on sale, which were almost the size of a baby's head. There were many carts coming into town on market day, drawn by oxen in their wooden headstalls. Sometimes, too, there was a pig market. The pigs here were different from the ones we knew. They had long, narrow backs and were black with wispy hair on their curly tails. They also had longer legs than our pigs in Silesia or those at Grandmother's.

What impressed us most was that whenever Mama bought something, or even when we stopped in the market just to look around, we were served with minute cups of coffee, of which there still seemed to be plenty about. That coffee was thick and very sweet. We used to drink Mocca at home, at least our parents had it after a meal, in small cups, but that was nothing like the coffee served here.

Once, at full moon, Papa gave us a treat. We walked to a ruin in a small wood about two miles away. We sat there on a broken wall and Papa told us to listen and be quiet. A bird was singing. We knew a blackbird's song and that of the lark, but this one was very different. 'It is a nightingale,' said Papa, and as we listened we felt very privileged.

As Papa spoke fluent Serbian, he had no difficulty in communicating with the lady of the house, whose rooms had, after all, been taken by one of the armed forces. This helped to maintain a friendly relationship throughout our stay. She was always friendly towards us children and helped us to learn Serbian. We, in return, taught Miksha some German. We would point at something and say the name in German, then he would say it in Serbian. We learned quite a lot in that way. But we did not really need to do that. Children understand each other much more quickly than grown-ups, whatever the language. It must be some kind of intuition, or a combination of imitation and guesswork, just as a baby learns to talk. We seemed to talk a lot with Miksha, and certainly got plenty of information from him.

Once he took us secretly to a film show in a private house where military films were shown. They were Serbian ones, of course, films about the occupying army and about punishments for civilians, which were all rather gruesome. I remember seeing there a film with some men shown hanging by their arms on cross-like structures. It was horrible, and that was 'war'.

We understood without being told that nobody must know about that little excursion. Miksha trusted us and we got on well together, although occasionally we had a good fight, but we quickly made it up again. A smile and a handshake and no words were needed.

9

WE HAD BEEN in Szabac all spring and summer, and in the middle of September we returned to Jaegerndorf as school was starting. Again we crossed the Save by night and caught a troop transport train. However, this train broke down and a local train came for us and took us only as far as Arad, about half way. We had to wait there several hours for the next long-distance train.

Papa had come with us and we all went to a hotel so that we could make up for our lost sleep. Only Lilly and I could sleep in the beds; Mama and Papa sat on chairs. They told us afterwards that nothing would have made them use the beds as bedbugs were crawling all over the place. They obviously did not like us because we slept soundly and, what is more, neither of us was bitten. We saw some crawling on the wall and thought them rather small and uninteresting for our parents to make such a fuss about. We had heard about bedbugs before, but they were supposed to be found only in the houses of the poor and not in a hotel. We certainly were learning that lots of things had changed because of the war.

The return journey took much longer than our first journey. Once we had reached the Austrian frontier with Moravia, Papa had to return. We continued with Mama and eventually arrived home, terribly tired. I had hurt my knee on one of the train changes, which stubbornly refused to heal until, one day, the doctor sprinkled some powder on it and to my surprise it was healed the next day. The doctor told Mama that this was one of the new remedies they used for the wounded soldiers. So the war had brought some good things as well!

While we had been in Szabac Papa had bought two wooden boxes and had filled them with beans, sugar, prunes and some precious flour. These had been well locked and then sent off separately as luggage when we travelled. After several weeks they arrived at our home. The locks seemed undisturbed — but the contents had gone. Two bricks were inside and a few paper bags; apart from that they were empty — all that lovely food gone. We were terribly disappointed.

Nobody knew how long the war would continue; there was no income from Papa now, and Mama had to use her private income. The sanitorium and my illness had cost a lot. Finally, Mama decided, with Aunt Marie, that we had better move to a smaller flat. One was found on the other side of the town. It was on the first floor and had only a very small garden at the back.

The day of the removal, 1 October, was cold and stormy and it rained all day long. Mama caught a severe chill and from then onwards she was never quite well again.

Our new home had only two rooms: a big bedroom and what we called the music room. There was a big divan in the music room and a divan in the bedroom across from the big double bed. While we were alone with Mama, Lilly and I took turns to sleep next to Mama and on the divan. We no longer had a maid; instead a woman came during the day to help Mama, who seemed to have little strength left.

On 21 November 1916, Franz Josef, our Emperor, died and Archduke Karl, his grand-nephew, was recalled from the Romanian frontier to succeed him as head of the Austro-Hungarian Empire.

We had seen the Emperor Franz Josef before the war, on a visit to Vienna, and he had looked like a benign old grandfather. I had intended to write to him and ask him to release Papa from the war, so that he could stay at home with us, but I had always postponed it. Now it was too late.

The new Emperor, Karl, was married to an Italian princess, Zita, and there were rumours that she wanted Italy to win the war. I remember the day of the old Emperor's funeral. We saw Karl's little son Otto walking gravely behind the coffin, and were more interested in him than in the funeral proceedings. Emperor Karl was never crowned as Emperor of Austria, only as King of Hungary in St

Stephen's Cathedral in Budapest. Not long afterwards he had to leave the country.

Meantime, the war was still going on. We no longer believed that it would ever end. There were very few victories now, but nobody celebrated. As food became scarcer we seemed always to feel hungry, especially Lilly, in spite of chewing prunes. We still had more or less normal meals, but there were some drastic changes. Breakfast, for instance, now consisted of a plateful of *klunkersuppe* (lumpy soup). This was just salted water, brought to the boil, with some coarse flour stirred into it, but only lightly, so that lumps formed. The more lumps there were, the more interesting was the soup. Lilly and I actually quite liked it and, what was more, could easily make it ourselves. We also learned how to make a kind of baked beans. The beans were boiled, after soaking, and then mixed with a dark roux. That and boiled barley became our staple diet. We had a little rhyme we would sing: 'Beans, then barley and prunes and prunes and barley, then start it all over again.'

Lilly invariably felt more hungry than I because she had always had a bigger appetite. However, she also had a friend whose father was a butcher, and whenever she visited her friend she got a much nicer meal there than she did at home. Our meat ration was only for Sunday, but there they seemed to have meat more often. When Lilly complained about this to her friend, her parents thought it might be the fault of our stepmother — not giving Lilly enough to eat.

We had never before thought of Mama as a 'stepmother'. Now Lilly thought of the stepmothers in the fairy tales, and this new realisation damaged her good relationship with Mama. She became stubborn and cheeky and tried to annoy her whenever she could. She came to regret this behaviour in later years, when she recalled how selflessly Mama had looked after us, by herself, at a very difficult time.

One night we had a burglar. We heard some strange noises in the flat, when we were already in our beds, and then we noticed the light of a torch through the upper part of the glass door, leading into the hall. Before Mama could get up, I started to cough and shout for Papa, who of course wasn't there. The light disappeared and we could just hear a slight noise on the stairs and the closing of the outer door. The hall door had been tampered with, but otherwise we had a lucky escape. Nevertheless, it was something to talk about in school — and we made the most of it!

Not long afterwards, something really exciting happened. There was a terrible thunderstorm late one night. My divan was between the window and the tall, tiled stove in the corner of the room. Suddenly I saw a fiery ball come in through the window, narrowly pass the divan and disappear in the stove door. Lilly just caught its disappearance. At first I thought I had dreamt it, but then we found the burst glass cylinder from the lamp near the divan, and there was a funny smell in the room.

Nobody believed my story at school to begin with; even the teacher, who was very young, looked doubtful. Then I was called to Reverend Mother and she believed me. She called what I had seen a fireball, and said that I had witnessed something very rare.

Just before Christmas, Papa came home on leave again. I remember looking down the staircase and all I could see was a cage with three live turkeys in it. Then I realised it was Papa, with the cage strapped to his back. Round his neck, and hanging down over his chest, were small sacks which contained beans and prunes. I could just imagine what his train journey must have been like.

As the turkeys were alive, the woman who came to help Mama during the day took them down to the wash house to be killed. Within minutes she rushed upstairs again, shouting that they had escaped into the back garden. Lilly and I would have loved to keep them there, but they were eventually caught again and one was to provide a marvellous Christmas dinner, even if it was not the more traditional goose. It was shared with Aunt Marie and lasted us for days; the other two were preserved in *weck* jars, divided up into reasonable portions, to be rationed over the weeks to come.

Papa took Lilly and I shopping while Mama was busy at home with the Christmas preparations. We had realised at last that there was no real Christchild, at least that he did not bring the presents, which really had to be bought by parents. That meant that we could no longer wish for whatever we liked; presents depended on the money available and the goods in the shops. That was a pity! However, we were not greedy for presents; crayons and painting books and paints, and another of those building sets with which to build houses and bridges and even cathedrals, were all that we wanted.

We had a lot of snow, more than usual, that winter, and it was very cold. Papa had returned to the war, yet I remember those winter evenings with pleasure. We had a covered bench, the end of which was against the tiles of the *kachelofen* (tiled stove). I loved sitting there with my back against the warm tiles and knitting, as usual, all those endless warmers of whatever part of the soldiers' bodies they were meant for. When I became tired I could always read a book — without anybody urging me to do something useful, as had usually happened in the convent.

On other evenings we sat around the table, where a paraffin lamp gave a mild light. Mama would read us stories and the shadows in the corners of the room came to life in my imagination with the people of the story. Life seemed good and peaceful — only Papa was missing.

We were no longer allowed to go into the woods without a grown-up, after some nasty incidents. We were told again and again that bad men were in the woods because of the war. Some, of course, might have been deserting soldiers.

Mama did seem to be well in our eyes, but she complained about pains in her chest and back. An oldish woman, a Frau Biefel, came once a week to our house to massage Mama and bring her homoeopathic medicine, as Mama said the doctor was too fussy and she did not want to worry Aunt Marie. Frau Biefel also washed our hair and then, when all was done, she laid tarot cards for Mama, trying to tell her when the war would end and Papa would come home.

In spite of the shortage of food, we still had our hair washed with an egg yolk instead of soap. There was no shampoo by that time, and soap was also rare; nearly everybody, including us, made their own soap, but it took a long time to collect the necessary fat.

Frau Biefel supplied the eggs and, as a treat, brought one extra egg for each of us to eat. The dried camomile flowers we used to rinse my hair had been collected on our walks during the summer. Only my hair was rinsed with a camomile infusion because I was darkish fair, but Lilly's hair, a lovely chestnut colour, was rinsed with vinegar added to the water.

That spring, Aunt Marie bought another small mill, not a steam-powered mill this time but a water mill, out in the country. It was about two hours' drive in the landau. There was a small cottage nearby in which we often stayed for weekends. We went there with my cousin Fritzl and his Nanny. Although he was now nearly five years old, Fritzl was still a whining little nuisance.

Nanny insisted that he was the most pleasant of all the children. He was very delicate, she maintained, but he had such a sweet nature. Sweet nature or not, he spoiled our games; he always wanted to join in whatever we were doing and then got us into trouble, because he either

My second Mama, myself and Lilly

fell and hurt himself or started to cry because we had shouted at him. Lilly and I disliked him intensely. Even Christl, his sister, got annoyed with him and sometimes I almost hated him. Nanny said that Lilly and I were too wild for him the Hungarians were a wild race!

At the old mill we used to paddle in the clear stream. One afternoon while paddling I suddenly felt something wriggling between my toes. It was a fish, a trout, about six inches long. I was thrilled at my discovery and raced into the cottage to show it to Nanny. 'Oh,' she exlaimed, 'how nice! Fritzl can have it for his tea. Would you like that, darling?' She turned to my cousin who had come in after me. 'A little fishy on a little dishy?' Of course Fritzl would like it.

I was utterly disgusted. That was too much! I couldn't even have the fish I had caught myself for my tea, because of Fritzl. At that moment I not only disliked him, I positively hated him. I decided that I didn't want any tea.

I went outside and sat on the swing which had been put up for us between two trees. Slowly I started to move backwards and forwards, higher and higher, and began to feel better. As I looked down I noticed Fritzl walking into the stream. He usually disliked water and never wanted to paddle, certainly not on his own. There were big pebbles in the water; he might fall . . . and he did. Suddenly he was lying in the water and not getting up.

I was off the swing and in the water in seconds. 'You little fool,' I hissed and pulled him out. He had his eyes closed and lay quite still on the grass. I screamed for Nanny. 'Dear God,' I prayed silently, 'please don't let him die, please.' Then Fritzl opened his eyes. 'I wanted to get a fishy for you,' he stammered. I nearly cried with relief. Then I realised that I loved this little cousin of mine, and did not want to lose him, even if he was so often a nuisance. We have been friends ever since.

Towards the end of May Mama was ill again. She coughed a lot, often stayed in bed, and seemed to be very weak. She stopped playing the piano because the smallest exertion brought her out in a cold sweat.

One evening, we were sent to the May evening service in the Dominican church. That service was held throughout the month and we had become rather bored with it by then. So we played marbles instead, outside the church, so that we could set off for home as soon as the congregation came out.

We had just started our game when Bertha, Mama's daily help, arrived, breathless. She stopped us playing and said: 'Get home quickly. Your mother has had a haemorrhage and I am off for the doctor.' We rushed home, convinced that Mama's sudden haemorrhage was a punishment from God, because we had played marbles instead of going to church.

However, Mama recovered this time, but then became worse again. My eldest cousin now spent a lot of time in our flat nursing Mama. We were sent for hours to our aunt's, so that Mama chould have complete rest. From then on everybody seemed to send us for walks. 'You need fresh air,' we were told, and my cousin explained that it was to prevent us catching Mama's illness, whatever it was.

Papa was unable to get compassionate leave because he himself had dysentery. We became accustomed to finding Mama still in bed when we returned home from school — but then there were again days when she seemed very much better. Surely she would soon be quite well again, we hoped.

During the summer holidays we had to spend nearly every free moment out in the fresh air, 'to keep healthy', as we were repeatedly told. It was then decided that we should go back to the convent in Gross-Herrlitz for the school term, and Mama would be moved to Aunt Marie's home. The flat was locked up.

10

WE WERE GREETED very warmly by the nuns at our old convent; they seemed pleased to have us back with them once again. It was almost like coming home to us — to a previous home. Nothing much had changed, but we had now to join in with the everyday routine. We were no longer the 'Sacred Heart children' who enjoyed special privileges. There was one exception, however, that we did not go to the village school but had private lessons with the two daughters of the estate manager, the doctor's daughter and, of course, Maritschel, who was still at the convent and was delighted to see us again.

There was also another private pupil, the Comtesse Elisabeth, one of the daughters of Count Bellegarde. She was the same age as Lilly, but she sat at a separate table. She arrived every morning in a donkey cart, accompanied by a groom, who came back at the end of the morning to collect her and bring her back again in the afternoon.

She was very pretty, usually dressed in white, and wore her hair long, unplaited, falling over her shoulders. That was something special for those days. We ordinary girls were no longer allowed to wear our hair loose, not even on Sundays, but had to have it in two plaits, called nests, wound round our ears.

At the convent we were all told to address the Comtesse in the third person, such as 'Has the Comtesse slept well?' and other such idiotic questions. During her first morning when we went outside at playtime, Lilly and I were told to take the Comtesse Elisabeth to the back garden, which was normally used only by the nuns and was out of bounds for the boarders. At the end of this garden was a wall, onto which the Comtesse promptly climbed. We, of course, followed, and before we could commence our well-rehearsed polite conversation, she pulled out of her pocket a bag of cherries and offered them to us. Cherries were a rarity so late in the season.

'Who can spit the stones farthest into the road?' she challenged. And from that moment on she was one of us. We had a good giggle about her being addressed in the third person, but we promised to keep it up in front of the nuns.

Apart from our normal lessons we now learned the piano from Sister Kasiana, needlework and embroidery from Sister Agnetis, and there were also painting lessons for those who wanted them. In addition, every week we had two *anstandlessons* (lessons in polite behaviour) taken by Sister Firmina, our 'home mother'. These took place after school and were for all the girls in the convent. We learned to make polite conversation, how to behave at the table, how to lay a table, how to greet guests; the younger ones, that included Lilly and I, had to learn how to make a little curtsey towards older people, which we had already practised since we had been very small. We also had to learn how to introduce and be introduced. Those little curtseys were made not only by children towards all grown-ups, even their parents, but also by young girls when greeting older ladies. They were called *knicks* and we were very good at them.

Later, we also learned how to treat servants and what to expect of them, and how to act in a reserved manner with strangers. We enjoyed these lessons; there was so much giggling when we had to bow and curtsey to each other and when being introduced to each other, but Sister did not seem to mind.

The meals in the refectory were still the same, with Sister still reading the lives of the martyrs. There were the same tables, the same benches. Lilly remembered to send the fat meat, of which there was now very little, and I sent her stewed fruit, of which there was still enough. We had, of course, chosen to sit on our old bench against the wall, so we could not be noticed by Sister.

The meals were much simpler now, although the convent was fortunate in that it received quite a lot of food in lieu of school fees from those of the boarders' parents who were farmers. I well remember most suppers, which consisted of potatoes with an apple sauce. This was not apple sauce as we understand it now: the apples, windfalls, were quartered with the skin left on, boiled and served with a rather watery roux sauce. However, we loved it. The vital thing was to watch out that nobody took too much, or rather fished for too many apple quarters, otherwise those who were served last would not get many.

Then again, just like at home, we would have barley, with the now well-known accompaniment — prunes — which Papa had provided. Occasionally we had a treat: barley with tiny pieces of bacon. This, of course, we liked best of all and after the war, years afterwards, I once became quite nostalgic and asked for barley with bacon. It was a great disappointment.

We could serve ourselves with as much as we wanted, with the proviso that whatever was put on the plate had to be eaten. Lilly was rather greedy. One day a white, thickish, creamy sauce was served. Somehow Lilly thought it was custard for afters, and served herself an enormous helping. Unfortunately for her it was horseradish sauce, which she hated. Poor Lilly! She could not possibly eat it all at that meal, so she had it for the next three meals until the hateful stuff was finished. I tried to eat it for her, but Sister prevented me.

In spite of the scarcity of food, some was found one day outside the refectory window. It must have been thrown out. How this had been managed was a puzzle to us all. Sister Firmina and Reverend Mother were very cross. A terrible inquisition followed but no culprit could be found. We all finished up in the chapel and then, in the evening, as nobody had owned up, all of us had to go to confession. Sister was probably hoping that God would decide the proper punishment.

Lilly and I had already taken our First Communion while we were living at home. We thought we knew all about the sins to confess, but one of the boarders brought a prayer book with a kind of checklist of sins for confession at the back. The prayer book was specially printed for 'maids' and there was quite a lot in it about the Sixth Commandment, which in Austria was about the sins of the flesh: *'Du sollst nicht Unkeuschheit treiben'* ('You shall not indulge in unchastity'). Lilly, Maritschel and I wondered if we had been leaving something out of our confessions.

We were not quite sure what it all meant, but Maritschel said it had something to do with the lower part of the body, so it could only mean, we concluded, whether or not we had wetted our knickers, even when we were quite small. At that time we had done it quite often, when we played outside and had not been quick enough to reach the toilets. Sister had then always been very cross, so it must have been a sin.

Oh horror! We had never confessed to that sin. It seemed such a dreadful sin in the prayer book that we were rather afraid to do so now, especially as we had not confessed it previously and had gone to communion with that sin still unforgiven. What would happen to us now? Perhaps we could get no absolution. I was the oldest and was chosen to go first into the confessional box. Lilly and Maritschel waited anxiously to hear what the priest would say.

I first confessed all my little sins, then I took courage and admitted that I had 'sinned against chastity'.

Father Franzl leaned forward. 'Repeat that again,' he commanded. 'What is it that you have done?'

'I have sinned what it says in the Sixth Commandment,' I tried to explain.

'Alone or with others?' came the stern question.

'With Lilly and Maritschel,' I replied.

Now he was really shocked. 'Come here,' he said and motioned me to the little door of the confessional. 'Now tell me exactly what you did,' he demanded rather sternly.

I took a deep breath. 'We played in the garden and it was so far to the toilets and when we got there it was too late.' I did not have to say any more. He understood, but was now obviously very upset. He put his hands to his face and his shoulders shook. Quite alarmed, I knelt in front of the little window again, to receive my penance. To my great relief it was only five Our Fathers and five Hail Marys. I nearly danced out of the confessional! I held five fingers up to let Lilly and Maritschel know the extent of the penance.

We were very glad to have been let off so lightly; we had thought that we might perhaps be reported to the Pope. It may seem ridiculous today to recall that we were so naïve at eleven and ten years old, but we were all like that in those days.

We soon settled down once more to the daily routine of our life in the convent. This was somewhat changed now that we were big girls. We had to get up every morning at six o'clock, open our beds to air, and disturb the straw in the mattress. After breakfast, the bed had to be made within fifteen minutes.

Those who wished could go to a quiet mass every day at six-thirty and take communion. I resolved once to go to communion every day without having to go to confession, meaning to live a whole day without the tiniest sin. However, my attempt did not last beyond the first day. Lilly did her best to make me lose my temper so that I would have to go to confession. I did lose it and was so furious that I tried to strangle her. Her shouts brought Sister running to her aid — and we were both sent for confession.

On Sundays at high mass we sang in the choir while Sister Kasiana played the organ. I loved to sing, but unfortunately I was incapable of doing so in tune. I pushed myself forward until I stood right in front of the raised choir and sang as loudly as I could. When I saw people turning their heads and looking up, I was sure that they liked our singing.

One day, Sister Kasiana, who probably did not want to hurt my feelings, showed me how to work the organ bellows and asked me if I would like to try it myself. It was easy. A bar had to be pressed down by standing on it while holding on to a higher bar. It was like a see-saw going up and down. I was delighted. This was now my job; it prevented me from singing but I did not mind. This job had also another advantage: I was called out from the classroom on many occasions to attend to the organ for a wedding. Sometimes at those weddings the boys' choir from the village school sang.

One morning I disgraced myself and nearly lost my job. While the priest was joining the young couple together, one of the boys sat down on the little bench beside me. When the priest pronounced: 'What God had joined together, let no man put asunder,' the boy whispered: 'I know a joke about that', and proceeded to tell it to me in a quiet whisper.

A school inspector was once visiting a village and saw some boys maltreating a cat by pulling its tail. When the inspector was in the school-room he related that incident then asked what saying would apply to this behaviour. There is in German a children's rhyme which they usually learn in school. Roughly translated it goes like this: 'Don't maltreat an animal, even in play, because it feels the pain just as you do.'

However, the inspector was not given the right answer. Instead, a little boy put up his hand and said: 'What God has put together, let no man take apart.' I broke into a giggle when I heard this and then a most gruesome noise was heard. It sounded like many cats caterwauling, but it was only the organ. I had forgotten to watch for Sister Kasiana's sign to start the bellows, and an organ without sufficient air sounds dreadful. Furthermore, when I frantically tried to make up for it, I jumped up and down on the bar far too quickly and made an additional clatter. Sister Kasiana was displeased to say the least, but I managed to keep my job. She probably thought that even the prospect of another incident like this was better than listening to my singing!

At the weekends we went for long walks with one of the novices. One day in May we were taken to a larch tree plantation, where there were many young trees. We were told to shake them vigorously. Hundreds of *maikaefers* (cockchafers) fell off. The trees were full of them in that year. The novice had brought a sack and a brush with her and we all helped to sweep them up and into the sack.

Once we had returned to the convent the sack was handed to the nun in charge of the kitchen, who beckoned us to follow her. She went into the kitchen yard and emptied the contents of the sacks for the hens. They polished off the whole lot in minutes. It seemed a special treat for them and we stood and watched in surprised horror. From all that would grow eggs, we marvelled!

Then came the time for cherry picking. Reverend Mother had bought a number of cherry trees that spring, which we had planted along the main road from Gross-Herrlitz to Skrochowitz. We were to climb the trees or climb up a ladder and Sister Kasiana would stand down below, giving good advice and pointing to branches which we might have forgotten. We were told that we could eat five cherries each. Probably she wanted us to learn not to take or eat what was not ours and for which we had not been given special permission.

However, I must confess that we suddenly found it very hard to count up to five and many a stone fell to the ground, which proved that more than five cherries had been eaten by us. I tried to be very clever and swallowed my stones and told Lilly to do the same, but she was afraid that the stones would all hide in her appendix. Our cousin Otto had had an appendix operation, which is how she knew about it. She therefore hid her stones in her knickers (those with elastic above the knees), but she had to be careful that Sister did not see her lifting her skirt, however carefully — and I continued to swallow mine. Nothing untoward happened to me, but Lilly was worried about me for days.

During the summer holidays that year we stayed on at the convent, as Mama was still far from well. Maritschel and we were the only boarders left there and, although Maritschel had to help in the kitchen for part of the time, we were more or less free to do what we liked. For the first time ever we could go out of the convent on our own for long walks.

There was a pond not far from the village, just deep enough in the middle for swimming in. This became our favourite haunt. There was a float in it, consisting of several wooden planks and, holding on to it, we improved our swimming. We had already learned more or less the right movements from Mama in the swimming pool in Szabac; now we could practise on our own.

At first we moved only our legs, holding onto the planks, then we gained the confidence to let go and began to swim freely. It was great fun. Nobody ever came to the pond during the week, so we just went into the water in our knickers and vests, which dried on the way back to the convent.

One day, however, when we climbed out of the water we could not see our dresses. Then we heard giggling in the bushes and our dresses were waved like flags — horror of horrors — by some boys! We were back in the water in seconds, and from there we pleaded for our clothes. Only when Lilly burst into tears and became almost hysterical did the boys put our dresses down and leave us to get dressed in peace. However, that incident put an end to our enjoyment of the pond.

11

THE MONTHS HAD passed by and it was now November 1918. One evening we were in the study in the tower room quietly doing our homework. Suddenly, Reverend Mother entered the room looking extremely serious. We had to put our pens and books down and pay attention to what she had to say. We looked at her expectantly. Then she announced: 'The war is over.'

We started to clap and shout, but she quickly motioned us to be quiet. 'We are no longer an Empire; we no longer belong to Austria. We are now a Republic. I don't know yet what we will be called. There will no longer be an Emperor: Emperor Karl has left the country. We must never sing the Austrian National Anthem again .' She was just about to leave the room, when she turned round again. 'There will be a thanksgiving service in the church tomorrow morning.' Then she left and closed the door behind her.

At first we all sat quite still. We were stunned. Then we all stood up. I don't know what suddenly happened to us. Amongst us were older girls, some even eighteen and twenty years old, who were doing the domestic science course. They and some of the younger ones came from the surrounding farms near Troppau and were Bohemians. They didn't seen surprised and shouted 'Nazdar!' when we others started shouting 'Hurrah, hurrah, the war is over!'

I cannot remember who started it, but suddenly inkpots, rulers and books were flying all over the place, aimed at each other, or rather the Bohemians against the Austrians, and vice versa. For the first, and not the last time, we experienced mass hatred, kindled by a few nationalist remarks which infected the atmosphere and exploded into that unexplainable hatred.

Reverend Mother returned, shocked and angry. She had to call another of the nuns to part us. Sister Firmina was helpless with shock. It was incredible that her 'nice girls' could behave in such a violent manner.

It appeared that the Czech girls (as the Bohemian girls were to be called from then on) had known what none of us had suspected, what had long been in the air. They had known that the Czechs had planned for some time to have their own country and government. They had known that the Legionnaires, the Czech regiments in the Austrian army, had deserted in Russia during the Revolution and that Masaryk was in America to sign the treaty which made part of Austria into a new country, later called Czechoslovakia, that is Czesko Slovenska Republika.

Masaryk became the first President of the new country. His daughter was the first to return to Prague from America and after she had declared the new Republic on the steps of the Hradchin in Prague, somebody started the beautiful old Czech song *Kde Domov muj?* (Where is my home) and that was to become the national anthem.

Later we also heard that there had been a kind of revolution in Prague, where the professionals and the shopkeepers were mostly of German origin. The Czechs lived mostly in the country in Bohemia and Moravia, and Slovaks in Slovakia, but there were very few in Silesia. The Czechs had assembled in Prague and as soon as peace was declared they stormed into the main square, smashed down monuments and damaged shops.

We listened to those accounts with excitement. Apart from that initial incident in the study room there were no more fights. Nevertheless, from being all friends together, we had now become 'we and them'.

Not long afterwards Papa returned home. He had survived the war, due to our special prayers we felt sure, even if we had neglected to say them in the convent. How he had managed to get back to us from Serbia amid the chaos of those days, through Hungary and Moravia to Silesia, can only be guessed.

One afternoon he arrived at the convent, but not to take us home, as we had hoped, at least not for the time being. We were to stay on until the end of the term. His homecoming must have been a very sad one. He found Mama very ill with 'Spanish influenza', which was rife at the time. She was still at Aunt Marie's, but he took her home as soon as she could be moved and engaged a housekeeper, who also had some nursing experience.

We were able to go home for Christmas. Neither Lilly nor I remembers that Christmas at all. It must have been a very sad one, in spite of having Papa at home.

After Christmas we had to return to the convent, although we had secretly hoped that we could have stayed at home. Mama needed rest and quiet. Shortly after we were back in school I overheard Sister Renate saying to Sister Agnetis: 'How dreadful for the poor man to lose his second wife through the same illness as his first wife. I feel sorry for the girls, but even more so for their father!' Then I heard Sister Agnetis reply: 'Yes, it's a dreadful thing, that TB.'

I knew that TB meant tuberculosis. In those days many people died of it and we had heard of a family where three daughters had died before they were twenty years old. I was devastated by the news. I had felt so sure Mama would one day be well again and, especially now that Papa was home again, that everything would be as it was in that wonderful year before the start of the war.

I went to the little chapel and prayed. I promised God that if he made Mama well I would enter a convent and, to make it really hard for me, I would choose the order of the Carmelites, which was a silent order. I left the chapel with a happy heart. Surely God would hear my prayers and make Mama well.

Meantime the chaos of the immediate after-war conditions went on. There was revolution in the Banat which, as a result of the carving-up of the Austro-Hungarian Empire, had first come under a French Protectorate, and was then given to Romania.

Papa heard from Uncle Lajos how Grandmother had come through the revolution. Moldova was a smallish town, where nearly everybody knew everybody else. The Germans were the better-off families, but had always lived quite happily with the Romanians and Hungarians and even the Bohemians. The latter were quite poor and lived mostly in the adjoining hills.

Now, with the end of the war, and with the revolution in Russia as an example, the least well-off people thought that the Golden Age had come —

and that now it was their turn to have an easy life. Groups of people broke into the houses of the wealthier members of the community and carried away what they could. They damaged property, looted and caused enormous havoc. Grandmother did not escape this treatment.

One night a screaming mob banged on the big gates at the entrance to Grandmother's house. Grandmother instructed her maid to open the doors to let them in, before they broke them down. The mob rushed into the house and seized whatever they could lay hands on. Lenka, the maid, led Grandmother, through the front door, to her daughter's, who lived nearby and who had a husband and a grown-up son, just returned from the army, who could at least give some protection. Uncle Lajos soon arrived from Graz and took her to his home until the excitement and trouble had died down.

When she returned to her house, much later, it was nearly empty. The huge wine barrels and tubs in the cellar had been broken open, and the wine stood knee-high in the cellar; she was told that two people had drowned in the wine, when they drunkenly fell in.

All the furniture had been taken from the house, as well as the crockery, kitchen utensils, almost everything, in fact. Only a round table and a rocking chair stood forlornly in the salon.

One woman, who usually helped at the vintage, told Grandmother that two men had wanted to take the round table through the door but found that it was impossible. They did not know that the table top could be taken off; so the table was left behind. She also heard how, inadvertently, someone had pushed against the rocking-chair, setting it in motion. When the two men saw the chair rocking silently without anybody in it, they crossed themselves and shouted to God for help, as they were sure that it must be the Devil sitting there. They left the room in great haste and terror. Unfortunately, the other furniture had already been moved.

We heard of another little incident which was quite comical. My aunt met a man on the little bridge which led to Grandmother's house. He was carrying her hip bath, over his head and down his back. When she asked where he was taking it, he replied that the 'Lady' had long enough washed her . . . in comfort; now it was his turn to give his . . . such nice treatment. A few days later, my aunt saw him again, this time taking the bath back. 'Have you had enough of washing in comfort?' she asked him. He replied gruffly that as far as he was concerned, the 'Lady' could sit in this contraption as much as she liked, he'd had enough of it.

When Grandmother returned home, the revolution was over. People had realised that the Golden Age had not yet dawned after all. Grandmother, who was nearly eighty years old, tried to retrieve most of her things, at least the bare necessities. Much help was given to her. Several people brought furniture and other things back without giving an explanation, just an embarrassed smile, saying they thought she might want them. Others needed a gentle reminder.

As life returned to normal, Grandmother was once more often called to a house when there was a new baby or some difficult problem to solve. As she was leaving, she might point to a bucket, picture or chair, and say: 'I used to have something like this and liked it very much.' Immediately it was offered to her and even carried to her house. In this way nobody lost face. Unfortunately, the more valuable things were never seen again, such as a pewter dinner service for twelve persons, her best china and, most regrettable of all, the box containing the various things belonging to our mother. Nobody seemed to have seen them.

The vinepress had also suffered in the disturbances but, in time, everything was restored and the whole affair forgiven and forgotten. However, the Banat belonged now to Romania, and that brought new problems for my father.

Papa was a Hungarian of the Austro-Hungarian Empire, which no longer existed. His place of birth was Uj-Moldova, whereas mine and Lilly's was Budapest. However, we all now lived in a new country, Czechoslovakia, yet we were not Czechoslovakians because we were not born there and had no home town there. In order for a town to be your 'home town' you had either to have been born there, or have bought the right to call it so. The latter option was necessary before you could apply for the new nationality.

Papa was still employed by the Vacuum Oil Company, whose policy was that their employees should be nationals of the state they lived in. Therefore my father had to decide whether he preferred to be transferred to Romania or to become a Czechoslovakian. He did not want to leave Silesia, so he applied for citizenship for himself and his daughters. Mama had automatically become a Czechoslovakian because she had been born there. My father, though, had to pay a considerable sum for himself and us for the right to call Jaegerndorf our home town. Unfortunately, this was later the reason for losing everything after the Second World War.

Meantime life in the convent went on as usual. The German and

Bohemian boarders forgot their quarrels and were friends again, but there was still a distinction made between them and us. We were now a minority in the new Czechoslovakian Republic. We learned the new borders and realised that Jaegerndorf was still bordering on Germany, or rather Prussia-Silesia, and that the north-western part of Silesia belonged now to Poland. We heard of some peculiar cases, where the frontier ran right through the buildings of a farm, or where the fields were in Poland and the farmhouse in Czechoslovakia. We made fun of these facts, expecially when we were told that the frontiers had been decided upon in America.

There was a new boarder at the convent, an eighteen-year-old girl from Troppau, called Victoria — Vicki for short. She came from a very rich family — and her underwear was not of this world. In spite of the regulations, she wore only silk and lace and her dresses were all the latest fashion and must have cost a fortune.

We were all intrigued to see these beautiful things. One evening, when Sister had left the dormitory, thinking we would be soon asleep, Vicky proceeded to show us her treasures. We sat together on the bed and she paraded in front of us in her underwear, making little dancing steps; we forgot where we were and ooh'd and ah'd, laughing and exclaiming loudly, when suddenly Sister came in and just stood there — like the Archangel Michael in the garden of Eden. She was almost speechless with shock. We fled to our beds, but Vicky was in disgrace. To prevent the rest of us from becoming depraved, she had to go to bed half an hour before everybody else from then on; however, she didn't mind as she could now read in peace, probably books Sister would never approve of!

We were now old enough to go the Rorate Service during Advent. It took place in the church at six o'clock in the morning. The church was dark and only lit by special candles which each person carried in with them and then put on top of the pew. This candle was very thin and long and was intricately wrought, like the bottom of a basket. Only the end stood up and was lit. Each of us got such a candle and it lasted throughout Advent. It was a lovely sight, just before entering the church, to look back and see hundreds of flickering lights coming up the hill.

We sang Christmas carols for about an hour, but all were expressing the longing for Christ, the Light of the World, to come. I remember that we all enjoyed that service so much that we did not mind getting up so early. It gave a wonderful pre-Christmassy feeling. There was also the added bonus of having more time for making the bed after breakfast, when we could laugh and talk together because, for once, we were without supervision.

Christmas came and went, a sad time just as the previous year had been. We spent the holidays at home, and Papa took us for long walks as Mama was mostly lying on the sofa or in bed. On Christmas Day itself there was a great family reunion. All the aunts, uncles and cousins were invited, even those from across the frontier. The huge dining table was opened up in the dining-room; the same one at which, five-and-a-half years ago, Mama had sat at the head of the table as a happy bride. Now she was just a shadow of her former self.

In the new school term Sister Firmina started a course in the 'History of Art'. In our schoolbook there were pictures of naked ladies and a picture of 'David', the sculpture by Michaelangelo. Unfortunately, somebody had covered some parts of their bodies with an ink pencil though previous pupils had, of course, licked their fingers to rub this out, to see what was underneath. Now only a few dark-blue patches remained, two on top of the Venus and one at the lower part of the body of David. Maritschel, Lilly and I were very curious. Luckily, in a few years' time we would stay with a family where I found in their bookcase an illustrated anatomy which had no blue patches. I was to be rather disappointed!

Easter was a happy time for us, in spite of Mama's illness. Papa spent most of the time at home. Although he was still with the Vacuum Oil Company, there was no oil available, so he had plenty of time for us. We again went for long walks with him and, of course, on Easter Sunday we followed the old custom of watching the sunrise on top of a hill. Mama could not come with us. We went straight to the old ruin and, predictably, Lilly again insisted that she saw the sun jump with joy and the Lamb of God mirrored in it. Papa just laughed but did not contradict her. I felt sure she was making it up. I had grown far too sophisticated for such a tale. The people round us laughed and smiled at Lilly and she beamed back at them.

We walked over to the hill with the holy picture and prayed for Mama to be well again; I hadn't told Papa of my promise to God, but Lilly said something about me wanting to enter a convent. 'Grow up first,' he said, 'and don't promise your life away.'

For the first time after the war we had the traditional breakfast again: ham, hard-boiled eggs, egg flip and *osterstrietzel*, a white loaf with nuts and raisins. You might almost have thought that there had been no war, if it wasn't for Mama's illness.

On Easter Monday we took part in the traditional *schmeckostern*. This is one of the ancient fertility rites. Specially made Easter birches were used by young men, brothers, fathers and cousins and their friends, to whip the girls and young women. So as not to embarrass the very young as to the purpose of this old custom, a little verse was sung or spoken: '*Leibes Maedchen lass Dich peitschen dass Dich nicht die Floehlein beissen*' ('Dear little girl, let me whip you so that the fleas do not bite you').

Throughout the morning cousins and their male friends arrived at our home brandishing their Easter birches and we ran all round the flat screaming and pretending to be terribly frightened. It was great fun. Papa had already used his early in the morning to get us out of bed very quickly.

It was the custom, too, for all the men and boys to give a bottle of perfume, or, for those who could not afford it, or were not close relatives, spraying with perfume was enough. The younger cousins, of course, took delight in spraying us with water. However, my father always gave Mama a large bottle of perfume and, as we grew older, we would receive from him a large bottle of eau de cologne.

In spite of the fright we had suffered, we were supposed to give the boys coloured eggs in return, according to the old fertility rites. Older girls, if they liked a boy, would give him a red egg. Lilly and I had coloured several dozen eggs on Saturday afternoon. Some of the eggs were hidden in the garden by the parents, and their children would spend the morning looking for them.

Any eggs which were left over would be used by boys for the 'egg cracking'. This was very much like the game I later saw played in England, with conkers in the autumn. The hard-boiled egg was held between forefinger and thumb and the partner tried to crack it with his own egg. If he succeeded, the cracked egg became his. One of my young cousins once started with a single egg and by the time he had played with all his friends he finished with fourteen eggs. The family probably had egg salad for the rest of the week!

In the afternoon there was dancing in the park, and in the evening there was the 'Easter Ball' to look forward to. In both cases the boys and young men would stand round the circle of dancers, trying to hit the legs of the young girls. We were, of course, too young in 1919 to go to the ball, but my older cousin Hannic went and told us so much about it that we longed to be old enough to enjoy such pleasures.

The summer term in the convent passed uneventfully. We went home again for the summer holidays, as we were still unable to travel to

Moldova. It was a glorious summer and we spent most of our days outside. We went to pick wild loganberries, then whirlyberries and blackberries and brought bucketfuls home to be made into condensed fruit juices or conserved in special jars.

Our housekeeper was a real treasure. Mama by now almost never left her bed or the sofa. On some afternoons Papa and the housekeeper carried her downstairs into the garden, and then we felt sure that she was really getting better.

I had developed a nasty cough and I think Papa very much feared a return of my TB attack. The doctor again ordered goat's milk and I had to go every morning to a neighbour's house to drink that horrid stuff there. Unfortunately, the lady was very proud of her goat and stood by while I drank — what she called — her 'beautiful' milk. Then I had to spend at least an hour after lunch sitting in a deckchair. I was not supposed to read at those times, but I often did so secretly, as Mama could not see me. I always had a bad conscience.

Papa often looked worried and sad, although he tried to be cheerful with us. Sometimes he became quite irritable, even occasionally with Mama. Then we criticised him between ourselves, that he did not have more patience with poor Mama. Only now do I realise how very patient he really was. Mama usually looked quite happy and when she had been down in the garden she would insist that she would soon be well again. I waited for the miracle God would certainly soon perform.

During the second half of August Mama became steadily worse, and then, suddenly, seemed to be much better. In spite of that, a nun came every evening in the last week of August to watch at Mama's bedside during the night.

Early in the morning on 3 September 1919, a day before Papa's birthday, Mama died. Some noise in my parents' bedroom woke us. I had experienced a bad dream and without knowing why, I turned to Lilly and said: 'I think Mama has died.' We both sat up in bed and had a dreadful feeling of something unexplainable. We heard the front door close — the nun had left for morning mass — then we heard the sound of suppressed sobbing, and we knew.

A little while later, Papa came in to our room and said: 'Children, we are alone again, you no longer have a mother.' He led us into the next room, where the nun had covered Mama with a sheet. As Papa pulled it away, we knelt by the bedside and tried to pray, but we just cried and cried.

Suddenly, my eyes fell on Mama's initials on the corner of the sheet,

111

embroidered in blue, and I remembered a nightmare I had had when Mama had still been well. I had dreamt that she had died and we were kneeling by her bedside, just as we were now, and I had noticed the blue initials. At the time I had woken up, crying, and when I told Mama my dreadful dream she had laughed and said: 'You must have seen the sheets of my dowry which are always kept for such an occasion, and they have blue intitials.' She had cheered me up and had assured me that she had no intention of dying.

Now I was seeing those intitials again — and there was no Mama to cheer me up, although she was still there, looking very peaceful. She was smiling, but her eyes were closed for ever.

The next few days were so busy that they passed as in a grey haze. We had to go to the dressmaker's for a black suit and a black crêpe dress to be made for the funeral. All our other suits and dresses were sent to be dyed black. Aunt Marie went with us to choose suitable black hats with black veils. In spite of the overwhelming sadness, we were quite excited with all the new outfits, especially the hat with the veil, which made me feel quite grown-up.

Everybody treated us with an almost reverential kindness. This made us feel very important, until we reached home again to see Mama, who was still laid out in the dining-room. It seemed incredible that she would never get up and say that she felt so much better for her long rest.

The funeral was a big affair. Through the glass of the hearse we could see such a long, long procession, as the hearse wound its way through the town to the cemetery. We thought the whole town had come to the funeral. Everybody walked, except for the horse-drawn hearse, as there were no cars. Amazingly, I don't remember what happened at the graveside as vividly as I remember my first mother's funeral. But I do remember the desolate feeling when we had to go home again, just Papa, Lilly and I.

When we got home there was Papa's favourite cake on the table. It was for his birthday, which we had forgotten. Apparently, Mama had given orders to the housekeeper to bake that cake just a few days before she died. None of us could eat it now.

Papa kept on the flat, but the housekeeper left as soon as school started. Papa would be busy again, doing a lot of travelling, so Lilly and I were now sent to the convent in Jaegerndorf as boarders. It was not really a boarding school, but they accepted a few special cases.

It was not much different from the convent in Gross-Herrlitz. The dormitory was more modern. There were no boards between the beds, but we had instead cubicles with curtains all round, like Sister had in Gross-Herrlitz.

The refectory was more like the dining-room we had at home, with just one long table in the middle, and chairs instead of benches. We took our meals without having to listen to the lives of the martyrs, which was a great relief, and we were allowed to talk quietly.

We stayed at the convent until Christmas, when we went to Graz, south of Vienna. Uncle Lajos and Aunt Ilona had invited us to spend the Christmas week with them. Before we left we gave Papa our special present. We had saved our pocket money and had a photograph of Mama enlarged and framed. Papa hung that picture over his writing desk but it made us all very sad. Luckily we left for Graz the same day.

We spent one day in Vienna and Papa took us to the *Prater*, a great park with lots of entertainment. The biggest sensation was the 'Great Wheel', at that time the biggest in Europe. Little cabins turned round and round in the big wheel and gave a marvelous view of nearly all Vienna.

In Graz we were welcomed by Uncle and Aunt and our cousins: Lola, nineteen, Elsa, eighteen, Gretel, eight, and Hans, twelve years old, the same age as Lilly. Hans was told to look after Lilly, which he categorically declined to do. I, although I was only one year older, paired up with Lola or Elsa. Lilly was furious and she and Hans quarrelled until Sylvester, New Year's Eve.

The days passed quickly. Our cousins showed us Graz, which is a beautiful town, but I am afraid we did not much appreciate it. The best treat for us was not the architecture or the town, but the big barrel of apples which Aunt Ilona kept near the entrance door, and from which we could help ourselves as much as we liked.

On the morning of Christmas Eve all of us girls helped with polishing the parquet floor. Aunt Ilona gave each of us a pair of felt slippers and then we danced to a certain tune, right and left along the parquet boards, as if we were dancing on ice. It was a delightful pastime and the floor looked like a mirror by the time we had finished. Luckily, the rugs were heavy enough or they would have slipped clean away.

Then came New Year's Eve. I was allowed to go with the grown-ups and Lola and Elsa to a New Year's Eve variety show, whereas Lilly, Hans and Gretel were sent to bed. Gretel went to sleep, but Lilly and Hans were suddenly drawn together in complaining about the unfair treatment they had received. In sharing their utter contempt of the grown-ups they became firm friends.

Before we set off for the theatre, I found Lilly looking somewhat apprehensive. There is a superstition, not only that what one dreams in the twelve nights after Christmas will come true in the coming twelve months, but also that young girls will see their future husbands in their dreams. That seemed to worry her.

I enjoyed the variety show immensely. I had never seen anything like it before: dancing girls, a magician, comedians, jugglers and lovely music. At midnight everybody seemed to go mad with shouts of *Prosit Neujahr!* and good wishes for the next year. Even strangers wished each other a 'Happy New Year'.

The journey home was yet another delight. We walked after we had taken a so-called early breakfast of *goulashsoup*. This was supposed to be good after having drunk a lot of wine. It had been snowing all day and the snow was piled up on each side of the pavement, so that we walked between white walls and could see nothing but the starry sky above. Now and then we could hear some late revellers singing, otherwise it was very quiet. I wondered what the next year would bring.

When we reached the house there I discovered Lilly, wide awake in bed and crying. Whether it was tiredness or despair, I don't know, but she kept saying: 'I don't want a husband ever.' We convinced her finally that she did not need to have a husband in the far-away future if she did not want to. She then went quite happily to sleep.

The Christmas holidays ended and we went back to the convent. The days seemed now rather monotonous. Furthermore, we could not go every weekend because Papa did not always come home; sometimes he visited us, took us for a walk and was off again. I missed Mama more and more. As we were allowed to go out on our own, I went regularly to the cemetery to Mama's grave. It did not seem to help me much. The cemetery gardener had already provided flowers suitable for the season; there were also flowers in a vase, probably from Aunt Marie, and all I could do was to change the water. I tried to speak to Mama, hoping that her soul might hear me, but I had no feeling that there was any answer.

One day, as I was changing the water, a woman approached me. 'Are you the stepdaughter of Hedl Sehors?' she asked, and when I replied 'Yes', she looked surprised. 'It seems funny,' she said, 'that you come here so often. She was, after all, only your stepmother.' I had never thought of Mama in that way and it seemed to me like a betrayal. I could not have loved Mama more, even if she had been my own mother. After all, I could not remember my mother and it hurt me that people should think I had no right to mourn her successor.

At the end of April it was the turn of Uncle Lajos and Aunt Illona to come from Graz to visit us. They took Lilly and I to a cafe and asked us later what we would like as a present. It would have to be money, because it was Sunday, but we could say what we wanted to buy with it. Food was still not too plentiful and I had a great longing for sardines. I was saving for a tin of that delicacy, as it was still a great luxury. Of course, Uncle Lajos gave me the money to buy a tin. Lilly wanted chocolates and was told to buy a big box and share them with me.

When we went for our usual Wednesday walk I bought a tin of sardines. We made our way through the woods to an old tower at the top of the hill. The tower was a favourite picnic spot and would have given a beautiful view if we could climb to the top. We took our hats and coats off and started exploring. First we tried the door. It was locked. We looked through the barred window into a small room and could see in the dim light some old guns and armour, and when we banged on the door the noise made an echo, which we tried out again and again, shouting louder and louder.

I tried to hold on to the bars of the window to climb right up when suddenly we heard heavy running footsteps from the other side of the tower coming towards us. To our horror, a big man appeared, looking like a tramp, but wild and furious. He was swinging an axe and shouted: 'Have I got you at last, you damned bastards?'

Lilly grabbed our hats, the novice and the other two girls our coats and they all disappeared, but there I remained, hanging on the bars of the window. The man tried to run after them, while I watched fascinated as some of my friends jumped over a fence in their panic. Then the man turned towards me. I had, meantime, managed to jump down and I ran as fast as I could down the other side, but the man followed me. It is astonishing what hidden powers we have when we are really frightened.

I stumbled and pushed through the thicket and trees, down towards the main road. I daren't look back; I was panic-stricken and even jumped a fence, as the others had done. Finally, I reached a point just above the main road, where there were some houses. Then I looked back and there was the man close behind me, swearing and still swinging his axe.

I rushed in through a garden gate towards the first house and reached the back door, but it was locked and there was apparently nobody at home. The man followed me through the gate. Then I saw, next to the back door, a washing basket and, in desperation, I crouched down and put it over my head.

My feeble attempt to hide was in vain, because the man lifted the basket and there I stood, a few inches away from him, and he still brandishing his axe, swearing and cursing. Suddenly I saw, sticking out of his breast pocket, the tip of my tin of sardines. I must have dropped it in my flight.

That was too much! Never mind the terrible fright and panic. Never mind the horrible threats of that man. How dare he rob me of my sardines, for which I have saved so long and, thanks to the generosity of my Uncle Lajos, I had at last been able to buy! I forgot my terror and said in my most accusing voice, looking the man straight in the face: 'These are *my* sardines.' The result was astonishing. The man dropped the axe, looked stupidly at his breast pocket, took out the tin of sardines and gave it to me. 'You should not steal,' I said sternly, as I took them, turned and walked away. I did not even look back to see what the man was doing.

When I had nearly reached the main road, I found the novice and one of the girls, who were waving at me. They had seen both me and the man going through the garden gate and were greatly relieved when they saw me coming out, obviously unhurt, and the man not following me.

When we at last reached the convent, Lilly and the two other girls had returned before us. They had been almost hysterical when they reached the fields below the hill and a man working there had given them a lift in his cart back to the convent.

At first the nuns did not believe our story, even when the novice confirmed it. They probably thought that our imagination had been working overtime. Later, the police made enquiries and we were told that a dangerous lunatic had escaped from the asylum in Troppau; he was caught the same day by the police. Apparently he had been under the illusion that the tower contained treasures which belonged to him and he had probably thought that we were trying to take them away.

In May I was in serious trouble with religious arguments. We were supposed to go every evening to a special service, in honour of Our Lady. One evening I declared that I did not want to go. This was unheard of. Why? We all needed Our Lady's help. She would intercede for us with God to help us in our troubles and forgive us when we had sinned.

I declared that I did not need any help at the moment and when I did need help I would rather speak to God himself. Sister's arguments were that most children usually first tell their troubles to their mother and then she would smooth things out with father if it was necessary. That argument had no effect on me.

'I have no mother', I insisted, 'and even if I had, I would rather tell whatever I had done to Papa.' Sister was not satisfied. After many more arguments I was told that my ideas were seriously wrong, and Sister wondered if she should not write to the Pope in case he could persuade me to change my mind. That did it!

I gave in reluctantly, but was then so enthusiastic that I joined in the hymn-singing, loud and clear — but out of tune. As there was no organ in the school chapel, only a harmonium, the noise I made sounded even worse. However, no complaints were made, because only the Sisters and the boarders were there. I wonder if they regretted that I had finally joined the service.

I often got into trouble for saying exactly what I thought, as long as it was true. There was only one thing about which I was always deceitful. We were not encouraged to read, except at the appointed times. I loved reading and so I always carried a book in my knickers, behind the elastic at the waist; even it if slipped down, the elastic above the knees would still prevent it from falling out. I read in the loo; in the dormitory while the others undressed and then shed my clothes in the dark; at mealtimes, when I balanced the book on my knees while eating and sometimes I read in the more boring lessons.

One day Sister Hugo caught me during class and confiscated my book. A few days later I asked for the book back and Sister Hugo told me that she did not have it. Later on, while Sister Hugo was marking homework, I happened to see the book in her drawer when she opened it to take something out.

I lost my temper. I turned to Sister and almost shouted: 'You have told me a lie. You have my book and you said you did not have it, you are a liar!' Then I came to my senses, but it was too late. Sister Hugo just looked at me very sternly, stood up and walked out. I felt sure she went to Reverend Mother.

We had always thought that nuns would never lie and my respect for Sister Hugo was greatly shaken. However, I was still in disgrace. Reverend Mother wrote to Papa and asked him to come and see her. He first saw Reverend Mother alone, but as he was very just, he insisted that I should be called in to give my side of the incident.

When I came in he told me what he had heard from Reverend Mother about my terrible accusation of Sister Hugo. How could I have said such a terrible thing? Nevertheless, when he heard my side of the story he had to agree with me.

He tried to excuse the nun, by saying that she probably had meant that she did not have the book on her when I asked for it. What he said to Reverend Mother I don't know, but neither she nor Sister Hugo ever mentioned the matter again.

I told the other girls that I felt sure that whatever excuses Papa tried to make for Sister Hugo, a lie was a lie and God would not accept such a flimsy excuse! I was very righteous-minded in those days and very intolerant!

The next time Papa visited us there was another upset. I had given up the idea of entering a convent when Mama had died. Lilly decided that, as God had been deprived of a nun, she was going to make up for it. So she informed Papa of her intention. I had never seen my father so angry. He told her in no uncertain words to put the idea right out of her head. I thought Lilly was secretly quite pleased because she never really believed that she would make a good nun. A father's prohibition can sometimes be a great relief, as it was in Lilly's case!

12

WE HAD FINISHED the education the convent world could give us and Papa decided to send us to the lyceum in Troppau to continue our schooling. We would lodge with a private family, as we had been exposed long enough to the convent influence.

The first family we went to was that of a widow, Frau Sedlacek, who lived with her daughter, a girl of our age, and her mother, who was a baroness — a fact she was very proud of and mentioned at every possible opportunity. Lilly and I were given a pleasantly furnished room and felt we would be very happy there.

We had passed the entrance examination for the lyceum; Lilly went into the fourth form and I entered the fifth form. A big change for us were our teachers. Most of them were male — and very different from the Sisters. The first time we had a lesson taken by the physics professor I was thrilled to hear him explain the beginning of our world. The big fireball circling around, cooling out and then evolving into the Earth as it is today. I had never understood why God, having created Adam and Eve, made a rule and then put temptation right in front of them. I hadn't dared to voice all my doubts to the nuns at the convent, but here was a man who knew.

Although Sister had forewarned us that the world was a sinful place it was still difficult for Lilly to accept the different atmosphere we found ourselves in. She still used the convent greeting 'Praised be Jesus Christ', fully expecting the answer 'In all eternity, Amen' when entering the classroom, but as the teachers were never present before the pupils, nobody took much notice. One day she was late for class. She had been helping an old man across the street, which made her feel quite saintly, and the lesson was already in progress. When she entered the room, she announced in a loud voice: 'Praised be Jesus Christ!' The professor ignored her greeting and shouted: 'Why are you late?' As the whole class laughed at her unusual greeting, Lilly replied quietly: 'You should have answered "In all eternity, Amen".'

Everyone laughed even louder and the professor was furious. 'You are impertinent,' he said sternly, 'and you will get a bad mark in "Behaviour" in your report.' Lilly was terribly upset and could only murmur: 'Yes, we were told that we would have to suffer for our belief.' Yet in spite of her apparent calm she was desperate.

In our termly reports we were given marks for 'Behaviour' and 'Diligence' as well as for all the other subjects; a bad mark for 'Behaviour' was a terrible shame and seemed something which could only happen to us. Lilly would disgrace Papa — and that was unbearable.

During the break she came to me and asked me whether she should kill herself by hanging, either in the toilet here at school or wait until we returned to the Sedlacek's. (Some time ago we had seen on our walks in the woods, a man who had hanged himself.) I told her, when I had heard the whole sad story, that she should do neither. I would go to the professor and explain that she had not meant to be impertinent. I did just that and he turned out to be very kind and sympathetic. He talked to Lilly and explained that it had all been a misunderstanding. He had not known that she had spent years in a convent and he certainly would not give her a bad mark in 'Behaviour'. He added that now, being in the 'world', she should perhaps choose another greeting for entering the classroom, especially when she arrived late.

Our teacher for religion was an extremely young priest. Because he always said that we were like 'God's little flowers', we called him 'Little Flower'. His was a very noisy class, which I found difficult to get used to after the strict discipline in the convent; most of the girls said that they did not like religious instruction. Of course, I knew the usual Bible stories inside out and was always bored, but kept quiet.

One day, the Director of the lyceum came into the classroom and announced that from the beginning of the next term, there would be no religious instruction unless the parents and the pupils definitely wanted it. We were no longer in the devoutly Roman Catholic Austro-Hungarian Empire. I thought that the girls would all rejoice. Instead, we thought of 'Little Flower' being deprived of us, and we all voted, indeed demanded, to carry on with religious instruction.

We promised 'Little Flower' to be as good as gold and we kept our promise — even when we had to learn Czech, as he was a true Czech, and also had to teach us this language.

The history teacher, a Frau professor, was a mournful looking, pale and very slim lady. After telling us what page to open in the history book, and asking one of us to read the text aloud, she would stand by the window, looking into the school garden, with an extremely sad expression on her face. The story went round that she had lost her fiancé in the war and I could well sympathise with her. She would never marry now, I thought, and it must be like losing one's husband or wife.

Anyhow, the history lessons themselves were not very inspiring as we now had to learn Czech history, full of strange names of battles and kings we had never heard of before. Nothing more was ever mentioned about Austrian or German wars. We also had a judge come to teach us about the new laws and regulations, in this our new country — especially about things one should not say as one could go to prison for it. For instance, to call Czechoslovakia *Tschechei* (a German abbreviation) was regarded as making fun of the name. Neither must one criticise the new regime, or the Czechs themselves or sing German patriotic songs — and definitely not the old National Anthem. It was also frowned upon for girls to wear white knee-socks, as they were regarded as emphasising the German bias. This I found difficult to understand, as I had never seen any girl in white knee-socks. Perhaps they wore them in Prussia!

We also had lessons in world history. Of British history I remember very little. It finished, or began and finished, with the Normans conquering Britain. Then there was a king who had six wives and was Henry VIII, or had eight wives and was Henry the VI. We were never quite sure. Then there was the powerful queen who was extremely cruel and was called Queen Elizabeth I. Then there was Mary Stuart, the tragic queen; we all loved and admired her. Schiller had written a play about her and we took, of course, her part. She was killed by the cruel Queen Elizabeth. So it is that history can be mixed up in the heads of young girls, who have to learn strange stories in a new republic with a new language.

121

Our time with Frau Sedlacek was not as happy as we, or rather Papa, had expected. He paid a lot of money for our board, but we did not get enough to eat. Everything in the household was high class: silver on the table, damask table cloths and a maid, suitably dressed, who would bring in the meals on a trolley, apparently for everyone to serve themselves. But then Frau Baronin would place a tiny portion on our plates. When we had finished she would ask if we wanted a second helping, directing the trolley towards one of us. Every time, as soon as we eagerly said yes, she moved the trolley away again — and we were both too shy to insist on a second helping. Her granddaughter, Vera, always insisted that she was not very hungry. She was a quiet girl, slim, very pale with dark eyes and long black plaits hanging down her back. I never knew what to say to her and even Lilly could not become friendly with her although she was in the same class. We bought stale buns with our pocket money to eat secretly in our room. Then one day, towards the end of the autumn term, we surprised Vera having a substantial meal in the kitchen. No wonder she never had much appetite at the table! Papa decided we would go somewhere else after the Christmas holidays.

We stayed at home with Papa for Christmas. It was again a rather sad time for us, only lightened by one amusing incident. It was the afternoon of Christmas Eve. Lilly and I had decided to bake the customary 'nut-strudel'. Everything went well: the dough was rolled out, then stretched to almost the size of the kitchen table, filled with ground nuts, sugar, butter and raisins and then rolled into a long sausage shape.

Now came the question of how to get this thing onto the baking sheet. We had forgotten that it should be rolled up with the table cloth on which it had been stretched, and with that rolled on to the baking sheet. In that way the 'sausage' could easily be lifted and turned to form a 'double' sausage. We therefore stood helpless in front of this long, rolled-up 'strudel', with no idea of how to get it into the oven.

At last we called in Papa. First, he rather crossly told us not to attempt to make something we were not sure how to do. 'First think,' he said, 'then act'. However, he tried to help us. 'How stupid you are,' he addressed me, 'this is such a simple matter.' 'You,' he pointed at Lilly, 'stand at one end of the strudel'. Then pointing at me, 'You will stand in the middle and I at the other end. When I count three, we lift the dough and place it on the baking sheet.'

Alas, even Papa did not know everything. At the count of three we lifted the thing and found ourselves standing, each with a messy lump of dough in our hands from which the filling of nuts and raisins protruded. With an angry exclamation, Papa threw his portion of the dough on to the baking sheet, muttered something incomprehensive, and left the kitchen. I threw my bit after his, relieved Lilly of hers and smoothed it all out, but it still looked terribly messy. Nevertheless, I took a cake tin, greased it, put the whole lot into it and deposited it in the oven. It was by now completely mixed up, dough and filling. I did not mind; somebody would eat it.

After Christmas, when the shop-bought strudel was finished, I brought this so-called 'cake' out. 'Only for Lilly and me,' I assured Papa, as he looked at it suspiciously. However, he tasted it himself, found it excellent and helped us to finish it off. In fact, we were sorry when no more was left!

After the Christmas holidays we went to lodge with a couple called Jantner, who had a comfortable flat near the park. The husband was a director of an insurance company. He was short, thick-set, with such a protruding belly that it was impossible for him to tie his shoe laces and his wife had to do it. She was much younger than he, a pretty and vivacious woman. When she was cross with him she refused to do up the laces and would leave him sitting on the sofa, trying in vain to reach his shoes. Lilly then took pity on him and tied his shoe laces so that he could go out.

Shortly before Easter we came back from school one day to find that Frau Jantner was not there; neither did she come back to give us our evening meal. We waited and waited until at last Herr Jantner informed us in a shaky voice that his wife had left him. A friendly neighbour came in to cook for us. 'Frau Jantner has gone off with that travelling salesman; I saw it coming ages ago,' she told us. That was another puzzling 'way of the world', I thought to myself.

Papa had to look quickly for another place for us. There was a so-called 'Young Ladies' Home' in the town which was run by a women's organisation and it was decided that I would live there. A middle-aged widow, Frau Benesch, was in charge of the 'young ladies'. There were about twenty girls, aged from fourteen to eighteen or nineteen. We all slept in a large dormitory and ate in a large dining-room, which also served as a study. It was a bit like the convent, except that we could talk whenever we liked and go where we liked, after school. Unless we went to the theatre, when Frau Benesch collected us, we had to be in by eight o'clock at the latest.

123

Lilly did not want to come to the 'Young Ladies' Home'. We both thought it would be nice to live separately. One of Lilly's school friends stayed with a family called Kossak. They had two daughters, one of whom had gone to a finishing school in Switzerland, so Lilly's friend had her room. Now the other daughter was going to Switzerland and there would be a room free for Lilly.

Frau Kossak was a smart, beautiful and fashionable lady, but, as it turned out later, she was also a kleptomaniac. We had always thought that stealing is stealing, but this apparently was different, an excusable illness. She brought home all sorts of things, sometimes completely useless, and either the cook would take them back to the shop or her husband would pay the bills. All the big shops knew about her peculiar illness. Lilly, however, had heard all this from the cook.

Lilly had a lovely time there. Frau Kossak took the girls to the theatre and to concerts and provided all kinds of treats for them. Then the parents of Lilly's school friend moved to another town and an older girl moved in. She was seventeen years old and a student was very much in love with her. When she broke off the affair he tried to shoot himself, but he was only wounded and spent a lot of time in hospital. Now the girl was so upset that she cried every night and became almost hysterical, so her mother fetched her home. When Lilly told me all this we were both convinced that everything to do with love should be avoided and we had already realised that even marriage was often a sad affair.

At the end of the term the question arose as to where we should spend our summer holidays. Of course, we deperately wanted to go to Moldova. It had been impossible to go there during the war, the year before Mama had been too ill to go anywhere and now we could not get a visa. I thought it incredible that we needed special permission to go there; it was our real home and it had been bad enough for us having to stay away during the war years. Now the Banat belonged to Romania and we were regarded as 'foreigners' who needed special permits. Try as he might, Papa could not get a visa. The Romanian authorities were still suspicious of any foreigners.

I lay awake sometimes at night, feeling sure that Grandmother was missing us. I could visualise the way there, past the vineyards and the gypsy camp and finally to Grandmother, welcoming us with open arms.

All my longing did not help. Back we went to Gross-Herlitz to the convent, which we still regarded as a second home. That summer stays in my memory as one of endless days of hot sun and blue sky, with the lake shimmering in the heat. We went swimming in the lake, took long walks through cornfields with thousands of poppies and enjoyed our leisure time free from all duties. It was the first time in the convent that we could do what we liked without supervision. At nearly fourteen and fifteen years old we felt quite grown-up. For the first time I watched the birds, noticed the wind playing 'waves' with the grass on the sloping meadow and made friends with the cows and horses in the fields. The church bells would ring at twelve o'clock for the midday meal and the Angelus bell would ring, calling us back for the evening meal. But it still was not Moldova!

After the holidays Lilly could not return to the Kossaks' as both the daughters had returned from Switzerland. So she joined me instead at the 'Young Ladies' Home'. I was delighted. Although we did not admit it, we had missed each other. Lilly had come every day to visit me and I usually greeted her rather crossly with: 'Why are you here? What do you want?' But if she ever missed a day, then I would greet her with 'Why did you not come yesterday? I was very worried.' Now I was glad that we were together again.

Frau Benesch was a kind, motherly soul. Every evening she went round the dormitory to each bed to say goodnight, especially to the younger ones, sometimes even with a kiss. I felt very embarrassed by this, but Lilly needed this type of affection as she was very warm-hearted.

When the lights were out, we talked quietly. Once the question of sex came up. It was not called sex in those days, one only spoke of 'it', but none of us seemed definitely to know what 'it' was. The two eighteen-year-old girls kept quiet and we younger ones puzzled about 'it'.

Then Louise Kleiber, who had been brought up by her grandmother, told us one evening: 'I have asked my grandmother and she told me I must not worry, because if I do it before I am married, it is a sin, and if I don't do it after I am married, it is also a sin, but my husband will tell me what to do.' This was not really a satisfactory answer but it would have to do. Papa had given me two little books, *What a Little Girl Must Know* and *What a Growing Girl Must Know*, but there was nothing about 'it' in those — only about hygiene and such matters.

Papa was generous with our pocket money. Apart from money to spend on ourselves, he also gave us money to pay for the various things we might need in school, such as new books, pens, pencils and, of course, toiletries; but we had to keep a strict account about these expenses. Lilly was always careful, not only with her pocket money, but also with her other expenses and her accounts were always right. I usually forgot to put down what I had spent and then tried to remember later and to balance the account. Papa had stressed the importance of keeping a strict account of all expenses. Every month we had to reckon up with him, either when he came to see us or when we occasionally spent the weekend at home.

One day I could not get my accounts right. It seemed that I had less money than I should have, although for once I *had* made a note of all my expenses. In the end I invented the absolute need of a new atlas, coloured pencils and a notebook — and at last got my figures to balance.

Papa examined my bookkeeping carefully and then he said: 'I knew you were a clever girl, but this is quite remarkable. You have been able to buy things from money you never had.' He explained that when handing me the money some weeks ago he had made a mistake and given me less than I should have had. I was terribly embarrassed. This was worse than if Papa had been very cross. I had to confess that I had made up the account from memory and put some extra expenses in to make it balance. I promised to stick to the truth in future.

Frau Benesch was a member of a group of spiritualists. 'Table tapping' was widely practised in those days. Every week, on two or three evenings, her friends came to see her and they held a session while we slept. Sometimes they needed some people to form the circle round the large table and several of the 'young ladies' were asked to join in. Lilly and I were amongst them. We sat around the table with our hands on the table top, little fingers and thumbs touching, to form a chain. The lights were put out, except for a covered light in a corner of the room, and the table tapping began.

The table was supposed to rise slightly and come down again with a quiet knock. One knock meant 'no', two knocks meant 'yes' and, if we wanted a whole word, the alphabet was recited and the table 'knocked' at the right letter.

After several meetings, the name of our second mother was given. At about the same time there came, in a long chain of letters, the news that Papa was thinking of marrying again. For some time we had found, when we were at Jaegerndorf for weekends and went into town, that several ladies whom we didn't know would stop us and enquire after

My third Mama

Papa. Aunt Marie had told us that several of her acquaintances, some of them rich young widows, wouldn't mind marrying Papa. I wasn't surprised by this. As far as I was concerned any woman would only be too happy to marry Papa. I even suspected that Frau Benesch was quite interested in Papa.

Occasionally Papa had asked us what we would feel if he were to marry again, so that we could have a home for always and not just for short visits. He said he wanted to find a wife who would be a mother to us and treat us like her own children, and, of course, we ought to like her as well. I considered this to be reasonable. I was fed up with living with strange families or in the 'Young Ladies' Home'. The message from the 'other world', therefore, did not surprise me much, but I was puzzled.

Shortly afterwards was the feast of St Nicholas and to our great joy and astonishment a big parcel arrived for us. We never had had a parcel before. It contained home-made biscuits and sweets, with a card saying 'Greetings from St Nicholas', but no indication of the sender was given. When we told Papa about it he just smiled and said he thought he knew the lady who sent it.

Then he told me that he would like me to learn sewing; I could go once a week in the afternoon (school finished at one o'clock) to a Frau Bayer who taught young girls sewing and needlework.

Frau Bayer lived just outside Troppau and it was a pleasant walk there. The first thing I started to make was a new bathing suit. It was the very old-fashioned kind — printed cotton, trousers below the knees and a sleeveless blouse long enough to cover the bottom. Frau Bayer smiled when she saw this and persuaded me to at least make it short and in one piece, with no skirt and no sleeves. I agreed but was afraid that I would be too ashamed ever to wear it.

One evening, Frau Benesch asked us again to a session of table-tapping. Again the name of our second Mama was spelled out. Frau Benesch asked if and who our father would marry again. Then came the message that Papa would marry Frau Bayer. I must admit that when the message about Papa's marriage was tapped out, I could not help thinking of Frau Bayer and when her name came up, I felt sure I must have been influencing the table without really meaning to, perhaps pressing my fingers harder on the table when the right letter was called out.

We heard nothing more for some time. As Christmas arrived, and passed, and another new year began, we decided to wait and see.

In January 1921 we had our first dancing lesson. After school we took the train to Jaegerndorf and went home. Papa was not there, but a big jar of home-made noodles was left on the table and plenty of preserved fruit had been stored in the pantry, still from Mama's time. I made a fire in the tiled stove, cooked the noodles and we ate them with brown sugar and butter. A dish of preserved fruit was for afters. Then we changed and waited for Aunt Marie to take us to the dancing lessons.

From one dancing lesson to the next we had to wash and iron our silk blouses. Lilly did the washing as soon as we arrived and I ironed them while stiil damp. This happened twice a week, on Tuesdays and Thursdays.

We enjoyed these lessons immensely. There were about twelve couples, but the partners had to be changed after every dance. We learned the tango, minuet, quadrille, polonaise, the waltz, laendler and the most modern dance of all, the charleston. Papa found that dance most peculiar when he came to the final ball. 'Kicking your legs like young horses!' he remarked.

One young man managed to dance more often with me than with the other girls. He was working in Jaegerndorf but came from Karlsbad. He seemed very sophisticated and I was flattered by his attention. One day Hanni, my older cousin, confided in me that he had asked Aunt Marie (who, of course, was our chaperone at all the functions) whether Papa would allow him to take me out. Unfortunately, I learned that Aunt Marie had answered that she was sure Papa would think me still too young to go out with a young man. From that moment on I felt sure that I was in love and that my young love had been thwarted by my stern father. I felt very romantic and used to stand by a window in school and in the 'Home' looking as sad as our history teacher, and confided to those who asked what was the matter with me that I was in love but that my father forbade it. Luckily I soon got bored with this tragic role!

Half-way through the course during the *Fasching* (carnival time) we held a *kraentzchen*, a kind of small ball, but without a dinner. For this we had to learn how to accept invitations to dance, note down the partners for later dances, move gracefully when being led back after a dance and also to make small talk. Then on *Faschingdienstag* (Pancake Tuesday) we had a real ball — with our first ball gowns. How grown-up we felt! We all had a beautiful ebony or feathery fan, but also a simple wooden slatted fan, on which all our partners could write their name, with a little verse or a few words with it, or even do a drawing. We had to prepare *kottilons*, small presents for our partners made of silk ribbons, which we were to pin to the partner's lapel.

Lilly could not make a *kottilon* and I was not even sure how to start. Papa suggested that we should go and ask Frau Bayer to help us. So, one afternoon, we went to see her. Frau Bayer received us in her customary warm and friendly way and showed great interest in our *kottilon* dilemma. She asked us to buy some cigarettes, little trinkets and various silk ribbons and to bring them to her on our next visit. Then she offered us a big bowl of fruit preserves and home-made cakes. Lilly was as keen as always on sweet things and so looked forward to her next visit. I could not go on this occasion because I had some other private lessons, but Lilly promised to show me what to do when she got home.

Frau Bayer not only showed Lilly how to make a *kottilon*, she made many herself and at the end of the afternoon Lilly had more than twenty, enough for every dancing partner. She was again treated to cakes and preserves and she told me later that she found Frau Bayer the nicest lady she had ever known. Her *kottilons* were a great success and Lilly felt sure they were the best of anyone's. She even gave one to the dancing master.

Our first ball was the most exciting thing that had ever happened to us. We could not sleep the night before. The parents of the young people, in our case Aunt Marie and Papa, were seated at tables round the room in order to watch that nothing undecorous should happen. The ball opened with a polonaise round the room; to be the leading couples was a great honour. The lucky pair, of course, was chosen by the dancing master, who in turn was greatly influenced by the parents. The girl chosen was the daughter of the most prominent manufacturer in town.

At the end of the dancing a formal dinner was held. We were led ceremoniously by our partners to the table. We did have wine, but only one glass. The dancing master then made a speech, thanking everyone present and especially his pupils for their co-operation and he congratulated us all on our excellent dancing. The parents or chaperones sat at a different table and seemed to enjoy themselves every bit as much as we did. It was a very, very happy evening and we felt quite sophisticated — until the following Wednesday, when school started again.

Just a few weeks later, when we were both at home, Papa had a serious talk with us. He said he intended to marry Frau Bayer, but as he wanted a peaceful family life he wanted to know whether we thought we could get on with her and behave ourselves. He spoke to me again separately afterwards, pointing out that I could influence Lilly in this respect. I in turn promised that there would be no trouble.

We both liked Frau Bayer. It would have been hard not to do so, although she was quite different from our second Mama. She was bonny, not as slim as Mama had been but just right. Her hair was already turning grey even though she was only thirty-five, but it suited her young, fresh-coloured face. I thought that she was the kind of person who, although so much older, would understand how a shy sixteen-year-old girl felt. I for one was looking forward to the wedding, and Lilly assured me that she was also very pleased. Then, too, was the fact that the summer term was our last term at the lyceum and then we would go to finishing school. It would be a complete new life for us. We just wondered if we would be able to go to Moldova for the summer holidays. Papa had told us some time ago that no special permits were now necessary for travel to Romania. Another mother and a holiday in Moldova, what more could one desire!

The wedding was planned for August. I realise now that it must not have been an easy decision for Frau Bayer to take on two teenagers and give up her independence. She lived in her own flat near her parents and taught needlework to a small group of girls, but that was only a few afternoons a week. Now she would have to look after Papa, Lilly and I every day.

Meantime we were introduced to our new relations-to-be. There were more grandparents, two uncles, two aunts and five cousins — and all living practically next to each other. Frau Bayer's father had an iron foundry in Jaktar, on the outskirts of Troppau. The family house was near the foundry and had a large garden and orchard. The orchard was full of apple, cherry and plum trees. Grandmother-to-be kept hens, geese, turkeys and two goats in the orchard and there were at least three cats running about the place. Frau Bayer had had a Doberman but he had died the year before and I wished he were still alive. The cats were all too shy to be cuddled, and the goats too big and not interested.

Unfortunately, there were difficulties to overcome first before the wedding could take place. Frau Bayer had been divorced in Vienna four years previously, in 1918. Vienna was in Austria and the laws in the new Republic of Czechoslovakia were different; her divorce was not accepted here.

She travelled to Vienna to find a lawyer to sort it all out. Papa explained to us that if she was unsuccessful, they would not be married.

Our life would have to go on as before. We were terribly disappointed and prayed that everything would turn out well. I must have been already broad-minded, or ahead of the times, because I implored Papa to live with Frau Bayer as though they were married if the wedding could not take place. I assured him that Lilly and I would not mind. He was somewhat horrified at my extreme views and declined my suggestion.

Fortunately, Frau Bayer came back from Vienna with various new documents and went one morning with Papa to the Registrar's office at the Town Hall. They were still unsure whether these new documents would be accepted. Lilly and I waited in Frau Bayer's flat. We had been told to go across the road to the house of our grandparents-to-be, but I felt too shy; perhaps they would not be our relatives after all. I sat desolately in front of a bookcase and tried to read, while Lilly prayed. Her prayer was answered. Papa came back with Frau Bayer as our new Mama.

13

LILLY AND I accompanied Papa and his new wife on their honeymoon to Moldova. We had not seen Grandmother since before the war and now we went there as 'foreigners'. It seemed incredible, but we felt sure that Moldova would still be the same.

We travelled via Vienna to Budapest and stayed there for a few days. We visited the castle on the hill, and the Cathedral of St Matthias where the Hungarian kings were crowned. When Austria and Hungary had been one empire, the ruling monarch was declared Emperor of Austria, but still had to be crowned as King of Hungary. The last Emperor, Karl of Habsburg, had been crowned there before he had to leave the country for Spain to live in exile with his family when Austria became a republic. We saw, too, that famous crown of St Stephen, which was used at all the coronations. St Stephen had been one of the first kings of Hungary.

Papa took us to Rakos Palota, the district in Budapest where we had been born and we visited the churchyard where our natural mother was buried. It was a sad sight. The church was badly damaged, and most of the gravestones and monuments had been broken during the revolution after the war. The gates had been smashed down and now sheep were everywhere. Papa looked thoughtful

'It is strange,' he said, 'your mother never liked gravestones and monuments. There should only be grass, she told me, so that sheep and lambs could graze there. Now she has her wish.'

I particularly remember going swimming on Margareten Island in the Danube. In the swimming pool there artificial waves were created at certain times. It was like swimming in a rough sea. Margareten Island was also famous for its hot springs. We sat on stones, hot from the spring underneath, and paddled in the naturally warm water.

During one of our walks through the town we passed the monument to Dr Semmelweiss. 'You ought to be specially grateful to this man,' said Papa, pointing to the statue. 'He saved many women from death in childbirth.' I did not realise what he meant at the time, but I looked in awe at the statue. I never forgot the name, and remembered it later when I learned that it was he who discovered the cause of puerperal fever and how it could be prevented through the strict sterilisation of hands and instruments by doctors and midwives.

Before we left Budapest, Papa went to collect the insurance which was due for both of us. He had paid this from the time we were born, to provide for our further education or for our dowries. The premium had been deposited in a bank as it had proved impossible to transfer it to Czechoslovakia. Unfortunately, because of recent inflation it was now only a very small sum — just enough for a meal for the four of us in a decent restaurant. Even then Papa had to pay for the wine and the tip out of his own pocket. 'Now you have eaten your fortunes,' said Papa, 'and I had better start saving again.' I wanted to study to be a doctor, but as matters stood Papa could not afford it. There were no grants in those days. The war and Mama's illness had taken all his savings, even the capital from Mama's dowry.

On our final evening we went to a restaurant where gypsies were playing. They cannot read music, yet they can move one to tears and laughter with their violin playing. They also are gifted at sensing the atmosphere or focusing on certain people in the audience. They will play especially well to a couple in love, for instance, and I, who could not sing and was regarded as tone deaf, was moved almost to tears by their playing. When they had finished I had to bring myself back from another world.

We continued our journey to Moldova by train. It was a beautiful sunny day. As we crossed the vast Hungarian Plain, the Puszta, I suddenly saw the rooftops and spires of a town in the distance. I exclaimed excitedly that we were approaching Debrecsin. Papa came over to my side of the window and looked out. 'No, we are not anywhere near it,' he said. 'What you see is a *fata Morgana*, something to do with the sky reflecting the town so that we see the picture as in a mirror.' It seemed strange to me to realise that what we were seeing was only a picture in the sky. Papa said it was quite a rare phenomenon and occurred on exceptionally hot days. In fact it took us another hour to get to Debrecsin.

Shortly after midday there occurred a slight collision. Our carriage stopped abruptly and we were all thrown forward from our seats onto the laps of those opposite. Nobody was hurt, apart from a few bumps from the suitcases which fell from the racks, but we had to leave the train and walk to the next station as the line could not be cleared until the following morning. There was no path next to the railway line so we had to continue on foot with our luggage, between the rails and over the sleepers, which did not make walking any easier.

Some people in other carriages had been badly hurt and waited for the ambulance men, who later arrived in a workmen's wagon. I wondered why this had to happen on Mama's first journey to Moldova, when we had done the same journey so often before without any incidents. Then I suddenly realised that I was thinking of Papa's third wife as 'Mama'. It had taken me a long time to get used to always saying 'Frau Bayer' but the happy atmosphere had made it easy to address her as 'Mama'. Lilly had done so right from the beginning, immediately after the wedding.

After we had crossed into Romania yet another incident happened. The guard warned us that the train would proceed very slowly over a bridge which had been damaged and was still not quite repaired. Those who preferred could get out and walk across the dried-up river bed and then rejoin the train at the other side. We preferred to stay on the train and Lilly prayed loudly to St Anthony, to the great embarrassment of Papa and I, as we moved at a snail's pace across the bridge.

This was our first experience of travelling in the new Romania. The majority of the people in our carriage were still resentful that this part of the former Empire now belonged to Romania; there were great arguments in progress and the Romanian Government was blamed for everything. There would be more to come.

At the next station some Romanian peasants got in. I had noticed on the window the usual warnings, such as 'Do not put your head out of the window', 'Close the window when going through a tunnel'. However, one notice was missing: 'Spitting is forbidden'. Instead, there was a new one in its place: 'Do not remove your shoes'. We had travelled in many trains and spitting had always been forbidden. Now, apparently, it was allowed but shoes were not to be removed. We always wore cotton gloves in a train, but we had never bothered about shoes, unless we were in a sleeper, when we undressed anyway.

I was still puzzling about this new regulation when a man in workman's clothes, sitting two seats away from me on the other side of the carriage, spit right past me through my open window. Luckily, he was a good shot, but I was disgusted nevertheless. I would have preferred smelly feet to this. Papa, who saw what happened and noticed my disgusted expression, shrugged his shoulders and his eyes told me to keep quiet.

Lilly seemed to have enjoyed all our adventures, even part of the walk. She whispered to me that she was already looking forward to seeing her teacher's face when she handed her essay in. (We knew in advance that we would have to write an account of our holidays.) I agreed with her that probably nobody else would have had such an adventurous time as we were having.

At last we arrived in Bascias and took a local train to Old Moldova. We left our luggage at the tiny station to be fetched later and walked the half hour distance to Moldova noua as Uj-Moldova was now known. *Uj* was the Hungarian for 'new' and *noua* the Romanian.

We were on home ground at last! We caught sight of the hut on top of the hill and the vineyards. The grapes in the vineyards were ripening and we pointed out to Mama the peach trees between the rows of grapevines. We passed, too, the gypsy camp and everything seemed the same as we remembered, even though we had been away so long. Soon we arrived at Grandmother's house and there she was, with outstretched arms and her lovely warm smile. She looked smaller — or had we grown taller?

In the front room behind the glass in the wall cupboard were two large plates with her customary *apfelpitta*, cut into diamond-shaped pieces. Lilly took a piece straight away. Then we sat down in the salon to coffee and cake and talked and talked. So much had happened since our last visit to Moldova.

Then Lilly and I went into the garden to 'tell the bees' that we were back and to give Grandmother a chance to have a talk with her new daughter-in-law. Mama told us afterwards that she had to promise Grandmother not to leave her son to be alone again, ever. Mama was to keep her promise. Many, many years later Papa died first, and she followed him several years later. She shared the Second World War years with him and the much worse years after the war.

We visited my Aunt Marie, Papa's only sister, and Uncle Gustav. There was a wooden bench in front of their house, next to the steps leading into the shop. Sitting there in the evening one could watch what was going on, greet the passers-by and have a little chat with them. It was a bit like sitting outside a café in Paris, but drinking wine instead of vermouth, cassis or coffee.

Aunt Marie told us about the revolution and the changes which had been made. 'Everything has changed for the worse,' she kept saying, 'since we have belonged to Romania.' She definitely did not like the Romanians; to her they were still peasants.

For a long time I had been begging Papa to let me have my hair cut in the fashionable *bubikopf* (little boy's head). His answer had always been the same: 'No daughter of mine will wear short hair. Long hair is something to be proud of.' Papa's generation seemed to think that a young girl's honour, whatever that meant, would fall with her tresses. Yet now here was Aunt Marie exclaiming quite indignantly to Papa: 'How can you let your girls still wear their hair long. It went out of fashion ages ago. I will ask my hairdresser who's coming tomorrow, to do my hair, to cut the girls hair, in a more up-to-date style. She has been trained in Bucharest, the Paris of the Balkans.' Papa agreed; after all she was his elder sister. Mama just smiled. She had not been married long enough to start arguments with Papa.

So we had our hair cut the following morning, and then had our first water wave. Even Papa had to agree that it suited us and Grandmother said to Papa: 'If Marie hadn't done it I would have asked her hairdresser next week.'

Papa intended to show his new wife the beauties of his homeland; Lilly and I of course, went with them. It was our homeland too. The first trip we made was by boat to Orsova, through the 'Iron Gates' — so called because huge rocks reaching down to the river banks on both sides resembled a gate through which the Danube could squeeze most dramatically.

While the river flows gently near Moldova and around the fortification of Golibac, now in Yugoslavia, but in Serbia in those days, it becomes increasingly wild and further down, through the 'Casan', it is really fierce. The word *casan* means 'kettle' in Serbian, but 'cauldron' would have been a better name. The river swirls and bubbles, and there are dangerous whirlpools which have pulled many a small boat down. The pilots do not have an easy task guiding the passenger boats through the Casan.

Just above Turn Severin there was an island in the middle of the river called Ada Kaleh. It was still inhabited by Turks, who had been left behind when the majority of their countrymen were driven to the southernmost part of Europe, the present-day Turkey. In 1878 the Congress of Berlin forgot about this island when they were dividing up the Danube shore amongst Romania, Bulgaria and Serbia. It remained a Turkish possession for the next forty years, when again it was forgotten, even by the Turks themselves. After the First World War it was not even mentioned in the peace treaty, when the main part of the country became Romanian property. The island of Ada Kaleh did not actually belong to any country.

This island was only accessible by means of a narrow, flat-bottomed boat, able to carry half-a-dozen passengers. This needed a skilled oarsman to manipulate it, as the Iron Gates were not far away and the currents ran strong. I felt quite excited as we were being ferried across.

Ada Kaleh was quite small and therefore easily explored on foot. There was a small mosque at one end of it and I remember there being an abundance of fig trees and roses. The Turks who lived there sold sugar, coffee and tobacco extremely cheaply as they paid no customs duties and, of course, no taxes or rates. They made and sold a kind of Turkish Delight. There were several stalls where we could watch how those sweets were made. Rose petals were used to give it that special flavour. We watched a man pounding and rolling a mixture of sugar, rose-petal juice and something else and then slicing it into half-inch squares. I didn't like the taste nor did I particularly enjoy watching it being made. The rest of the male population, those who weren't watching the stalls, seemed to spend their time sitting at small tables, drinking coffee and smoking in the sun.

These Turks still maintained their traditional customs and their wives lived in a harem watched over by a eunuch. By that time, in the mainland Turkey, Kemal Ataturk had more or less freed the women when he took over from the Sultan's regime. No longer did they have to keep themselves completely veiled and live in harems. But here nothing had changed.

The women were used to being looked at by curious tourists and Mama, Lilly and I were allowed to visit a harem. I was most disappointed by what I found there. The few huts where several women lived together were sparsely furnished. Rugs and mats were laid out on the floor, obviously for sleeping on, and there were cushions everywhere. Two women were preparing meals on tiny charcoal ovens and on a tiny stove. It was hardly as exotic as I had hoped.

We were told later that when Kemal Ataturk visited Romania he was surprised to hear about the Turkish community on Ada Kaleh, but by then it was already doomed as a huge hydroelectric dam was already planned. When this was eventually built the whole island was submerged, like Atlantis.

On the way back to Grandmother's from Ada Kaleh, we visited a small chapel on the side of the road which followed the banks of the Danube. Here I had yet another lesson in history. Although I had never shown much interest in history at school, here I found it all to be real and exciting.

Hungary had revolted in 1848 when the Emperor Franz Josef came to the throne as an eighteen-year-old youth. That much I knew. Kossuth Lajos was the leader of that revolt, which was cruelly put down by the Austrians. He had to flee the country, but did not want to leave the crown St Stephen in Budapest — to be worn by the hated Austrian Emperor. On the other hand, the crown should not be taken out of Hungary, so he buried it near the then Austro-Hungarian frontier, hoping that he would come back to a free Hungary.

Instead he died in America. Only years later was the crown found by a ploughman, and reverently taken back to Budapest. To commemorate the place where that treasured crown had been buried, a little chapel was built. We all signed the visitors' book and left impressed by that piece of history which we had not learned at school. We did, however, know the song about that national hero, Kossuth Lajos, as Aunt Marie played it often on her ancient gramophone.

A little further down the river, opposite the tiny village of Ogradeno, could be seen 'Trajan's Tablet' cut into the rock. The inscription read:

IMP. CAESAR DIVI. NERVAE F. TRAIJANUS.
AVG. GERM. PONT. MAXIMUS.

This tablet celebrated the victory over the Dacians in AD 101, when the Emperor Trajan threw a bridge over the Danube and colonised Dacia. Some see this event as the beginning of the Romanian people.

It was said that the name 'Romania' comes really from Rome. It is true that there is a similarity between the Romanian and the Latin language and there are still many places where Roman origin can be proved. Nevertheless there are also many customs and place names which date back to the arrival of, or rather conquest by, the Turks.

When the hydroelectric dam was jointly constructed by Romania and Yugoslavia much was destroyed, not only Ada Kaleh and Trajan's Tablet. The holes in the rock, carefully bored by Trajan's legionnaires: to hold iron rods which were covered with planks to allow a path over the rocks, are now filled in with river water; so too are the large rings, on which the Turks later fixed a chain across the Danube. Everything has disappeared.

A few days later, Uncle Gustav suggested another trip, a special one such as we had never done before. It was to be a trip by cart right across the Carpathian Mountains to the other side. It would take a whole day and night then another half day. 'You might see a bear,' he promised, 'and there are still wolves there but we don't want to see them because they usually come in packs.'

The cart ride should be fun! There were wooden seats and the wheels had only iron rims. Nobody had thought of taking cushions. There was no inbuilt suspension at that time and the roads were more than primitive. We bounced along through the *urwald* (primeval or virgin forest) where the trees grew until they fell down of their own accord and then lay there until they rotted. 'It is extremely dangerous to go in between the trees because you never know what is under your feet,' explained Uncle Gustav. Then the trees grew sparser, until at last we reached a clearing on a plateau. It was by then quite dark, but there were stars in the sky and the air was still relatively mild. Uncle insisted that we make a fire 'to frighten away the wolves in case there are some nearby'.

We collected fallen branches from the edge of the so-called road, which Papa and Uncle Gustav broke over their knees into smaller pieces, and soon we had a lovely fire blazing. Long ago, we learned, merchants had to bring everything over the pass; they usually travelled in groups and then they put their wagons and cars into a square with a fire in the middle and then they felt quite safe. A bear might be curious but would not venture inside the square.

Then I remembered a story I heard as a child, about Uncle Herrmann going out to hunt a bear with his big spotted dog. 'Yes,' laughed Papa, when I mentioned it, 'he was always hunting bears but he never actually shot one. He just liked to stalk them and watch them at their antics; they can be quite funny, especially the young ones.' We kept quiet for a moment, probably all thinking of Uncle Herrmann. We had not talked about him in front of Grandmother as he was still missing, although Grandmother had never given up hope that he

The Carpathian Mountains

would return from Russia. Several prisoners from Russia were still arriving home. They had taken all this time as they were returning via China. Others had been reported by fellow prisoners-of-war who had returned as having married Russian girls and stayed there.

We drank our hot soup, warmed over the fire and ate fried chicken pieces and then it was time to go on. The horses had also had a rest and a feed. Lilly and I nodded on our seats. It seemed as if the journey would never end. It was such a long time since we had left Moldova.

I must have fallen asleep, when suddenly I heard Uncle Gustav's voice: 'Come on, out you get, we are here.' I realised that it was daylight. I tried to get up, but, oh, were my limbs stiff! They had to lift me off the wagon as they had already done with Lilly, and then they even had to help Mama. Papa and Uncle Gustav laughed. 'Never mind, said Uncle Gustav, now you know how all those travellers felt long ago, before Dunlop invented the rubber tyre — not that it would have been much good on these roads.

141

I don't remember much more of that journey, only stiff joints and an aching back, but the picture of the dark forest, the dancing shadows of the fire and the velvety starry sky are still very clear in my mind. Secretly, deep in my heart, I had hoped to see a bear and to hear the howling of the wolves and perhaps catch a glimpse of them as our cart raced away.

We also explored the more immediate surroundings of Moldova that summer. Before the war we had always gone to the vineyards, which we now proudly showed our new Mama, but there were other interesting places to visit. Moldova lies between the lowest hills of the Carpathians and is well protected from the rough winds which sweep down from the higher peaks. To the south, towards the Danube, the road led past the gypsy camp and the field vineyards. I used to be slightly frightened of the gypsies, having heard in school that they sometimes steal children, although these seemed to like us. Uncle Herrmann used to throw pennies to the gypsy children on the way from the vineyards and would let them have baskets of grapes. Now that I was growing up, however, I thought their life was most romantic, especially in the evening when the red glow in the sky told of their big camp fire.

Towards the north of the village was a forked road; one side leading past the Lilac Hill — a wonderful sight in spring — and the other road leading up to the Calvary Hill. At the top was a fairly large plateau, with a tall wooden cross in the middle. Under a few trees was a bench. From there could be enjoyed the most beautiful view. Across the top, further to the north, was unspoilt country with a big cave, the 'Gaura Tusaka,' which was the ideal destination for a day trip.

Soon Papa's holiday, or rather his honeymoon, was over and he had to return to Jaegerndorf. It was late September and as the vintage would probably start on 5 October Grandmother asked whether we might stay on, so that Mama could enjoy it for the first time. Papa agreed. He was to leave and we were to stay on with Mama until after the vintage. It probably was the only case where a man returned from his honeymoon alone to be followed shortly afterwards by his bride and two teenage daughters.

This was to be the last time that we helped Grandmother with the harvest. Not a year later, at the beginning of May 1923, Aunt Marie's son Oscar informed us that Grandmother was ill — some small tummy trouble, but nothing serious; she was, after all, eighty-four years old and had never been ill before. I dreamt that night that I was in Moldova and walking to Grandmother's house, when I met Uncle Herrmann.

'Oh, Uncle Herrmann,' I said, 'why couldn't you have come earlier, Grandmother always knew you would come back and now it is too late, she died a few days ago.' I woke up in tears. When I told Papa about my dream a few days later, he said that Oscar would surely send a telegram if anything serious had happened. Then came a letter that Grandmother was well again — and the next day a telegram that she had died.

I was heartbroken. The only consolation I had was that Moldova was still there and that Grandmother was certainly in Heaven and would keep an eye on it. Then there was talk that Papa and Lilly and I had inherited a share of the vineyards. They were to be divided between us and Papa's elder brother and his children. I longed to go to Moldova and take over. 'Why can't I learn how to look after vineyards?' I questioned and argued with Papa. 'Surely Uncle Gustav could teach me and I would work very hard.' It didn't help. Papa explained that I would have to pay my uncle and cousins for their share, and we wouldn't have enough money. Furthermore, even if I was grown up I would not be allowed to stay in Romania for good or hold any possessions there, as I was a foreigner. Finally, I would probably not like to stay there all my life, as I had been brought up totally differently.

I argued and argued. How could I ever not like to live in Moldova? However, what Papa had said turned out to be true. We were not allowed to keep the vineyards or the house, although Uncle Gustav promised he would look after them for us. The house was sold and Aunt Marie bought the vineyards, but we could not get our money out of Romania legally. I don't know how Uncle Lajos, Papa's elder brother, managed it, but I was to go many times later to Moldova and always paid with Romanian money for the return journey and several years later, when I travelled in other parts of Romania, Aunt Marie or Oscar would send me the money to spend in the country. It seemed the most outrageous situation that we were foreigners in the place where we really belonged!

14

WHEN WE HAD eventually returned to join Papa, a new life was starting for us. We moved to a bigger flat in the middle of the town. For the first time ever we had central heating and a shower in the bathroom, but there was still only gas lighting. It was the first three-storey house in the town and our flat was on the third floor.

The flat roof could be reached from a huge loft, which also acted as a drying area for everyone in the house. There was also a special wash-house at the back and a washerwoman came every three weeks; the maid would only help with the rinsing and hanging out. The house was not far from the church and Lilly and I were sure that the bellringers could probably look into our room. Unfortunately, on Green Thursday so called because the first green vegetable of spring, spinach, is eaten, the church bells would ring throughout the morning, saying goodbye before leaving for Rome until Easter Saturday when they would again return. The noise was deafening.

However, such criticism came later, for the moment we were absolutely delighted with our new home. We had our own room with a writing desk and big settee and our own bookshelves. Mama said we could invite our friends whenever we liked, even for weekends. Life was good.

We had left the lyceum and continued our education in a kind of

My third Mama in the field vineyard

finishing school in Troppau called a *familienschule*. Everything or almost everything was taught that a cultured wife, mother and hostess should know, including dressmaking, supervising a household, instructing the maids, giving orders to a cook, knowing how to furnish and decorate a house or flat, the arts in general and music, how to make good conversation and to encourage conversations as a hostess. So the list continued. At the end of the two-year course we ought to be fit to marry even the President!

We had practised light athletics and running all through the winter of 1922 at our twice-weekly session at the sports centre and now it was decided that we were to go to the First International Turnerfest, which was a forerunner of the Olympic Games, to be held in Munich in July 1923. Our club was to represent Czechoslovakia in the group for Silesia. I had trained specially for running and the double bars. Lilly was to come too, though not as a competitor.

As inflation was still rising in Germany and money devalued from day to day, the leader of our group, who was a bank cashier, took charge of all the money we needed for the week in Munich, with the understanding that he would pay all expenses and only charge what the money was worth day-by-day. We slept in a school and had our meals in a communal kitchen and that was to be paid at the end of the week. The big day of the opening of the 'Games' arrived on 20 July. For the first time ever we wore real shorts, navy blue and cut above the knee. With these we wore white short-sleeved blouses. We had to wear this outfit for the procession — without any skirt!

The procession started at 10 a.m. and we paraded for one-and-a-half hours through the town to the stadium. There were athletes from America, Poland, Russia, Romania, Hungary and many more; the French were missing and I don't remember there being any representatives from Britain. Only as we marched in wider and wider circles round the stadium did we realise how many had actually come. Nothing much seemed to happen then, except for some welcoming speeches, and each country sang their national anthem. Then we made our way home to the school to which we were allocated, but not before we had a good meal. Then early to bed to be ready for the next day.

I did my running and did my bar excercises, but I did not win anything, not even a third prize. I came fifth in the running, which was very disappointing, but I had at least received good applause for my bar excercises. Lilly took part in the group gymnastics and forming symmetrical shapes and flower pictures with their bodies and coloured scarves.

In the evenings we could do what we liked and we walked through the town in large groups. It was on one of these walks I heard Hitler for the first time. He was not particularly well known at that time; it was before the *Weimar Putsch* and we only had heard his name mentioned.

He was shouting his opinions on the street corner. I just saw a little man with a funny moustache — very excited and wildly gesticulating — yelling about something or other, the gist of which I didn't quite understand. I was not impressed, but was still curious to know what was going on as a small group of people stopped to listen. The older members of our group urged us to come away; three of us had stopped to watch, but we quickly had to rejoin the others. Somebody whispered 'This is Hitler', and we left him to his shouting.

The following evening, we witnessed an anti-Jewish outrage, the first I ever saw, which horrified me and nearly got me into trouble. We had just passed the famous *Hofbrauhaus* beer-cellar when we heard the sound of breaking glass and shouts. Several men wearing shiny black boots and a kind of dark uniform had smashed the large window and were pulling several other men out through the broken glass in an extremely rough manner. As the victims fell onto the pavement, the booted ruffians kicked them while they lay helpless on the ground. Impulsively, I made to try and help up one of the fallen men, when my friends pulled me away. The uniformed men were shouting: 'You dirty, filthy Jews! Get out of this country before we kick you out for good.' We were horrified, but had no idea that this was just the beginning of the horrors to come. I only felt ashamed of speaking the same language as they.

As the week of sporting events progressed, we forgot the incident and when on the last day of the Turnerfest the German National Anthem *'Deutschland Deutschland ueber alles'* was sung we joined in with the thousands who were there and felt only pride in being of original German stock, even if we did now belong to the Banat. Being part of a great crowd creates a compelling atmosphere and enthusiasm is contagious; unfortunately this works also in riots, when people will do things they would never dream of if they had been alone or in just a small group. I would witness this for myself later in Prague.

We should have gone home then as the week was over, but our leader informed us that because of the inflation in Germany we had now almost more money left than we originally brought with us. He suggested that we stay another week and visit the various lakes round Munich and also make excursions into the mountains. His bank had agreed to inform our parents and get permission. It was a wonderful week and we, at least, had cause to be thankful for the inflation. When we finally left for home we felt as if we had been away for a long, long time.

That winter brought a big sensation: radio. Posters appeared everywhere in the town. One of the leading cloth manufacturers then invited the general public to a demonstration of the new invention. Of course, everyone was talking about it. The demonstration was to be held in the biggest hotel in the town, which had a large hall, normally used for theatre performances. The hall was crowded on the day. There was a table on the stage and on this a large box. Herr Larisch, the manufacturer, explained that music was being played somewhere else but we would all be able to hear it.

There had been similar claims made before. Walter Kratochvil, the brother of Lilly's best friend, Hilda, had built himself what he called a crystal set. He was forever playing with it. He would put on a pair of phones and listen. From time to time he would shout: 'Come quickly, I've got it!' And if you ran there, by the time he handed over the earphones all you could hear was a crackling sound. 'Oh, it's gone off again,' Walter would explain — and the whole performance would start once more.

As we sat in the big hall we expected similar things to happen: perhaps a lot of crackling sounds and then an apology from Herr Larisch that the thing had gone off again.

Herr Larisch said a few words by way of explaining and then pressed or turned a button on the box and, to our great amazement, there was real music to be heard. It was unbelievable, incredible! After about half an hour Herr Larisch turned it off, and told the audience about the various radio sets which were on the market at the moment, before thanking everyone for coming.

We went home feeling very excited. Papa was deep in thought and then had a long talk with Mama. Within a few days a table radio was installed, complete with wires and knobs, and earphones for each of us. Papa and Mama managed to produce music and even some interesting talks. Most of the time the sound could be heard quite clearly, but then there would be nothing but crackling — and more knobs had to be turned. Lilly and I soon lost interest and did not use the radio much. On the other hand it was gratifying to be able to boast to friends: 'Yes of course we have a radio set'. The town was almost divided into those who had one and those who did not.

In the spring a great Radio Exhibition was held in Vienna. Papa and Mama went to this and the result was a Philips box radio, similar to the one we had seen at the demonstration. No headphones were needed with this one. Once it was turned on it could be heard all over the room. What is more, the volume of the sound could be adjusted.

Meantime, in the autumn, other exciting things had happened. At the beginning of October a notice appeared in the local newspaper: 'A club will be formed for skiing. A dry course will be held in the gymnasium at the sports centre. Those who are interested may borrow a pair of skis from the sports shop in Troppau. Women and girls must come in trousers.' Papa would have dismissed this idea, but Mama said that Lilly and I should go. It would be good for us and we would enjoy it. If she had been younger she herself would have joined; she had seen skiers on the hills outside Vienna and had always envied them. Now the sport had at last come to Silesia and even to Jaegerndorf.

Lilly could not accompany me on the evening in question as she was staying with friends. This was lucky for me because Papa had only one suitable pair of trousers, knickerbockers to be more precise, and I was going to wear them. The skis and the special boots were duly borrowed from the sports shop. The skis had to reach from my feet to the tip of my outstretched hand. I tried them on at home and I stood there with these long wooden things on my feet, unable to move. Two sticks with leather thongs to hold on to and spoked wheels at their iron tips went with them.

The evening for the dry course arrived. I shouldered the skis, as I had been shown to do in the shop, and set off for the sports centre. I felt slightly embarrassed. I should not have been. I met many more enthusiasts along the way. Once we were all assembled in the hall, the instructor asked us to form a long line along the middle. We were about two dozen, mostly young men in their twenties, but only four girls.

We fixed our skis and waited expectantly. 'Raise your right leg and put the end of your ski on the floor,' commanded the ski instructor. We had to lift our legs up high, to 90°, just like chorus girls. Then we practised. 'Lift the right leg, lift the left leg, make a quarter turn, make a half turn, turn a full circle. Try to walk, left foot forward in a gliding motion, as if you are skating on ice.' And we all tried to follow the instructions.

It was hilarious but in the end we could all do it. 'We'll meet at the station on Saturday,' said the instructor finally. 'There will be a sports train to Klein-Mohrau at three o'clock and from there we shall go up to the Altvater.' That is the highest mountain in the Sudeten, in the mountains of Silesia, about 1962 metres high. 'Bring two pairs of woollen mittens and an *erbsenwurst*,' he added as an afterthought. 'We'll stay in the hut overnight and come back Sunday evening. There will be coffee and *kuchen* available in the hut, but nothing else.' Then we said our goodbyes and went home.

I begged Papa to be allowed to go. There were difficulties: I would be with a lot of young men, without my parents' supervision and probably with all of us in the same room. That was something unheard of for a girl from a 'decent' family. My parents conferred with each other, Mama spoke to Papa in my favour and I was finally allowed to go.

The skis were bought and the special boots. I knitted two pairs of woollen mittens. Trousers and a jacket were ordered; they looked like a railwayman's uniform. A skiing cap was also bought, which looked like an army cap with ear flaps and shield, all in navy blue. Meantime Papa's knickerbockers would have to do again, until the trousers were ready. I was all prepared for my adventure.

From that day on I was completely taken up with skiing. Lilly was not yet interested in this new sport. The whole week I looked forward to the Saturday midday train. We skiers became special people, allowed to invade the mountains in winter.

First, of course, we had to practise on the slope outside the hut. We quickly learned to walk uphill with our skis, in long sliding movements, helped along by the sticks, which acted in the same way as the arms when swimming.

The hut we used was a converted hunting lodge, with accommodation for at least thirty people. We slept in a large annexe, on wooden beds which were placed in a row along both sides of the wall. They were placed so close to each other that we had to climb on the bed from the foot of it. Straw mattresses and rough blankets without sheets were provided and we slept in corduroy pyjamas. For the first few weeks we wore warm dressing-gowns, until the specially made pyjamas were ready.

Skiing was wonderful. Whenever we met groups from another town in the mountains we greeted each other with *'Ski heil!'* The word *'heil'* means 'good luck!, long life!' or similar good wishes. *'Ski heil!'* meant 'good skiing!'. We felt special, a band of brothers (girls included) who had discovered the beauty of winter. When we were sufficiently advanced we went further afield, across the mountain. It was glorious to make the first spoor in the newly fallen snow.

I mostly remember there being blue skies, sun and glittering snow crystals; the breath escaping in delicate clouds. Sometimes our eyelashes would freeze and our ears and noses had to be rubbed; but the cold was invigorating and the downhill runs exhilarating. Life was exceedingly good — and for the first time in my life I enjoyed friendly relations with young men.

Then I fell in love. It happened slowly. I liked Willy Machold: he was older than I, already working in his father's linen factory in Freudenthal, not far from Jaegerndorf. He was tall, broad-shouldered, and could ski excellently. He had brown eyes and a quiet, velvety voice. One afternoon, having come in from skiing for a rest on the bed, he came too. I was lying next to him and suddenly he very slowly moved his hand toward me and traced the outline of my face. I had closed my eyes and I lay there, strange feelings sweeping over me. From that moment on I was sure that I loved him. Nothing was said. A little later we talked about books. He was reading a book by Verlaine and I tried to talk intelligently about it, because I wanted to impress him.

Another time, we were skiing down a ravine; jump, turn, cross diagonally and again jump, turn, until we reached the bottom. As we were making our way back up, he started to quote a few lines of a funny verse by Morgenstern (a writer of comic verse). It was about a weasel which tried to be in a place which rhymed with his name. I felt I knew what he meant. My name rhymed with kiss: Nussi-Bussi. Then I stopped and turned towards him. He bent towards me, and I had my first kiss.

Unfortunately, Willy had not put his arms around me, neither had I around him and I had not placed my sticks firmly enough in the snow. My skis were not horizontal to the slope, but pointing uphill — and I went downhill. I had my kiss and the next moment I found myself sliding down towards his feet and before I could recover myself I was halfway down the slope. This should be a warning to all skiers: if you kiss on a slope, make sure that your skis are horizontal to the slope and your sticks firmly stuck in the snow!

Before long everyone we knew seemed to be going skiing, even the professors at our school. We had lessons on Saturday mornings, finishing at one o'clock, but the sports train waited until half past one in Troppau so that we could catch it. We would arrive in school, professors included, in our ski outfits and with our rucksacks; the cloakroom looked like some kind of strange forest.

The last lesson was always spent polishing our nails under the desk. There was no nail varnish; we had to use chamois buffers. We had been taught tatting and that had proved an excellent way of attracting attention from the young men in the sports train. Naturally, one had to have polished nails to make the art of tatting look really fascinating!

While the professors loomed large in the classroom, it was a perfect delight to show off our skills in skiing on the slopes. We could virtually run circles round them, whereas they still had to practice on the gentler slopes.

I have many happy memories of evenings spent in the hut. We younger ones still slept in one big dormitory in the annexe, whereas the much older skiers, especially the professors, shared smaller rooms for six or eight people, in a kind of barn separated by partitions. On some evenings we would give a show. A sheet was held vertically by two people with a paraffin lamp hanging on the wall. Two or three of us would dance on a bed behind the the sheet, so that only our shadows could be seen. Nobody knew who was dancing, so even I lost my shyness and joined in the fun. We really let ourselves go.

During the carnival season we arranged a masked ball in the hut. Costumes were carried there in rucksacks. An admirer of mine, whose father owned a delicatessen shop, brought Viennese rolls, caviar and champagne. We danced until two o'clock then, as the moon was shining, did a quick round tour with the skis to refresh ourselves, before finishing off with a large spoonful of caviar on a slice of Vienna roll washed down with a small glass of champagne. Then to bed for a few hours.

We felt sophisticated, grown-up and gloriously happy. We had no supervision, but nothing wrong was done. I didn't even have another kiss from Willy Machold. Yet on other Saturdays we would sometimes go to a ball at home, only to have Papa and Mama sitting at a table watching us dancing round and round. Even after these, at midnight, I would go home, change and take a train into the mountains. There I would walk nearly two hours up through the forest, to the hut on the top. After a few hour's sleep I would be able to ski all Sunday, returning home about eight o'clock and still have time for an hour's skating to music on the big ice-rink. It makes me tired now to think of all that activity — and yet we were always ready on Monday mornings to take the school train at 7.30 a.m. I loved those lonely night walks up the hill often on newly fallen snow, where I had to make my own spoor and had only the stars to guide me. I knew only the Andromeda constellation, which was always ahead of me on my left side and if I walked uphill I could not go wrong.

I was still in love with Willy Machold, very innocently, but when Papa heard from Lilly about him, he warned me: 'Willy Machold will take over his father's linen factory one day and he needs money to buy out his two brothers, so he has to marry a rich girl. I could never give you the necessary money for your dowry. Get him out of your head, it is hopeless.' Papa knew most of the local manufacturers, as he had to advise them on difficulties connected with oil for their machines.

I had heard some talk about Willy Machold and Paula Kudlich. She was in my class at school, and her father was a rich cloth manufacturer. She did not ski and I had never heard her mention Willy. However, one weekend, who should be on the nursery slopes, but Willy with Paula. He was showing her the beginner's routine. I felt stabbed to the heart.

'I'll show her,' I thought and went down the slope, did a Christiania stop, made a perfect little jump, and threw a *'ski heil!'* to Willy, pretending that I had never seen Paula. Such a cheap, unsatisfactory gesture! Even in the train home we acted as complete strangers; when Willy introduced us we still maintained our pretence. She was probably as jealous of me as I was of her.

'I will never fall in love with a man again,' I vowed to myself. 'Men have no sensitive feelings.' I learned that lesson early enough, but one never remembers such things!

15

WHEN AT LAST we had completely finished our education, we stayed at home. Girls of good families did not normally take a job. We would marry and then have a family; meantime we should enjoy going to dances and having parties at our house and at our friends' houses.

On Sundays we walked on the *Abee*, as we called it. It was one side of the main square reserved for promenading. In spring and summer it was in one part of the park and a band played while we promenaded. We girls walked one way and the young men the other, so that we could look at each other as we passed. Not that we did much looking, openly, but we could receive and give an occasional smile!

Sometimes a man would be brave enough to enquire whether he could accompany a girl. Of course, we always walked in twos, but on such occasions the other girl might discreetly disappear under the pretence that she had to get home early to help her mother with the dinner. I had an admirer who was only ten years older than I, but he seemed ancient in my eyes; however, I felt quite proud to be seen walking with him, even though there was no other feeling in my heart. I tried to talk intelligently and look sophisticated, but it was rather a strain.

One Sunday he asked me to come with him for a walk along the main street instead of the promenade. I agreed. Soon after we left the park he asked me to excuse him; he would be back in a minute. To my horror he went to the public convenience outside the park. That finished him for me! The man of my dreams would certainly have nothing to do with public conveniences, especially when he was in company. So much for prudery! I made an excuse to get home early and did not go to the concert promenade for several weeks. A few years later I learned that a friend of mine had married him and he made a very good husband and father.

After Christmas I was allowed to go skiing for a fortnight in the Tatra mountains with a special skiing friend of mine, Ella. Three friends of hers, young men, had invited her and she wanted another girl to join the group. It was planned to go up from the Hungarian side, walk along the top of several mountains, one of them 3000 metres high, and then come down on the Czechoslovakian side to a very small, lonely village where we would sleep at the schoolmaster's house. During the trip we would also use two woodcutters' huts and one old hunting lodge, to which one of the young men had been given the key. He was also a trained photographer and would bring his camera.

I was terribly excited. We went at the beginning of February: that is always regarded as the best month for skiing. The days are already longer and there is more sunshine during the day — the right weather to get really brown!

We travelled by train throughout the night and arrived at the small frontier station at about eight o'clock in the morning. In spite of our excitement we had slept well on the wooden seats of our second-class compartment. Only the first class had upholstered seats.

In order to reach the top we had not only to climb rather steep slopes, sometimes with no path at all, but we also had to carry the heavy rucksack crammed with provisions for a fortnight. We took *erbsenwurst*, (dried peas and smoked sausage) cocoa, prunes, crispbread, nuts, raisins and several bars of chocolate. During the daytime we carried in our pockets a small bag of nuts and raisins and little pieces of chocolate. That mixture was called 'students' grub'. We also had about a dozen red and green paprikas and some salami sausage. Chewing prunes during the day was better than sucking sweets, as it did not make you feel hungry or thirsty.

In the evenings we would prepare a hot meal. Melted snow was boiled and poured over the dried peas and sausage, which then made a thick nourishing soup. It didn't matter that this was to be our daily evening meal for fourteen days. We then had some salami on

155

crispbread and ate some paprika raw, which was not only good for the thirst, but provided us with the necessary vitamin C (although we were not aware of that).

We also carried in the rucksack a bottle of oil instead of soap, especially for the face and arms, a few short-sleeved blouses, underwear, pyjamas and toothbrush and a tin of *hirschtalk* (stag grease), which is as hard as a candle but the best thing possible for blisters on the feet. When applied at night, the blister will have completely disappeared in the morning. The boys carried matches and bits of kindling wood. That was all we took with us and it was heavy enough! Whenever possible we piled our rucksacks on a kind of sledge which we improvised by tying the skis together. The boys would pull this up the steeper slopes.

We had spare mittens tucked into our belts and most of the time our caps were tucked in there as well. The weather was perfect and we were supposed to be careful not to be exposed to the sun for too long when we rested. However, the sun was so delightful that it was hard to do this.

In spite of the sun being so hot there was sometimes up to 30° of frost and we had to watch our noses and ears, or rather we watched each other's noses and ears. It can be quite disconcerting when you are walking or skiing along quite happily and feeling warm, when suddenly somebody rushes at you and rubs your ears and nose vigorously, but you have to be thankful for it. Frostbite cannot be felt, but it can be seen. The frostbitten part looks white.

In spite of all the precautions I had bits of my cheeks frozen and the tops of my ears. It is like a blistered burn and the new skin, of course, emerges a light pink. My father was horrified when I got home. 'All these years we have tried to keep your skin free from blemishes, and now I have paid all that money to make you look like a scarecrow,' he moaned. He wasn't far wrong. My face was sunburned to a dark brown and I looked like an owl, with big white rings round my eyes where my special sunglasses had been. On two parts of the brown cheeks, on the tip of my nose and the tops of my ears, the new skin looked bright pink. Certainly it was not a face to look at with pleasure, yet no hero could be prouder of his battle marks than I of my ugly face. It proved that I had been skiing on high places.

We slept during our trip in even more primitive conditions than those in the Sudeten Mountains. The Lower Tatra had not yet been discovered by tourists, whereas the High Tatra already had hotels. We

The Lower Tatra: skiing in February 1927

had to be satisfied with our, mostly empty, huts and neglected hunting lodge. They all had a big tiled stove in them. The woodcutters would come there early in spring in order to be ready for when cut trees could slide down into the valley with the melting snow.

The lower half of the stove was big enough to accommodate several pots in which to melt snow. Then there was the top where you could dry clothes or even sit on it, like the one in Grandmother's house in Moldova. We dried our wet trousers by just sitting on the top of the stove, so warming our bottoms at the same time. A rare and exquisite joy!

When we arrived at a hut, one of us had to collect snow for melting down. The others collected branches from the fir trees or spruces, which lay in abundance on the ground. When these are placed on the floor, piled high, and then covered with a blanket, several of which we always found in the hut, they form a resilient mattress. We would start out, when going to bed, by climbing up to reach the top of the 'mattresses', but by the morning it would be about the depth of a

157

normal mattress. Was it so comfortable because we were so tired? I have never tried it out under different circumstances.

At the end of the first week there was a full moon and we woke up with the moon shining on our faces. We could not resist it. We dressed quickly, went outside and put our skis on. There was a clearing outside the hut, sloping gently down to the trees. We pretended to dance on our skis, gliding and jumping. The shadows we cast on the snow created an eery atmosphere. We seemed to move in another world. That moonlit night was unforgettable.

At last, we reached the highest peak we were to climb, and then we walked along the ridge. This was no wider than a dual carriageway in some parts, and mostly just a few metres wide. We could look down into the valleys: Czechoslovakia on one side, Hungary on the other and far to the north was Poland.

Now came the best part of our journey. A marvellous downhill run.

Snowed in

An evening in the Tangoska Hut, Lower Tatra

Sometimes it was very steep, sometimes a gradual slope and then almost flat again. Just before the last run down to the village I broke the tip of one ski. In those days there were no spare tips you could easily put on if such an accident happened. As it was too dangerous to continue with a broken ski tip and yet too difficult, almost impossible, to walk in deep snow, I took off the broken ski and put it in my rucksack where it stuck out like a warning pole. Then I tied my calf to my thigh with my belt, as children do in a one-legged race, and skied down the slope on one leg and one ski. Luckily the sticks helped me to balance and nobody was there to watch the antics I had to perform to prevent myself from falling.

The village to which we came had only a few houses and a church. We could see no school, but one house seemed slightly bigger than the others. This was where the teacher and his wife lived. They welcomed us with open arms. They were delighted to have visitors from the outside world. They were a young couple and the sheets the teacher's wife put on our beds were new, from her dowry. We slept in the schoolroom and were told that some beds had been lent by their neighbours for the five visitors. The schoolroom had only five double desks and there were only eight children to teach. We heard all this later in the evening.

We enjoyed a delicious meal, after nearly a fortnight of pea soup. By this time the five of us were like brothers and sisters and we got on extremely well with the young couple. After the meal the man brought out his lute and we spent the evening singing folk songs, some of which we had not heard before.

The following day we had to ski about eighteen miles to the nearest railway station, from where we caught the connection to the night express, finally reaching home the next afternoon.

Now the normal routine started again: practising for the twice-weekly piano lessons which I took in Troppau. The music teacher was a friend of Mama's. She had suggested that if I practised well and took harmony and music lessons, I might become a piano teacher if I felt I wanted to do something in case I did not get married. I did my best, but not having a good ear was no recommendation for a music teacher. Although I was good at harmony and music history, I could never play the piano in the inspired way that Lilly could. She knew all the latest *schlagers* (popular songs) by heart; when she played Viennese music, especially Strauss, Mama really enjoyed listening to her. If I tried Strauss, however, I could only hear groans from her and 'Put a bit more swing into it!' Finally I gave up the piano lessons and started to learn Esperanto instead.

Esperanto is very easy to learn if you know some French, German and English. There is even less grammar than in the English language and the words mostly have roots in those other languages and are easy to remember. The spelling is phonetic. Hanni, my cousin, who was three years older than I, had joined me. We soon started to perform short sketches for our amusement. The students were mixed, mostly elderly businessmen — who were not very exciting. As the course was held in a hotel, the men would go for a beer and Hanni and I had to be satisfied with a glass of lemonade.

As soon as we could speak the language quite tolerably we became bored. 'Life is so dull, nothing exciting happens during the week,' I complained to Mama.

Sunbathing outside the Fichtlich Hut in February 1927

'You go to the Esperanto Club' she pointed out, 'which we didn't have when I was your age.'

'But,' I argued, 'when my mother was my age she was already married and I was on the way, whereas all I have is a bottle of lemonade and being allowed to say a few lines in Esperanto in a stupid little play.' Mama just sighed.

However, there was one thing to look forward to: our visit to Moldova. We went at the beginning of September. Papa would return home earlier and we would stay over for the vintage.

It was sad to pass Grandmother's house with her not there, but we spent most of the time in the vineyards. In the evenings Lilly shocked Aunt Marie with the words of the latest *schlagers*, which she would sing while playing the piano. They were words such as these:

'Only one night will you belong to me, until the morning dawns,'

161

or

'I know that you love me,
That you think I am the most beautiful girl you have ever seen,
That you will grant my every wish,
But tomorrow morning it will all be over and only faded flowers left.'

or, worst of all,

'I know a little hotel in a quiet street,
Spend a night there with me you little princess.
The day is short but the night is long,
And when you have kissed all night long
You will do it again and again.'

Neither Lilly nor I could understand why Aunt Marie was shocked! As I have said before she was Papa's elder sister and though she invariably looked stern she did have the kindest smile. Unlike Mama she was very slim, and always wore black. Her only daughter had died when we were still very small, but Aunt Marie had never got over it. Hilda was her name and she had only been married a few months when she died of cancer. Nobody had suspected. Aunt Marie had kept all Hilda's clothes and sometimes took them out and showed them to us. We never knew what to say.

We had to leave with Papa, after all, and could not stay for the vintage. We had reserved tickets on a Danube passenger boat and were advised that it would leave earlier than expected because of low water at certain places, due to the hot, dry summer, and the severe winter that was expected.

We had comfortable cabins but we stayed up until we reached as far as Budapest. The sight of its lights as we approached it was breathtaking. It was as if all the stars had fallen from the sky. I had stayed longer on deck than Lilly, to watch the lights disappearing again, when I was joined by several Bulgarian students. They were going to Vienna University. I wanted to surprise Papa with a few words of Bulgarian and asked them to teach me some.

The following morning I proudly declared that I had learned some Bulgarian. 'Dej me hubicky', I said. 'What?' shouted Papa. 'Do you know what that means?' 'Of course,' I said. 'It is a kind of greeting which will make me immediately liked wherever I go.' 'Huh', grunted Papa. 'I can believe that. It means "give me a kiss". In future you had better look up any new words in a dictionary.'

When we arrived home there was already snow on the mountains, so

I went skiing every weekend. Elsa came after Christmas to visit us. She was good at climbing mountains but had never been on skis. Now I introduced her to this great sport. Of course, she had to use Papa's knickerbockers and when she fell, which was quite often, I was more concerned about Papa's trousers than about her safety. Instead of shouting 'Watch out, there is a nasty bend!' all I did was shout 'Mind Papa's trousers!'

I complained to her about being bored at home. True, I had been skiing each weekend and done a lot of skating, swimming, athletics and, of course, dancing, but once the winter was over life would be very dull. Elsa was lucky. Both she and her elder sister Lola had been studying chemistry in Leipzig and now she worked at a chemist's.

She agreed with me that waiting for a young man of the right kind to propose was a tedious business. 'You like books, why don't you do something with books,' she suggested. We went to the Chamber of Commerce for information. If I did two years of practise at a bookseller's shop, I could then go to Leipzig and do a two-year course for Booksellers and Publishers, the only one in Europe. Then I would be a highly qualified bookseller or could work with a publishing house, or even become a publisher myself. That sounded exciting.

Before Elsa left, I went with her to one of the two bookshops in the town and offered my services free of charge in exchange for practical experience. This was also a stationery shop and I would have to serve behind the counter, but would still have enough time to read the new books in order to be able to advise the highly valued customers. I was delighted when I was accepted. No wonder, it is not every day that a shop gets a full-time assistant for nothing!

Papa gave his permission and I started my new job the day after Elsa left. Working without payment put me socially right with my skiing clique, who were somewhat snobbish. All sons and daughters of manufacturers of woollen cloth or linen were regarded as the social élite, at least in that part of Silesia.

I enjoyed working in the bookshop. I could do a lot of reading, but it also gave me an insight into the real cultural standing of some of the so-called élite, especially some of the women. There were those who would order books where the binding was more important than the content, of which they often had no idea and couldn't care less. Others would be very mean. We were told to send copies of the latest titles for them to peruse at home and then choose which they wanted. Many times the books were returned and not a single one bought; when I put them back on the shelves I might find a match or a hairpin between the pages, which had been used as a bookmark.

My two years' practical experience quickly passed and soon I was to go to Leipzig. The course at the university started at Easter. I had, of course, to have new dresses and Mama and I spent weeks ordering them at the dressmaker's and having some old ones altered.

Mama came with me to Leipzig and helped me to find a comfortable bedsit. The landlady promised to provide breakfast, but other meals only if I paid for them separately. Mama thought I would prefer to have the meals with my friends. When at last I said goodbye to her at the station, I wondered what I had let myself in for. I felt terribly alone in this strange town. I only wished that Lilly was here to share my new life. However, the excitement of the next day swept away all feelings of loneliness. The course was not at the university itself but at an associated college. All the students congregated in the big hall, then the course director bade us welcome and we were divided into two large groups. There were students from every corner of Europe, including several from Poland, but only two from England and one from Norway.

I talked with a girl from the Ruhr in Germany. She was very fair and the most beautiful girl I had ever seen. A girl from Stuttgart also joined us. She was as dark as Lore was fair and was called Ruth. She brought a young man with her, also from Stuttgart, who had a very unusual surname of Teufel, which means 'devil'. He was everything but a devil: full of fun and very clever. He took a liking to Lore. Then I met the Norwegian on the stairs one morning; he smiled, I smiled and soon he too joined our group. His name was Johan. We got on extremely well together.

I remember well the first lecture we had in literature. Our tutor was the head of the famous Leipzig library, where a copy of every book printed in German is kept. 'We will start with the German Romantics,' he began, 'and I will quote you a few lines.' He did. The last line was, roughly translated, 'that those who love and kiss know more than the wisest philosophers'. What more did we want? We were all young, it was spring and, of course, we were only too keen to know more than the wisest philosophers. That would be part of the reason that I never became a publisher. But that was much later!

We spent most of our free time together in the parks and, as summer approached, in the swimming pool. We loved to go to a restaurant for a really excellent meal. That was expensive so we thought if we skipped a meal during the day we could afford the restaurant in the evening. In

164

order to overcome the hunger at midday we would go swimming and then go home for a short sleep. Sleep, we thought, was as good as a meal. Unfortunately, before we went to the afternoon lecture we felt so hungry that we spent as much on coffee and cakes as if we had had a good meal. We had to learn the hard way.

I am not very economical. If I have money I spend it and then I try to save, which is never very successful. After a trip to the *Boehmische Schweitz* (the Switzerland of Bohemia) I had almost no money left and we had planned to visit Weimar at Whitsun. I wrote to my father, complaining about the high prices of everything, how much I missed home and especially Lilly, etc. — a really moaning epistle. Papa reacted marvellously. He realised what the real trouble was.

'Before you do anything else, my dear,' he wrote, 'take your two best friends and invite them for a meal in a nice restaurant. That will cheer you up. And then try to be a bit more economical. Put some money away in your desk and think hard before you buy anything which is not necessary. Then you will have a good time without worry. Try to stick to your allowance. You might be a bit short at the moment, so I enclose a cheque.' Then came the phrase Papa always used: 'You know I am not made of money'. Dear Papa, I could have hugged him.

We did go to Weimar. We visited all the places Goethe had made famous and in the evening we wandered through the park. I went off with my Norwegian friend and Lore with hers. Suddenly as we turned a corner, we came across a statue of Shakespeare among the bushes. The moon shone straight in his face and he looked almost lifelike. I had grabbed Johan's hand and then we sat down nearby on a bench, hand in hand.

I told him about my disappointment with Willy Machold who was now lost for me and he told me about a girl in Norway who was also probably going out with somebody else by now. We finished our tales with a kiss. Suddenly the world was wonderful; the moonlight was especially provided for us. When we met Lore and her friend it seemed, at least for me, as if we were returning from an enchanted wood; it was the same park we had entered a short while ago, but it was now transformed.

This all sounds as if we did not work at all. We did. Sometimes we would meet and study together in Lore's room; sometimes we took our books with us to the swimming pool and tried to study while sunbathing and sometimes we would study alone in our own rooms. On the other hand, studying did not seem the most important thing during that summer!

I also remembered what I had read in a book by a Swedish philosopher when I was working at the bookshop. Amongst other things he wrote that when we are feeling rather low, don't feel like doing anything, we should not call ourselves lazy and feel guilty; we are having what he called 'a creative pause'. We should just bide our time and in due course renewed energy and mental vigour would return. I loved that idea and it has been a great help to me, both then and in my later life. Not lazy, but having a 'creative pause'. How comforting!

Unfortunately, I really fell in love with my Norwegian friend. Weimar had been the beginning. I became very touchy. Why? I don't know. Small remarks which normally I would have laughed off, I now took too seriously and was quickly hurt. I also realised that Johan as a partner for life was not for me. He was fiercely independent and the last thing he wanted was somebody clinging to him. I tended to be the clinging type, but also extremely proud. The slightest sign that my loving attention was not wanted at any particular moment made me feel wounded.

So it was that after a quite ridiculous quarrel, not even a quarrel, just a hurtful remark — I was off. Literally off. I packed my bag, left a note and went home, although the summer holidays were not due to start for another week. I even left my passport behind. On my arrival in Leipzig I had needed to send it to Berlin and it had not yet been returned.

Jaegerndorf was on the German-Czechoslovakian frontier and the passport and customs officials were at the railway station. As soon as I got out of the train from Germany I should have produced my passport. I told a pathetic story. I was a student and I had to get home in a hurry and could not wait for my passport to be returned from Berlin. I gave my address in town and the official was very kind. 'We shall inform Berlin,' he said, 'and they will send it to us. We will then let you know and you can come here to collect it.'

Lilly was delighted when I arrived home so unexpectedly. Mama was astonished and Papa was even more astonished. 'Why must you always be so impulsive?' he queried, when I informed him that I had merely felt like coming home earlier, as there was not much to do in the college in the last week before the summer holidays. I did not tell him the real reason. He looked quizzically at me, probably because in my recent letters I had written, somewhat poetically, about the years of youth and love and spring, and more such nonsense. However, he asked no more questions. 'You are here now,' he said, 'and I hope you don't miss much at the college.'

Of course, no sooner was I home than I regretted bitterly that I had left Leipzig in such a hurry. But it was too late for regrets. There was one consolation. Lore and Johan had wanted to visit Prague in the holidays for its famous architecture and historical buildings and it had been planned that they would then come to Jaegerndorf and stay with us for a fortnight. I swore to myself that I would not be so touchy in future.

I received a letter from Johan in which he said how sorry he was to have hurt me. I was crying over this when Papa came into the room. He must have understood when he saw the letter in my hand. He put his hand on my shoulder and said: 'Never mind, there will be many more tears in your life but a lot of happiness too, so don't worry.' Lore and Johan did not come after all. Lore's mother died while they were in Prague and Johan went straight home to Norway.

How fickle is the human heart! Or was I just driven by fate to reach the road on which I was meant to go? I soon got over my disappointment. Everything would come right after the holidays, I told myself. Then my younger cousin Christl introduced me to a friend of hers, a Dr Lange, who practised in Troppau. Apparently all the girls were mad about him. He was young, good looking and a bachelor. When he invited me out I was flattered and soon became quite a regular visitor to his surgery after hours when he was 'on call'. He seemed to be serious in his attentions to me and I was dreaming of marriage. The man himself did not play such a big part in my dreams, but to be able to have my own household was a tempting idea.

When I returned to Leipzig, Johan and I felt a bit strange with each other. I tried to make him jealous and started to talk a lot about Dr Lange, which had the opposite effect to what I had planned. Lore was no longer friendly with 'Teufel' and spent more time studying with Johan. Meanwhile, I received long letters from Dr Lange and became more and more confused in my feelings.

The lectures now seemed dull and the thought of having to spend my life in a bookshop or even as a publisher no longer seemed the slightest bit desirable. I wrote home that I thought the course was just a waste of time. I would like to get married, but did not tell them to whom. However, they must have guessed. The trouble was that nobody had asked me yet!

Papa wrote back: 'Think it over carefully. Finish the course — at least you have then something worthwhile to do whether you marry or not. Think of all the time you have already spent in the bookshop; now you have only another year to go and then you can choose what you want to do. Marriage can wait that long.' Mama also wrote: she pointed out that I should make use of the opportunity given me. 'Think it over carefully,' she repeated. 'I would have been happy if I had been given your chances when I was young.'

It was no good. I was restless. I wrote and informed my parents that I was coming home and told the director of my course that I was leaving. He was very surprised and asked for the reason. I told him that I was thinking of getting married and he looked even more surprised. 'Not to one of the students?' he asked, and was visibly relieved when I denied it. He eyed me rather suspiciously. Perhaps he thought I was pregnant and had to leave in a hurry. This, of course, had not occurred to me at that time, only later, when I remembered his puzzled, questioning face. He pointed out that Papa would have to pay for the full course. Poor Papa, having such a restless daughter!

As it turned out in later years, the very fact that I had left Leipzig and had continued to be restless enabled me many, many years later to give Papa and Mama a refuge from tragic happenings in Czechoslovakia after the Second World War. Fate weaves a tangled web.

16

DR LANGE, IN spite of all his letters, did not seem overjoyed by my return from Leipzig. It was a frustrating affair. We had lovely meals together and went to the theatre, but very often he seemed preoccupied. I wondered if he had met another girl. I had expected to be asked the all-important question, but nothing of that sort happened.

In the middle of October I had a brainwave. Why should I not go to England to learn English, which I had not studied at the lyceum. I had concentrated on French because we had already been taught some French at the convent. Now would be an opportunity to learn English and where better than in England. By chance, I had been given an address from one of the girls in Leipzig, whose sister had gone to work in a children's hospital in Brighton. Why I had noted down that address I don't know. Fate had probably pushed me again. The only chance to get a British visa in those days was to work in a hospital. If I couldn't be a doctor, then the next best thing would be a nurse.

However, it took some doing to persuade Papa to let me go. 'I am not made of money,' he kept saying. 'Do you realise what that will cost?'

'I only need money for the journey,' I argued. 'I will get some pocket money if I become a probationary nurse.'

'I don't want you to be taking chamber pots round a ward,' insisted Papa — and I could only try to assure him that it was quite different when it was done for children.

Then I had another brainwave. 'You would give me a dowry,' I told Papa. 'What if you take some of the money which would go towards my dowry and let me use it for going to England?. You see, I could do all sorts of things if I could speak perfect English, and I don't think I will ever marry.' Papa sighed. Mama implored me to let the matter rest, but I was stubborn and Papa finally agreed. A letter was sent to the Royal Alexandra Hospital in Brighton and before long the answer came back that I would be welcome, and could start straight away.

I went to Maehrisch-Ostrau, the second-biggest town in Silesia, to choose a travelling suit for my journey. 'If you can go to England by yourself, you can start by choosing your own wardrobe.' I came back with a grey-blue jersey suit, which had just come into fashion, and Papa was satisfied. Mama bought me a trunk and a small suitcase. She also gave me a small leather case for my toiletries; a brush and comb with silver handles and glass and silver containers for everything else. 'Every young lady needs one of these,' she said, and I felt wordly wise and very excited.

Papa gave me enough money for the journey: second-class train, first-class boat. 'Never take second class on a boat,' I was told. He also gave me enough money for meals on the train and on the boat and some more to keep in reserve. All this was put in a small bag which I hung on a thin belt around my waist underneath all my clothes. Later, when I had a dance with an elderly gentleman who had been sitting opposite me at dinner on the boat, I could feel the bag banging against my thighs. What he thought about it I cannot imagine!

This gentleman had promised to take me from Waterloo Station to Victoria Station, where I would catch my train to Brighton. When we arrived there he asked me to look after his luggage while he phoned his family. There I stood, full of anticipation. 'This is London,' I thought, 'the biggest city in Europe and I am here. How marvellous!' I was rudely awakened from my ecstasy by a lady who was wearing some kind of uniform and who looked extremely stern.

'Are you waiting for somebody,' she asked in three languages. 'Yes,' I replied eagerly. 'The gentleman has just gone to phone and then he will take me to Victoria Station.'

'Is he your father or brother?' she enquired.

'Oh no,' I replied naïvely. 'I only met him last night on the boat, over dinner.'

'Then he certainly will not take you to Victoria Station,' the lady announced in a determined voice. 'I will do it instead, and see to it that you don't come to any harm.' Before I could reply the gentleman returned and the lady showed him a metal disc, whereupon he took his leave, wishing me good luck at the hospital.

The lady then hailed a taxi. I was surprised to see that they were inside the station, just where one got out of the train. No sooner had we sat down than she pulled my skirt further below my knees, as I crossed my legs. She pointed to some landmarks; then another pull at my skirt, which, being jersey, slipped up again and again. 'Stop smiling, you are in England now.' She had to repeat it — but how could I stop? It was a lovely day, we were driving through London, which I had never dreamt I would ever do, and this lady wanted me not to smile. Perhaps she thought all continental girls were out to catch men with their smiles, but that was the last thing on my mind.

We reached Victoria Station all too quickly. The lady told me how much to pay the driver and then led me to the Brighton train. She also told me to buy one of those huge English newspapers, double the size of those we had at home. When she handed it to me I explained that I could not read it as I spoke practically no English. 'Never mind,' she told me, 'as long as you hold it in front of your face.' She installed me in a window seat in a small compartment and made me hold the open paper in front of my face.

'Now, don't talk to anybody, don't look at anybody, just pretend you are reading the paper and *stop smiling*,' were her last instructions. She had a word with the guard outside, and then disappeared. I guessed that she must have told him to make sure I got out of the train at Brighton. I had the address of the hospital written on a piece of paper which I would show to a taxi driver at the Brighton station.

As soon as the lady had left I put the paper down and peeped out of the window. Yes, she had actually gone. I returned to my seat quite relieved, but still felt compelled to take hold of the paper again and pretend to read. After all, I was in England now, and, as I had been told so frequently, 'other countries, other customs!'

A gentleman got into the compartment. Of course, I had a peep above the paper to see how he looked. He was young and looked just as we had always imagined Englishmen to look: tall and slim, small oval head, a bit like my Norwegian friend. I was sure that I did the peeping very discreetly and then I pretended yet again to read the paper.

After a while, a hand reached over the top, pushed the paper down and there I saw the stranger, with a big smile on his face and pointing to the newspaper. I quickly realised the reason for his mirth. I was reading the paper upside down. Now we were like children, who can understand each other without being able to speak the same language. I soon found out that even in England people did smile. Luckily, the 'lady' could not see me. It was easy to make him understand that I was going not only to Brighton but to a hospital. The journey seemed to be over in no time. When I said goodbye to him after we left the train and he had hailed a taxi for me, I am sure that the driver thought we were old friends. I was looking forward, yet again, to a new life.

At the hospital I found that I was not the only foreigner. Luckily there was a Swiss girl, Veronika, called Vroni for short, also a probationer, who was able to act as my interpreter. She took me into town to buy a uniform. It was a very simple one; a plain, long, white cotton overall with short sleeves and a pair of extra sleeves to slip over the bare arms when the doctor came, or visitors. A wide belt clinched the rather voluminous overall at the waist. I had what the Scottish people so charmingly call 'a bony figure', but in that overall I looked like two sausages still twirled together. On our heads we had to wear a white, well-starched square of cotton, which was laboriously formed into a kind of crown to sit on top of the hair, making me look like a chef's apprentice. I was now fully equipped for my duties and started on the wards the following morning.

There was one ward for the babies, one for the under-fives, and a third ward with children of various ages, some of them up to ten years or even older. I was placed on the under-fives' ward, although the babies' ward might have been more sensible. I could have communicated without trouble with the babies, but I might not have always understood what I had to do with them.

What the children thought of me I cannot imagine. It can be difficult enough to understand a small child in normal circumstances, but when the child is ill and one is not sure of the meaning of the words, it can be very funny indeed. I remember a small boy calling, 'Bottle, bottle, nurse'. I ran and took him a glass of water. I made many such mistakes before my spoken English improved.

I carried a small dictionary in my pocket. How I guessed the spelling I don't know, but I usually managed to find the words I heard and ticked them off as the day progressed. In the evening I would look through the dictionary, read the meanings again and try to memorise them. It is extremely satisfying, when learning a foreign language, to be able to have written proof about how many words one already knows. I also studied a 'teach yourself' book and after some months I became

The probationary nurse at the children's hospital in Brighton

even more ambitious: I bought some of Thomas Hardy's novels to read in the evenings in bed.

It was a weird experience and often I fell asleep only to dream about withered arms and hangmen. However, I did make progress. When we later had an epidemic of measles at the hospital I was confined with a group of convalescents to look after. I amused them by telling them Grimm's fairy tales in my own special English. The children seemed to like this, because even the well-known stories must have sounded different from what they had heard before.

My daily work consisted mostly of cleaning, bed-making, handing out the meals and helping with the feeding where needed. Bed-making was difficult; it needed two people to do it quickly. The child was wrapped in a shawl and, if not too ill, placed on a chair. Then the bed was stripped. What a lovely expression! Once a week the mattress was turned. Heave ho! Our mattresses at home were in three parts, even a child could turn and exchange them. Here, too, two sheets and two or

173

three blankets were used, plus another thin one under the bottom sheet. The only blanket we ever used at home was a thin one over the mattress and even then a chamois leather or skin was often used instead. Then we only had a duvet, with its own washable cover. No corners to make, no tucking in on all sides: we just shook the duvet and replaced it on the bed.

I felt sorry for the British housewife. Life must be very difficult, especially with a big family, I thought. In my own room I never bothered about 'the corners'. Anyhow, I could not bear tucked-in blankets and in the morning my bed looked a real mess of tangled blankets and sheets.

Sister was extremely strict about tidiness in her ward. The beds had always to be in a straight line, not even a few centimetres out. They had to be tidy all the time and, as the children were often restless and upset their perfect arrangement — with even the bedspread tucked in — the probationers had to see that they were continuously straightened.

The rest of the time Vroni and I carried bedpans and bottles into the ward and then, of course, they had to be cleaned in the sluice room. Then the bathroom had to be cleaned and scrubbed every day and, once a week, all the bedside tables were emptied and scrubbed.

To me it seemed that there was almost too much cleanliness. Yet Vroni complained that everything in England was dirty. I hadn't been to Switzerland and wondered if they perhaps even scrubbed the pavements. She told me that if they had a white fence they would wipe it down regularly. One lives and learns! I was glad I had been living in Czechoslovakia. I was sure that we were a clean country. There was no litter on the streets and our homes were certainly clean and, best of all, I did not have to do it.

There was one thing we both agreed about and which we found both strange and amusing — that was the importance of the 'sleeves'. No dress or only a sleeveless one was worn under our white overalls, which had short sleeves reaching to the elbows. The rest of the arm was bare, 'the better to be cleaning with'. However, as soon as a doctor came in sight, the sleeves had to be put on, even in an emergency.

We were never allowed to run but had to take quick, short steps. Once, as I rushed to the door to call the doctor quickly, Sister's voice boomed after me: 'Nurse, your sleeves!' Back I had to come to take a pair from the shelf where they were kept, as the pockets of the overalls were too small. Afterwards I confided to my friend: 'I think the sleeves are more important than life or death. What is the matter with the

174

doctors? Can't they bear, the poor things, to see a girl's bare arms? Surely they must be used to seeing much more than just an underarm?' But who were we to complain? The English were certainly different!

As the days went by I thought longingly of home. The big cleaning would now be starting in preparation for Christmas. The carpets would be taken down into the yard and put over the *teppichstange* (a horizontal pole over two upright poles) and then thoroughly beaten with the carpet-beater.

If there was enough snow on the ground the carpets would then be placed face down on the lawn, beaten and shaken and replaced in the rooms. The snow took out all the dust and dirt and the carpets looked fresh and like new. It was all so easy.

Mama had probably already started to bake our Christmas specialities, all those different kinds of biscuits and sweets. Suddenly I realised that I had not heard from my family for some time and they had probably forgotten me. That same evening I wrote a most pathetic letter home, from which they must have guessed how homesick I was.

However, life was also interesting. On one of my days off I had travelled to London to go sight-seeing. With a guidebook clutched in my hands, I did a tour of the whole city. I even went to the zoo. In the afternoon I saw something quite unusual: a man seated in a carriage, wearing a fancy hat and a golden chain round his neck, and followed by several more carriages. Crowds of people lined the streets to watch this procession, the meaning of which I couldn't fathom. Then somebody explained that it was the Lord Mayor's Show. I was most impressed. Unfortunately, I did not manage to see the King, but I saw Buckingham Palace. The feeling of awe and grandeur and that I was privileged to see it all never left me. I also remember feeding the pigeons in Trafalgar Square and went to the National Gallery. When I finally took the train back to Brighton I was utterly exhausted but very happy.

Christmas in the hospital was different from ours at home, but an enjoyable experience nevertheless. A week beforehand I had received a parcel from home with a box full of Christmas baking. All my favourite pieces were there and each one was carefully wrapped in tissue paper so as not to get broken. I kept the box until Christmas Eve when I shared the contents with Vroni, my Swiss friend. Nothing special happened on Christmas Eve in the hospital. The wards were decorated; small dishes with sweets and nuts were put out on the big table in the middle of the ward, and we were allowed to help ourselves.

On Christmas Day a record player played Christmas carols. I played some hymns on the piano and was praised by Sister. Parents came with toys and presents for the children. A tall Christmas tree stood in a corner of the ward and there was a cheerful atmosphere which left no room for any homesickness.

In the evening a Christmas dinner was held for all the staff, except the night sisters who had to stay in the wards. Matron presided at the head of the table. For Vroni and me it was very different from home. I had never seen crackers before; they had to be pulled apart and inside were fancy paper hats which everybody put on. We all sat there among the decorations, looking somewhat ridiculous, reading the jokes found in the crackers. Then there were long periods of silence when everybody just quietly chewed away.

We were quietly amused to watch how the others cut a piece of meat — it was turkey — then loaded the wrong side of the fork with the other good things, gravely took it to their mouths, then folded their hands on their lap and chewed. We used the curved side of the fork like a shovel and admired the skilfulness of the English way. Why use the easy way when it can be done with difficulty!

Vroni looked at me. 'Let's do something different and pretend it is a custom at home.' She dipped her finger into her wine glass and then rubbed the rim of the glass. I followed her example. Very solemnly we rubbed and, sure enough, we produced sounds which could be called music, or a kind of singing. In a little while everyone noticed what we were doing.

There was a hush and then Matron asked: 'Nurse Haller and Nurse Stiller what are you doing?' We looked surprised. 'It is the custom in our countries to do this on Christmas Day to bring good luck for the whole year,' I lied, and Nurse Haller confirmed it. 'Surely,' Nurse Haller added, 'you have a similar custom here?' Matron denied that this was so, but soon, starting with the doctors, everyone was dipping a finger into their wine and then making the glass sing. That was better! Once we were all giggling and laughing, all formality was forgotten.

Afterwards we had a dance. When it was the ladies' choice I asked one of the doctors, with whom I had been trying to flirt all evening. The Scottish sister from my ward pulled me aside after the dance and hissed: 'You should not dance with a doctor, you are only a probationary nurse.' I took no notice of her and continued to enjoy myself. In my country I would be considered a woman first and the doctor just a man, at any social function. It didn't matter whether Sister thought me a cheeky foreigner — I was happy.

After Christmas we had some snow. I was in the sluice room when it started, I saw the flakes falling outside and my heart rejoiced. How great was my disappointment when I looked out of the window and saw only slush on the ground! That night I dreamed of snow-covered hills and fir trees, the loaded branches forming intricate patterns of icy lace. My homesickness returned with a vengeance, only to become worse when I received letters from my skiing friends enclosing photographs of the winter forest and the Altvater. I cried and cried. I felt terribly alone.

Fortunately, my English was quite good by now. I had made friends with an English nurse, Rosie, who had a room next to mine and then even with a sister, Eva Alexander, known also as Alec, who invited me to her home in Hove. Rosie was an orphan and Alec's parents had more or less adopted her. Alec's father reminded me of my own — he was kind and understanding — and her mother did everything to make me feel at home.

All this helped me to improve my English. By now I could hold a discussion with my friends on almost any subject. I had signed on to train as a nurse and I felt sure I could do it. We had lectures about anatomy, various illnesses, first-aid, etc. and, of course, we took notes at these. Everyone seemed surprised that I could spell the difficult words with Greek or Roman roots, like psychology or physiology. It was easy for me because we pronounced them almost as they were spelt. It was the same with words which came from the French. That was one plus for me!

Fortunately the so-called winter didn't last long. By February I could walk along the beach wearing just a dress and cardigan. Then came a lovely summer by the sea. The hospital had a chalet down on the beach and we could go there in our free time. I was a strong swimmer and, as I was used to a river, swimming in the sea was easy for me. I loved every minute of it and my homesickness seemed cured.

A wing had recently been built onto the hospital, providing rooms for nurses and another children's ward. The opening ceremony was to be performed by the Duchess of York. We had made a little doll dressed as a nurse for her daughter, Princess Elizabeth. Vroni and I were told to provide ourselves with new overalls, as we would probably be introduced to the Duchess.

The great day arrived. An hour before the honoured guest was expected all the children were put on potties or bedpans; all the taps were turned on to make it easier for them to perform. Then the beds were straightened to perfection. The children were told not to ask for a bedpan or bottle while the Duchess and Duke were in the ward. When all was ready, the nurses stood in a row to greet the Royal guests.

The Duchess walked in front of the long procession. She was lovely, very much as she is even now, in a flowing gown, smiling and gracious. I was introduced, and made my curtsey, which I found easy, as a result of my early training at home. The Duchess took my hand and said a few kindly words to this stranger from an even stranger new country.

Behind the Duchess was a jolly, much older man, rather pompous looking, whom I took for the Duke. He wore a gold chain round his neck. Then followed the consultants, Matron, the doctors and sisters. We nurses, of course, remained in the line to let the procession pass. At the very end, was a young, slim gentleman. He looked rather forlorn, as if he did not quite know where he belonged. When his eyes fell on me I smiled at him and he smiled back. It was a friendly, but rather shy smile.

I wondered who he was, and decided that I liked him better than the Duke. No sooner had the guests departed, watched by the nurses through the windows, when excitement broke out. 'Wasn't the Duke lovely, isn't he nice, and the Duchess, so pretty, so gracious and kind', were the remarks.

'I don't agree,' I argued. 'How can you call the Duke lovely? He is far too old and fat for the Duchess. How could she have married such a pompous fat man.'

Indignant denials broke out. 'How can you call the Duke pompous and fat? He is slim and shy,' several nurses shouted back. Then it became clear. 'The man you call the Duke — he is the Mayor of Brighton,' they explained. 'The young man at the end of the procession was the Duke.'

I was even more surprised. Who could understand the English? Letting a Duke go last in a formal visit! True, it was the Duchess who was actually opening the new wing at the hospital, but the Duke should certainly be in front with her. However, 'other countries, other customs!'

In spite of enjoying such a glorious summer, and a beautiful September, which made me think of Moldova and the ripening grapes in the vineyards, when October arrived I began to dread the winter. We had several days of fog, rain and winds, which brought back to me the miserable little bits of snow we had the previous year. Most of my friends at home were probably already making new spoors in the snow on top of the Altvater. My homesickness returned. I heard, too, that Lilly had meanwhile also left home. She also had become restless.

Her friend, Grete Rathmann, had a cousin in Slovakia, and suggested that Lilly should go there for a while as a change. The doctor's wife wanted a companion and also some help with her little girl and it had to be somebody from a good home. Lilly agreed, Papa permitted, and Lilly was off to Slovakia, to Spiska Nova Ves at the foot of the High Tatra mountains. Mama wrote to me that Lilly sent very happy letters home. She got on extremely well with the young doctor's wife and apparently also went out a lot with Grete Rathman's cousin, Max.

I was thinking of Lilly and the good time she was having, while here I was spending my days still cleaning the bathroom and carrying bedpans. Of course, by now I did other things as well, such as changing bandages, taking out stitches and I had even been two or three times to theatre.

The first time I was told I was to go to the theatre I truly thought it would be the 'real' theatre — with plays and operas — and did not quite understand how that could happen in the middle of a morning in hospital. I was soon to find out!

I hadn't expected what I was going to see. It was a throat operation and suddenly the floor seemed to come up to meet me, the next minute I was on the floor and being pulled rudely out of the theatre like a sack of cut grass. However, I was told that I would soon overcome this weakness and my next visit to the theatre proved this theory right. I became very interested in the circumcision operation and the next time an appendicectomy, so I had no time to faint.

Unfortunately I blotted my copybook the next time. We had a surgeon who was rather short of stature. Just as he was going to start the preliminaries to the operation, Sister whispered to me: 'Bring a breakfast tray.' She meant a tray on which one could have breakfast in bed. I had not quite understood the word 'tray' and had no idea what she wanted it for, so I asked the Ward Sister for the thing on which the breakfast is brought in. She pointed to the trolley which was used to transport the breakfasts for the whole ward.

Naïvely, I took hold of this and pushed it to the theatre, which was on the same floor. Luckily, I had to open the door wide to get the trolley through, so the theatre Sister saw me in time. Never have I seen such an irritated, annoyed expression as that worn by Sister, as she unceremoniously pushed both me and my trolley back and hissed into my ear: 'It is for the consultant to stand on, you fool.' I am afraid that Sister never regained her good opinion of foreigners, if she ever even had one!

As autumn advanced, so increased my homesickness. It is an illness. I dreamed again of our mountains, of snow-laden fir trees, of those exhilarating runs down the slopes and woke up crying. Any kind word spoken to me only made me dissolve into more tears. Finally, I wrote home that I could not stand the prospect of another winter in England: 'anywhere in the world I would go, but not to England in the winter'. The dear God must have heard me, for here I am now, after over forty years in England and half the time spent in the north on the east coast! However, I now wouldn't want to be anywhere else.

Mama wrote back a very sympathetic letter. 'Come home if you feel unhappy,' she wrote. 'Papa will send you the money for the journey, as you have probably not much money left,' she added, understandingly. Dear Mama, she always understood.

I told Matron that I wanted to go home. There were some difficulties. I had signed on for three years and had been receiving the monthly salary of five pounds. As usual I had spent it all, plus the money Papa had given me for emergencies, or in case I needed it for the return journey if I was unhappy. All this had been spent and Mama had guessed correctly.

There was a meeting of the Governors at the hospital and I was called in to tell my sorry tale. All I could say was that I had been treated with great kindness. Everything would have been all right, if only winter wasn't approaching. Snow was already covering our mountains and I was terribly homesick. I was in tears as I spoke about how I felt.

Everyone eyed me curiously. Then one Sister and a doctor saved the situation. 'Homesickness is serious,' said the doctor, and the Sister told of a case where a girl had been homesick for Scotland and had to be sent home. It was decided to forget about the money I had received and to let me go. Soon Papa sent me the money for the journey and I was on my way home.

17

WHEN I ARRIVED home exciting news was awaiting me. Papa had become a Director of the Vacuum Oil Company and we would have to move to Prague. Mama was looking forward to the move. I remembered that years ago, during the war, there was a girl at school who had come from Prague, and I had envied her and thought it must be lovely to live there. Would that all my wishes came true like that!

Papa came home at the weekend and although he told me, rather sternly, that he hoped that I would now settle down, and not always be wanting to do something else, I felt he was glad to have me back at home.

Lilly was still in Slovakia, and wrote glowing letters about her young man, Max. She wanted to become engaged, but would return home meanwhile and move with us to Prague. Max would then come to Prague to ask Papa for her hand. We expected her the following week, at the end of which we would move.

Lilly duly arrived and there was a great reunion. We spent half the night talking. Lilly had just enough time to say goodbye to all her friends before we were off to Prague.

We found a small villa which looked, to me, rather like an English family house. There were two flats on the ground floor and two on the first floor. In the basement was the caretaker, who also looked after the large garden. Fields and woods were not far away and in between was a cemetery. From our flat we had a lovely view over the river and could see the *Hradshin*, the famous castle on the hill, from where 'Good King Wenceslas looked out'. The flat opposite looked towards the fields and the cemetery. The rent was higher, it appeared, when one had a lovely view. Papa used to say: 'Look at that glorious view, I paid enough for it.' The rooms were rather smaller that what we had been used to in Jaegerndorf, but they were still big enough for us. There was central heating and, at last, electric light instead of gas.

As soon as the flat was in perfect order and we had settled down, Max was expected to be introduced to the family and to formally ask for Lilly's hand. One morning the bell rang and I opened the door. There was a good-looking young man standing outside. He was tall, had curly dark hair and a twinkle in his eyes. 'Am I at the right house?' he asked. 'I hope so,' I replied, 'and you must be Max.'

'And you must be Nussy!' he answered, whereupon we shook hands and laughed. 'I wish I had known before that you had dimples,' he continued, and that nearly ended the engagement, before it was even officially announced.

Max had previously confided in Lilly that he preferred girls with a dimple in the chin. Now his remark upset Lilly. She was very jealous of me, although we mostly understood each other so well. This was not the first time. Hilda's brother in Jaegerndorf had shown a preference for me and though I was not interested, Lilly did not believe it.

Quite often Lilly had preferred to go to Hilda's parties whilst I went skiing. However, when I returned I would always change quickly and still go to the party. As I was so busy skiing I had not much time to look after my clothes. I was also somewhat careless. I shared a big wardrobe with Lilly and it was easy to borrow her clothes, especially stockings and plissé skirts, which invariably suffered when I wore them on the bicycle!

One Sunday evening I grabbed a pair of her new stockings and wore them to the party. Lilly recognised the colour and accused me in front of everybody of having taken her stockings. I denied this vehemently. She then rushed towards me, pulled my skirt up high enough for everyone to see the suspenders, turned the top of the stocking over and there were her intitials — which we had embroidered in all our clothes. I was acutely embarrassed. I could have killed her. A sister is not always a blessing!

However, here in Prague her jealousy soon vanished when Max took her into town and bought her a beautiful ring. Papa had given them his blessing after finding out all about Max's work and his prospects. Max told him that he was working with his father, erecting and servicing tiled stoves and would finally take over the business. His family owned a large house in Slovakia where Lilly and he would have their own quarters. His only sister still lived with his parents but she would be well provided for. So Lilly's future looked secure. The only drawback was that she would be so far away. It took a whole night's train journey to get there.

The wedding was planned for the end of February. That gave Mama ample time to prepare Lilly's trousseau. Bed linen, table linen and other household linen was bought and sent to be hand-embroidered and initialled. The embroidery and the initials were quite elaborate. Plain initials were put on tea-towels, dusters and even floor cloths. Everything was provided in sets of a dozen, as it was supposed to last a lifetime. Most of it did.

There was also table silver and crockery to be bought and everything else necessary to keep a household, even a toolbox. Mama knew that in a small town a new bride's dowry was very important, especially as far as the neighbours were concerned. The washing lines were watched and the prestige of a young husband rose if his wife had been well provided for with a good dowry.

Lilly was to choose her furniture in Kaschau (Kosice), the capital of Slovakia, where she would be in a better position to know what was needed; the bills were to be sent to Papa. Poor Papa, he could never stop saving. As Lilly played the piano better than I did and as she had had her voice trained and could accompany herself, Papa let her have our grand piano. The dining room looked a bit bare now, so Papa bought a set of easy chairs and a couch, which had just come into fashion. We had only had a sofa before. Such a couch was called a *lotterbed*, 'a bed sunk on in indolence' according to the dictionary. It was usually covered with many cushions and had a drawer underneath in which spare bedding for a guest could be kept.

Meanwhile we explored the beauties of Prague. It is a magical, partly romantic, partly modern city extending on both sides of the river Moldau. The city lies between seven hills. On one of them stands the world famous castle dating back to the days of St Wenceslas. It is built in the rock and the lower windows are famous for the *fenstersturz* which started the Thirty Years' War, when the officials working there were thrown out of the windows. Luckily the windows are not too high, and the officials landed on the soft turf below with only their dignity seriously hurt.

Next to the castle is St Veit's Cathedral, which has a special chapel to hold the tomb of St Wenceslas containing the remains of the saint in a coffin made of lead, gold and silver. This Wenceslas was not the 'King Wenceslas' of Bohemia as in the well-known carol, but the patron saint of Czechoslovakia.

The year we went to live in Prague was the thousandth anniversary of the saint's death and Czechs had come from all over the world to see him in the opened coffin. I don't know what they were able to see, as the queues of tourists were so long that people had to stay in the queue overnight and sleep on the pavements. Those who lived in Prague thought they would see it all when the visitors had left, but then the coffin was closed. The chapel is full of precious and semi-precious stones found in Bohemia. They hang from the ceiling where they catch the rays of the sun, enhancing their beauty.

When Hitler marched into Prague in 1939 the Czechs were glad that the door to the Chapel had a treble lock. It needed three keys to open and the keys were kept by three different government officials. Only that fact prevented the art-lover Goering from carrying away the many other treasures also kept in the chapel. Some of those were taken secretly to Hungary and from there to America and only returned after the Second World War had ended.

Prague is full of beautiful palaces and churches; the old city has narrow twisting streets and ancient houses where you can walk in at the front door, walk along a passage and then emerge again in another street without the householder even being aware of it. The old market place has a monument to Hus, the Bohemian religious reformer, who was the first to insist that communion should be taken with bread and wine and the mass read in a language the people could understand. When the monument is lit up at night it resembles the huge fire in which he was burned at the stake as a heretic. There is also the little church where he said the first mass in Czech with the permission of Wenceslas IV.

There is the famous bridge with statues of saints on both sides, one of which is St Nepomuk looking down into the river, where he was thrown in by order of the King. Some say it was because he did not tell the King what sins his wife had confessed, others say that it was for political reasons. There is also a large cross covered in gold which, it is said, some hundred years ago the Jewish community were made to cover with gold, because a Jew had spit on the cross.

Seagulls fly about over the river, although Prague is in the middle of Europe and far from the sea. The river is frozen in winter, so that people can skate and lorries make a short cut across the river. We always said that when the wild ducks arrive, in early spring, that very night the ice would break. As far as I can remember, it always was the case. The river bank is planted with acacia and lime trees and I remember the scent in spring being intoxicating.

Lilly's wedding was quite a grand affair. She wanted a white wedding and she made a lovely bride. By the time the final list of invitations was complete, Papa had made his famous remark many times, 'I am not made of money', but always with a twinkle in his eye.

After Lilly's wedding I was alone again. I decided that I must prove to Papa that I was capable of earning my own living. I had been attending evening classes for a few weeks to prepare for the Cambridge Examination in English at the university and finally passed it.

I studied newspapers thoroughly, but nobody seemed to want anyone with a good knowledge of English. Then I found a rather intriguing advertisement: 'Painters wanted to paint unusual objects'. I had been quite good at art in school; the only drawback was when I had to use a ruler. We always had to draw lines with Chinese ink round a finished picture, to look like a frame. It was then that I made a mess of it. Blotches everywhere. I felt sure that painting 'objects' would not require straight lines with Chinese ink.

I went for an interview and got the job. There were three other girls in the workroom. The owner explained that we were using a very new paint. It was radium-based and would shine or glow in the dark. We were to paint small busts of sportsmen, for instance. They were made of plaster-of-Paris and would be exhibited in shop windows as advertising material.

However, the most recent order had come from Slovakia. Hundreds of crosses, about a foot long with the figure of Christ hanging from them, were to be painted for the prayer corner in Slovakian farms and cottages. There was a small dark-room attached to the workroom. We had to carefully check each finished article there to see that no part of the surface was left uncovered, thus making body or cross appear to be full of holes. We wore white overalls — my hospital ones came in handy — and I amused myself and my family at home by donning my overall and turning out the light. Nothing could then be seen except glowing splashes.

Papa was impressed that I managed to get a job, although he did not think much of a job where I received a weekly wage and not a monthly salary. It seemed a poor return for all the money he had spent on me. It sounded a bit snobbish to me, but he was right — anybody could do what I did.

Meantime I was learning international shorthand. I had learned the Gabelsberger method years ago at the convent, and I now found a private teacher who taught me the additions to that method. I would eventually be able to take shorthand notes in French, German, English or Czech. I also wanted to learn to type, which I should have done in Leipzig, but I had spent my time in more pleasant occupations!

I obtained a typewriter on loan from a shop, bought a book which taught the ten-finger method and practised each evening. When Papa realised that I was really in earnest he bought me a typewriter of my own and I promised to type his letters at the weekend, instead of the girl from the office who usually came to do them. I was extremely pleased when he called me his private secretary.

The painting job went well to begin with. Then when the Christ figures for Slovakia were complete we started on some special posters. I was called into the office and the owner offered me the job of supervisor. He wanted to take on more girls and I would have to train them. That would normally have been fine, but I was worried. The posters showed girls in national costume. The scarves and head-dresses were rather difficult to do, with bright colours and intricate patterns, and the advertiser wanted each pattern emphasised by lines in Chinese ink. How could I show the girls something I could not do myself? So I resigned from my job, with regret.

Again I studied the papers. Unfortunately the world did not know of my existence, or somebody would perhaps have provided a special job for me! Then I found an advertisement for a German-speaking secretary in a Czech firm.

I got the job, but when I started it did not take me long to find out that the word 'secretary' was an exaggeration. I sat in a room with three Czech typists who were very busy, whereas I had almost nothing to do. It turned out that my boss was the only German in the firm, there to deal with German correspondence, and as most customers were Czech, he himself had very little to do.

I practised my typing, read the paper or a magazine and felt bored, until a kind soul gave me a book to copy, the reason for which I never fathomed. It was a textbook about the art of building. The firm sold building materials. Now I found out how to mix cement, learned to distinguish the various kinds of bricks, how to build a wall, make corners — different from hospital bed corners — and various other items of interesting but useless information.

I copied that book almost all day long and then tried to impress my parents in the evening with my new-found knowledge. Mama remarked, practically, that she had no intentions of building a wall, let alone making a corner with bricks, and she doubted whether my new-found knowledge would help me in any way in a future marriage. However, I plodded on, until one day, idly skimming the newsapaper, I read: 'English secretary required'.

I applied immediately to the given address. It was a Czech company which had an English manager and a Czech/German manager. The Czech manager interviewed me while the Englishman sat quietly listening. I was given a German newspaper. 'Read it in English,' said the Czech manager. Then he gave me an English newspaper and said: 'Read it in German'. I did it, slowly, but I think accurately. Then somebody came in and said something in colloquial English, meant to be a joke. I smiled and the Englishman noticed. He remarked quietly: 'I think she will make quite a good secretary,' and he gave me an encouraging smile.

'All right', the Czech manager said, 'the job is yours. How much salary do you want?' I thought quickly. In my current job I earned Kc650 per month. So I answered 'Kc800'. Mr Hakl laughed: 'Your salary here will be Kc1500, but you must start next Monday.' It was already Wednesday and the middle of the month. I ought to have given a month's notice, but I did not mind if I had to lose half a month's salary; perhaps the boss might understand. 'I'll be here on Monday,' I promised, almost shaking with excitement.

When I informed my boss that I was leaving and starting the new job the following Monday he refused to let me go. 'You cannot leave until the end of next month,' he said. 'I don't care if you will earn more than double your present salary. I cannot find another secretary in so short a time and I can't possibly be without one.'

That lunchtime I went to the newspaper office and placed an advertisement for my job. The wording was as it was before, but instead of 'apply in writing' I gave the address of the firm and stated 'apply in person, morning or afternoon, during office hours'.

I did not tell my boss what I had done, but very soon he came into the typists' room. He was furious. 'Who has played that dirty trick?' he shouted and turned to me. 'Was it you? The staircase is full of applicants for the job. I have no time to deal with them all.'

'You said you could not get anybody in time for me to leave,' I quavered, 'so I thought I would help.'

'How dare you?' he shouted again, and left the room banging shut the door. I told the others what I had done and we all had a good laugh. 'Serves him right,' said one of them, 'he is far too pompous.'

Papa and Mama were on holiday when all this happened. I sent them a telegram, 'Got a new job. Kc 1500 salary' and received the reply, 'Congratulations and good luck'. I was as proud as a peacock.

The work was more interesting than anything I had done before. I sat in a Mr Davidson's room, which gave me a high status in the office, as I was the only secretary who had a boss all to herself.

Mr Davidson was tall, dark and slim. He looked about forty years old, had a sense of humour, went riding every morning at six o'clock, which made him different from everyone else and, as he told me later, was writing a book.

I soon found out that my international shorthand was not as perfect as I had imagined. Sometimes I could not read my own scribbles. It is always difficult to switch quickly from one language into another, but this is where Mr Davidson's sense of humour came in useful. 'You give the English language a bit of colour,' he said, 'and why should headquarters in London not have an occasional laugh!' So it was that most of my mistakes regarding the meaning of words were left uncorrected in letters.

As the first and second of November approached, Mr Davidson informed headquarters: 'The native population are having two holidays: one on All Saints' Day and one on All Souls' Day.' I could not translate 'All Souls', so I started to think logically to find the right word in English. All Souls' was a day to think of the dead, perhaps still suffering in Purgatory for their sins. 'That's it,' I thought, and wrote: 'The natives celebrate All Saints' Day and Sins' Day.' Mr Davidson was delighted.

I also made mistakes in the Czech language. The Czech director, Mr Hakl asked me to make copies of a contract in time for that afternoon's meeting. I had to do it in a hurry and he left me no time to correct any typing mistakes. 'Never mind,' he said, 'only the lawyer and I know Czech and the English gentleman from London will receive a translation anyhow.'

After the meeting he came to my room. He was beaming. 'You made a mistake all right,' he said, 'but you are not to correct this copy. My typist will make a new copy for the files. Your original will be framed and hung in the Gentlemen's Club.'

'What did I do?' I asked, puzzled. Then he explained. The Czech word for 'selling' is *prodavati*. I had written *prdavati*, which meant the sound of making a nasty smell. Mr Davidson and Mr Hakl laughed aloud: 'Ha, ha, the Dunlop Company is to have the exclusive right to "*prdavati*" throughout Czechoslovakia.' One vowel left out and laughter in the Gentlemen's Club! As far as I know, my mistake might still be hanging there on the wall.

With my first salary I bought myself a kayak. I was able to keep it at the swimming pool down on the river. I went there every morning at six o'clock, paddled to the small island in the river, ran round it and paddled back. That left me still plenty of time to go home, have breakfast and cycle to the office for eight o'clock. As the weather became warmer, the office opened at seven o'clock and we finished work at four in the afternoon instead of six.

I also bought a dog; I had always wanted a dog, but Papa had always refused. 'A dog is not for a flat, even if we do have a garden,' he would say. 'Mama would probably have to take him for walks and do all the work a dog entails.' However, once I began earning my own money I renewed my attacks with vigour, imploring Papa and Mama incessantly to change their minds. Eventually I wore them down and Papa, after talking it over with Mama, gave his permission.

I went with a friend to the animal centre to find a dog nobody wanted, so that I could make his life happy again. Papa's last words had been: 'Don't forget, only a small dog, please'. He had told me before that under no circumstances could we have a big dog and I had promised accordingly. Now I was surrounded by dogs of all sizes, all clamouring to be given a home. A small dog pressed against my legs. It did not reach my knees, so it definitely was a small dog. It looked appealingly at me and I could not resist. I had brought a lead with me and we walked happily home; at last I had found a pet to love and cuddle!

It was late in the afternoon when I opened the front door. Papa had just come home. 'What is this?' he exclaimed, pointing to my new acquisition.

'My dog', I said proudly. 'You told me I could have one.'

'What?' he shouted. 'I told you to get a small dog.'

'But it is a small dog,' I defended myself.

'Yes,' Papa agreed, 'but it will grow. This is only an Alsatian puppy and will soon be a big Alsatian.' I had known this, of course, but had thought if I didn't mention it nobody would object until it was too late. I hung my head, still thinking Papa may relent. He shattered my hopes.

'That dog,' said Papa, pointing an accusing finger at the innocent animal, 'will have to go back where it came from.'

'It is too late today,' I pointed out, 'and tomorrow is Sunday.'

'All right, Papa agreed, 'it can remain — but only until Monday, mind,' he repeated. 'Mama will see to it that the dog is taken back on Monday, as I have to leave early in the morning.' I was still looking round for a place to put the dog, when Papa brought an old cushion from the couch. 'He can have this for the time being and you can then use it for the small dog.' He put the cushion in the hall near the front door. It was quite a large hall and the doors from all the rooms, including kitchen and bathroom, led into it. My darling dog grabbed the cushion with its teeth and dragged it to one of the doors — the one leading to my parents' bedroom — where he deposited it and lay down contented.

Papa was amazed. 'Look Mama,' he called, quite excited, 'that little dog has chosen our bedroom door to protect us. Clever little thing!' and he patted the dog's head. I think that was the moment that the dog's fate was sealed. Now the only problem for Papa was how to save his face.

During that week while Papa was away, I postponed taking back the dog. I used all sorts of excuses. Mama was a dog-lover herself and was definitely on my side, but she bided her time. When Papa returned home, he admitted that it was only for Mama's sake that he had insisted on my having a small dog, in case I could not take him for walks and she would have to do so. Mama now said that she certainly would not mind, so finally the dog was allowed to stay.

He was not a pure Alsatian, so I called him 'Dingo'. Even Slava our maid liked him, as long as he did not invade her room, which was next to the kitchen, to lie on her bed.

The kitchen window was very large and had a deep windowsill outside. There was no fridge in those days and we sometimes put dishes there overnight to save going down the cellar. Now Slava had a brilliant idea. She put a blanket down on the sill and Dingo used that as his resting place. He was in nobody's way and was in the fresh air. He would gaze over the countryside in a lordly manner, watching the other dogs passing. Later, when he was fully grown and a dog came by he did not like, he would jump down from the first floor, right into the rosebushes, to the gardener's disgust. But even he forgave him because he was such a friendly, lovable dog — and also an extremely good guard dog.

Sometimes when I came home late after some party or the theatre I would find a note on the hall table: 'Please take Dingo out!' Sometimes the young man who had brought me home did not mind having a walk round the cemetery with me and the dog. There was, of course, no kissing in those days when we said goodbye. We would have regarded ourselves as almost engaged if that had happened and one of our parents had seen it.

Then one day I met my fate. It came in the shape of a Scotsman, a Mr Robertson, who was Area Manager of the Dunlop Company in London. He had to visit the various car manufacturers in Czechoslovakia who had concessions for the Dunlop hydraulic brakes for aeroplanes and he also had to settle complaints and problems. He flew a small aeroplane, a Puss Moth.

We had seldom seen him but on this occasion Mr Hakl came to ask me if I would type some letters for him. It was a Saturday, after one o'clock and I was ready to go home. However, I obliged. Mr Robertson dictated his two letters, I typed them and he thanked me. Nothing very special about that. Yet the impression he made on me was world-shaking. When he thanked me I suddenly felt as I had never felt before. It was love at first sight! I knew with certainty that 'this was the man for me!' It seemed as if I was looking into the future, where this man would play an important part in my life. I went home in a daze.

Mr Robertson was a tall, slim man with a crooked smile which I found enchanting. It came from plastic surgery he had to have when, during the First World War, he had crashed his aeroplane and had broken both jaws. He was only nineteen at the time, but that I found out later. The scar was hidden behind a small moustache. He had hazel-brown eyes with a twinkle in them and had looked kindly down at me as he thanked me for the work I had done for him.

The afternoon was free as it was Saturday. I went down to the river and took my kayak, rowing down the river the whole afternoon, dreaming about Mr Robertson. Paddling back upstream in the evening made me forget him for a while. However, on Sunday I was back on the river, dreaming again.

When I arrived at the office on Monday morning, Mr Hakl, who was a great friend of Mr Robertson, asked me how I had liked him. 'Very much,' was my enthusiastic reply. He looked at me with a serious expression. 'You have not fallen in love with him, have you?' he teased, half serious and half joking, 'because he is married.' My world collapsed. In those days a married man was definitely taboo. Mr Robertson was lost for me for ever. So much for trying to look into the future! I felt quite sad for some time afterwards, then I decided to spend my savings on a holiday in Moldova.

I travelled by train on my own and once I was in the German-speaking part of southern Hungary, the Banat, I felt as though I had come home. I had to take my holiday in the spring and for the very first time I realised how much work had to be done in a vineyard before the grapes ripen.

My uncle was looking after the vineyards for us and I stayed with Aunt Marie as Grandmother's house had been sold. She knew the new owners and suggested that I go and see them. It was disconcerting to see strangers in the house which still seemed to me my second home, and which had been in our family for over two hundred years. Few changes had been made, both inside and outside. The garden was still full of vegetables and flowers, but the beehives had gone. The lime kiln was covered up for good. 'Too much work,' said the new owner's wife, who was about forty years old. I thought of Grandmother, who at the age of eighty had done it all and organised the work in the vineyards. However, at least the vineyards were still there and Moldova was still the place where we really belonged.

When I came back from Moldova I had forgotten Mr Robertson and my disappointed 'love at first sight'. At Lilly's wedding I had met two of Max's friends who were living in Prague. I had become very friendly with them. They had introduced me to other young men. We went for hikes and cycle rides, to the theatre and dances, but were no more than good friends. One of them, a student of architecture admired me and kept on saying that he loved me. Unfortunately, I couldn't feel anything for him, yet we stayed good friends. There was another one, a teacher from Jaegerndorf who was studying to become a professor. He had taken me to the Giant Mountains skiing after Lilly's wedding, as we had been in the same skiing club in Jaegerndorf. He also said he loved me, but received no encouragement.

We had a special name for frustrated lovers, *kuemmerer*, which means the sort of person who will do anything for you but never gets any reward. Sometimes one of these two would arrive at our house when I was going out with somebody else. One in particular was an excellent chess player and Mama loved chess. I would persuade him to stay and have a game with Mama, which he did. What he thought about me I will never know, but Mama was a good listener and there was always coffee and cake, which for a student was perhaps sometimes just as welcome.

In July that year there was a theatre festival in Prague and a British theatre group came to play *Joan of Arc* by Bernard Shaw. Sybil Thorndike was Joan. It was a magnificent performance and a young man sitting next to me enthused about the play and the setting. It seemed natural that we should take a little walk along the river, talking and talking. He mentioned a lecture on English literature which would be given in a few days and I promised to go with him.

From then on we met several times to walk in the wood, up to the castle wall, along the river and in the little old streets on the *Hradshin*. One street is a cul-de-sac with a stone door at the end, behind which, so the legend goes, a hermaphrodite is encased.

This little street used to house the alchemists, who tried to produce gold from base metals. They lived in little houses, built into the wall which surrounded the castle, literally 'one up, one down' with just two little rooms of which the top one reached through the ceiling. It was still possible to see the primitive cauldron in which magic mixtures were produced, but never gold.

The last of these old houses was occupied by a fortune-teller, Madame Thebe. She was as famous as the alchemists' street itself, and was visited by all the tourists. We went there one evening, just for fun. The room was so small that both my friend and I could only just squeeze in! We didn't mind listening to each other's future.

Madame Thebe had no crystal ball. She gave us a long look then took my hand. She told me all sorts of things, which made me wonder, although I had entered determined not to believe anything she would say. Amongst other things, she told me that I would cross the 'little water', not the big one, meaning the Atlantic to America, but the little one, meaning the English Channel.

'You mean I have crossed it,' I interrupted.

'No,' she said firmly, 'you will go again and finally stay there for good. You will have hard times, very hard times.' She looked at me again and sighed.

'Financially, you mean?' I queried.

'Yes,' she said, seriously.

'But will I have enough to eat?' I tried to joke. Not to have enough to eat was the most impossible thing that could ever happen to me, I

193

thought. She became very serious now and said: 'Just enough'. I tried to suppress a laugh, but felt shaken just the same. Of course this is all ridiculous, I thought, how could I ever be so poor!

Madame Thebe continued on a lighter note: 'You will meet somebody, or have already met him, and in January in a year's time you will be married'. That was better. In the end we left the fortune-teller happily. I think my young man felt sure that he was the one, whom I had met recently. I could see by his cheerful, confident expression that he liked the prospect of being married within a year and a bit. It was already September, but I dismissed the whole thing as utter nonsense.

Just before Christmas, however, he made me a positive proposal, but I had to refuse. We said goodbye. He had already ordered a Christmas present for me from a cousin in Japan. It was a book of sixteenth-century Japanese poetry translated into English, handwritten on ricepaper. The binding and jacket were Japanese. It was a thoughtful present which I accepted with thanks and I was sorry that I could not feel any love for him. He must have thought me a very cold fish!

In the autumn I had joined the German ski club in Prague. They had their first meeting on 2 October in the 'German House'. Now my skiing fever started again. Every week from the end of October onwards we went to the mountains, the *Erzgebirge* (Iron-ore Mountains) and the *Riessengebirge* (the Giant Mountains). We had to take a lift because the sports train left late in the evening and we would have had to spend most of the night walking in order to reach the various huts.

One evening we became stuck in the lift. There were about eight of us and it was rather a tight squeeze. We had to wait until five o'clock in the morning before we were released. Next to me was a Dr Steiner, with whom I had spoken quite often in the ski club. It was bitterly cold and we stood even closer together than normally. There was only one bench against a wall, where two girls could sit at a time. Unfortunately, there was a draught at the back of the seat; it had been snowing on the way and my trousers were damp and nearly froze to the wall.

Later, I was often teased that the lift was responsible for my acquaintance with Dr Steiner. Whatever the case, we spent the summer hiking every weekend, with my dog as a third. As the fortune-teller had predicted we were married the following January. I rejoiced: I would not go over the 'little water', I would live in Prague.

Karl Steiner was ten years older than I. He was clever, charming, musical, good company and loved skiing as much as I did. He also loved going to the theatre and especially to operas, most of which he almost knew by heart.

Right from the beginning I felt flattered that he preferred my company to those prettier girls who were also in the ski club. I was probably longing to get married and have a home of my own. There was also some unintentional pressure from my parents. They always had an expectant look when I came home from a day's hike and I could read the question in their eyes: 'Has he declared himself?' I also longed to have a child.

Before the marriage he confessed to me that he had been gambling at cards a lot over the last ten years. His two elder sisters had always come to his aid to help pay for his losses. He insisted that since he knew me he had not gambled at all and was probably cured. It was only I who could make him stop gambling. So my acceptance of his proposal gave me the gratifying feeling that I was saving him from himself. We married at the Registry Office, but had a large reception and, of course, Lilly and Max came from Spiska Nova Ves.

However, Karl's good behaviour did not last long. Within a few weeks he was back with his cronies in the coffee house, playing cards for money and probably for high stakes. I had, like Lilly, been given a generous dowry and a substantial amount of money, which was deposited in a savings bank in Jaegerndorf. Papa advised me to leave it there; it was in my name and I would therefore never be entirely dependent on my husband.

Then came the Wall Street Crash, which involved many banks in Europe. Somehow, Karl persuaded me to take the money out of the little provincial bank in Jaegerndorf and put it in his big bank in Prague, where it might be safer. Although he didn't ask me to do it, I put the money into a joint account rather than in my own name. After all, I loved him and believed in the saying 'What's mine is yours and vice versa'.

Before very long I found out that Karl was losing more than he was winning. Money which we kept in a strong box disappeared; once I found that the quarterly rent money was gone and sometimes he could not give me any household money or pay the maid. He always promised this would be the last time. Soon I knew that when he brought me a book I had wanted or a box of chocolates or flowers, that he had lost again. He probably went to his sisters for money, who still spoilt him as he was not only the youngest in the family but had been born when his two sisters and two brothers were already grown up.

Although he was a Doctor of Law he had preferred to join his brother in an import and export business. I never found out what really happened, but he quarrelled with his brother and left. It was fortunate that I had kept my job in the office, because things became more and more difficult as he could make no more contributions to the household expenses. Yet he still had money for gambling. 'I win quite a lot,' he assured me, 'and as soon as I am out of this lucky streak, I will never play cards again.' I believed him. Nobody can be more stupid than a woman in love!

I realised that the marriage might not last, but I still wanted a child. That was the least I wanted from my marriage. Karl also wanted a child, but he said it would not be fair. He couldn't take on the responsibility. He said it would be much better if I left him; he realised he was no good for me and had finally admitted that he might never change.

I promised that I would never ask anything from him if we should ever part, if only I could have a child. Secretly I hoped that it might be the one thing to make him change. He adored children and finally agreed.

We went to Moldova for our holiday at the end of September and Karl was delighted. Aunt Marie and Uncle Gustav seemed to like him and we spent nearly all our days in the vineyards and lazing in the sun on the roof of the hut on the hill top. We could not stay for the vintage but the grapes were already ripe and the peaches. There was no opportunity for card-playing and Karl seemed to be quite happy without his daily card games. I hoped he was cured.

As soon as we were back home the magic of Moldova no longer worked. Karl was back in the coffee house each evening. However, as I became pregnant I felt sure that all would be well once the child was born and Karl would realise his responsibility. He had formed an agency of his own now, for furnishing material from Holland, and everything seemed to be going well — except for his gambling. It will be all right soon, once the baby is born, I consoled myself.

However, it did not work that way. In June my daughter, Evi, was born. Karl adored her and for weeks he stayed at home. I was happy. Then it started all over again. He spent the evenings in the coffee house and often returned with a worried, unhappy face. We had to give up the maid and moved into an attic flat in the same house where my parents lived. I had to make all kinds of excuses to my parents, who suspected that things were not as they should be. Then, in desperation, I went to

Lilly with the baby without telling him, to give him a fright. He was frantic and his enquiries to my parents, whom I had only told that I was visiting Lilly, made it quite clear to them that I was in trouble. Of course, Karl pretended that we had merely quarrelled and he came to collect me. It was such a pity. Karl was charming, kind and understanding; his only vice was his gambling. It was like an illness.

Then, one night I had really had enough. I went to the coffee house and implored him to come home, but he made the excuse that he could not leave honourably, as he was winning. His hands were shaking, his eyes wild. I realised there and then that there was no hope.

I returned home, took my little daughter and went down to my parents' flat. Papa was not at home, but Mama welcomed me without too many questions. They had guessed long ago what was the matter. 'Have you looked at your silver cutlery?' she asked, when I told her that the money in the strong box had again disappeared.

I was horrified to think that he might have pawned the silver. People like us did not pawn anything. But sure enough, when Mama came upstairs with me to look, the silver had gone, most of my jewellery and very soon I found that there was an overdraft in the bank. All my money had been spent. Still I felt no real anger, but only pity. I knew how he suffered from being unable to control his passion for gambling.

I let Karl stay in the flat until he could find other accommodation, while I remained at my parents'. To my surprise, he now stayed at home every evening, played the piano and sang my favourite songs. He even came home as soon as his work was finished.

I could hear him singing and playing, and finally went up to the flat. Mama was worried I might weaken and return to him. I only stayed for a couple of hours. There were chocolates and flowers on the little table by the couch. What could one do with such a man? Why could he not have been like that before I left him?

I had intended only a legal separation, but Papa insisted on a divorce. 'You are still young,' he said, and although I swore I would never marry again he wanted me to be free for whatever might happen in future. He felt sorry that he had not helped me more while I was with Karl. 'I will look after you and the child,' he promised, 'but I will not throw money away on a gambler. They never change; he can't help it.'

However friendly the partners are when they agree to a divorce, it is a traumatic experience. One feels such a failure. It was doubly painful for me because I knew how Karl loved his little daughter, Evi. Many times I saw him crying when he held her in his arms. Nevertheless, he admitted that though he loved her very much he would still be unable to look after both of us. His gambling habit was too strong. He had fought it for years, ever since he had left the army, but he had never succeeded in curing himself.

There was one funny side to the divorce. My lawyer was a friend of the family. In Czech law at that time it was possible for a woman to get a divorce if the husband insults her publicly. So the reason given for my divorce was that Karl had called me 'a stupid old cow' on the stairs — for all the other tenants to hear. This remark showed great disrespect and no wife could be asked to live with such a man again!

On my daughter's first birthday the divorce came through and Karl left the flat. I went upstairs with Papa. There I found our living-room full of red roses, the same as it had been when I brought the baby home from hospital. There, too, was a pair of little white shoes standing on the piano. It was heartbreaking, but had to be endured. Papa just patted my shoulder, a quiet reassurance that I was not alone.

Mama proved a great help. She looked after Evi while I was at the office and a more loving grandmother could not be found. 'I can enjoy with her now, what I missed with you two girls,' she confided. Slava, the maid, also adored Evi. The child could do nothing wrong. Slava could only speak Czech, so it happened that Evi learned to speak German and Czech at the same time. Children don't get confused if they learn two languages or even more at the same time. Later on, Evi would always answer in the language she was spoken to.

Meanwhile, I took her regularly to see her father and once she could walk properly he would collect her and then bring her back. She grew to love her *Vati*, as she called him. At that time she did not ask any questions.

Karl's family also kept in touch with me. Occasionally his eldest sister would invite me for a *jause* (coffee and cake in the afternoon), where the whole family would make a fuss of Evi, who was the only girl among the second generation.

18

SHORTLY AFTER THE divorce Mr Harry Robertson re-entered my life. One morning he came to the office and then disappeared again into the owner's office. I don't know what I felt. It seemed almost a lifetime since I had seen him for the first time. I was no longer the young girl who had spent a whole weekend on the river, dreaming.

The following day my boss, Mr Davidson, asked me if I would agree to have dinner with Mr Robertson the next night. He was too shy to ask me himself. Apparently it was not his custom to take secretaries out to dinner and perhaps he felt lonely in Prague. I agreed. I was, after all, divorced. My experience of marriage had made me slightly cynical. Why should I not have dinner with a man, even if he was married?

During the course of the evening, I learned that Mr Robertson was separated from his wife and that divorce proceedings had started. I respected the fact that he blamed only himself for the estrangement, and not his wife, as so many men did. Usually the men were the misunderstood ones! 'She might have felt lonely when I was away so much,' he told me, trying to excuse her, 'but she refused to come with me and it could so easily have been arranged.'

It was a pleasant evening and when he suggested taking me up in his aeroplane the next day, I was thrilled. He still flew the small plane, the Puss Moth. The next afternoon was sheer bliss. The Puss Moth was big enough for two, with the passenger sitting behind the pilot. I had never flown before, but had always wanted to. When we flew over our garden and I could clearly see my little daughter, then about three years old, playing in the sand and Mama sitting on the bench nearby, I felt so excited and happy that I could have kissed and embraced the pilot.

Years later I always said that I fell in love with the plane and not its pilot. Before he left, he asked me if I would go to Warsaw and then fly back with him over Vienna to Prague. I promised that I would try. I could go as his secretary, and it was arranged with Mr Davidson that I would be released from work for a few days. The following week I took the night train to Warsaw, and so began the first of many such trips.

Within the next two years I flew with Harry quite often. Mama looked after Evi, Slava did the housework, and I travelled all over Europe. As Harry worked for Dunlop, my boss always allowed me a few days off. Harry had to visit the countries from Norway, Finland and Sweden right down to Turkey, twice a year. There was a civil war in Spain, so I missed that. Sometimes I was afraid, but afterwards there was always the marvellous feeling of having overcome that fear.

I fell very deeply in love, but I did not want to go to England and was not too keen on a second marriage. Eventually we did get married, but meantime I enjoyed the flying and seeing the world. We had all kinds of adventures.

Whenever the plane was taking off, Harry used to sing the drinking song from the operetta *The Student Prince.* All my life I had tended to sing whenever I was happy, but tried never to do it in company. Now I felt so happy in the aeroplane that very often I could not keep quiet. That was when Harry's natural kindness would desert him. He would turn round — we were seated behind each other — and remark worriedly: 'There seems to be something wrong with the engine; it is making such a funny noise.' It was so humiliating for me!

Once, however, we did have some real engine trouble, on a flight from Bucharest to Belgrade. I wanted to see Moldova, at least from the air as there was nowhere he could safely land. Harry flew along the Danube, then right through the Iron Gates, low enough for the rocks to be on both sides of us.

I had written to Aunt Marie, asking her to go to the vineyard on the hill in the late afternoon, as we would fly over it. Unfortunately, there was a thunderstorm and the lightning flashed both above and below us. It was beautiful — but frightening. All of a sudden the lightning was right in front of the nose of the aircraft and at the same time the

Harry with the Puss Moth

propeller turned the wrong way, only for seconds, but long enough to make Harry look worried. 'Phew', he exclaimed. 'That was close. I thought the propeller would break.'

When the thunderstorm was over there was a rainbow, again both above and below the aeroplane, and we flew right through it. We could already see the outline of Belgrade in the distance when the engine began to splutter. Harry took his false teeth out and put them in his pocket. Then I began to be really worried. He always said: 'I'm damned if I'll choke on my teeth — for which I paid good money.'

In my imagination he had already crashed and I saw, as if a ghost, the funeral procession, and one of the mourners saying: 'That poor child,

201

and not even a photograph to show her what her mother looked like.'
What funny thoughts people have when they think they have reached
'the end'. We managed to reach Belgrade safely, but when I eventually
returned home, I had a studio photo taken of myself. Now I could die in
peace.

I remember another amusing incident. We were flying from Warsaw
to Bucharest. When we landed at the frontier to refuel I stayed in the
plane as they were doing a lot of rebuilding. Halfway to Bucharest I
said: 'Harry, I have to go somewhere.'

'You will have to wait,' he replied, 'my bottle would be no good to
you.' I promised to try and wait.

However, in a little while I had to confess: 'Harry I can't wait any
longer, what shall I do?'

'Perhaps you have something in your suitcase which might do as a
container,' he suggested. Then I had a brainwave — my bathing cap. It
was the kind which fastens tightly under the chin and was in the shape
of the head.

It was not easy to get my suitcase down but I managed, and then I
performed a very delicate operation. With a feeling of relief I sat there
with the wobbly container in my hands.'What shall I do now?' I asked.
'Throw it out of the window?'

'No!' But it was too late. The back draught blew the contents right
into Harry's face. Then I knew that he really loved me: he did not throw
me out of the aircraft! 'Jesus Christ!' was all he said, as he wiped his
face.

In 1936 the World Exhibition took place in Brussels. The Russians
had brought their training tower for parachute jumpers. When we saw
it, Harry asked whether I would like to have a go, thinking that I would
certainly refuse. He had maintained that he would rather go down with
the plane — as he did in the First World War — than risk his life with
those horrible things. He was obviously disappointed when I said: 'Yes,
let's try it'.

The training tower seemed incredibly high. The top was reached by
means of a lift with glass doors. Crowds of people were waiting for
somebody to jump as Harry and I went up in the lift. Halfway up I
regretted what I had said, but I was too proud to let all these people see
me coming down again in the lift.

We arrived at a platform which had a low fence around it with a small
gate. The man in charge first put a belt round my knees to prevent the
people down below seeing more than they had paid for and then he

fixed a harness on my shoulder. He opened the little gate and said: 'If you please, Madam'. Madam was shaking all over. I looked down, shuddered and jumped.

It was marvellous. For the first few seconds I fell. Then the parachute opened and I had time to take a good look about. There was a sea of faces down below, looking like pink pebbles on a beach. I was floating in the air. Then the ground seemed to come up to meet me and I landed.

It was a bad landing; I was sprawling on the ground like a toad. Nevertheless, the applause was music to my ears. Harry came floating down, also in an undignified manner. He too had liked the jump. 'I was luckier than you', he confided. No "If you please" for me! The man just opened the gate and gave me a push.' We both jumped twice more and finally came down with a perfect 'knee bend'.

In time, Harry gave up his job with Dunlop. He had bought a patent from a Hungarian. It was for an advertising gadget whereby anything could be made to move using only a light bulb. He and a friend in London became partners; his partner looked after the manufacturing side and Harry looked after the sales. Harry also took the agency for a French firm who supplied aeroplane parts. The advertising gadget sold well and our financial position seemed secure. I would miss the flights with the Puss Moth, but being with my daughter and having Harry all the time compensated me for the loss of that pleasure. After all, I had seen most of Europe and could stay at home now.

I had taken Harry to meet Lilly and Max and also introduced him to skiing in the mountains. Evi had been accustomed to skis since she was three years old and could glide smoothly down the slope, while Harry did it mostly on the seat of his trousers. At first he had refused to be out all day in the cold and was surprised how warm one gets when skiing. Then at the end of summer we went to Moldova. We took Mama with us and Papa followed a week later. I could now show Harry the place over which we had flown in the thunder and lightning — and I think he understood how much it meant to me. Evi was up and down the hill in the vineyards, showing *Oma*, as she called her grandmother, the different kinds of grape, as if she had known them all her life and climbing the peach trees just as Lilly and I had done. We had a glorious time, but it was to be the last time I ever saw Moldova. Luckily, I did not know it.

We returned to Prague just in time for the crisis in 1938. There were various causes for this. At the beginning of Hitler's régime many

203

changes for the better had taken place in Germany. First the school leavers, rich and poor, had to join the two-year *Arbeitsdienst*. That meant doing all kinds of work necessary for new projects, like building motorways, cheap cars to be available for everyone and various other smaller projects. Experts in that kind of work had to be re-employed. The unemployment figures in Germany at that time stood at about six million or more.

A bad custom had started recently whereby a young man was dismissed as soon as he got married, because married men received a higher wage. Under a new ruling, no man with children could be dismissed and there was also a limit set to the high incomes of executives, so that a larger number of men, at lower salaries, could be employed.

On marrying, young couples who could prove that they were healthy in body and mind received a certain sum to enable them to buy furniture for a kitchen and bedroom. A similar sum, which had to be repaid without interest, was given to them to start their married life. Rents for all flats had to be recorded, so that no excessive profit could be made. Under these conditions it did not take very long for the unemployment figures to fall. All this news made many in Czechoslovakia envious, especially as unemployment was rising there. It was mostly the German-speaking population, the industrialists and the industrial workers, who looked with envy at the German Reich.

There had always been occasional trouble between the German-speaking population and the Czech-speaking one, ever since the German craftsmen had been called into Bohemia from Germany hundreds of years ago. Even when Bohemia had been part of the Austro-Hungarian Empire the Czechs had wanted their own country and government. The irony was that it was a German, 'Vatar Jahn', who not only started the physical culture movement, but also instilled a nationalist feeling in the Czechs. Since Czechoslovakia had been formed the German speakers living there were now the minority — and did not like it — and the Czechs triumphed.

When conditions were bad in Germany after the First World War, and Czechoslovakia was comparatively well off, there had been only murmurs of discontent, but no open conflict. Now things were different. A political party was formed, the 'Sudetendeutsche Partei' (SDP), who wanted to be united with the German Reich. They got all the help they needed from Germany. They had special privileges if they went to a German university, and the only place in Europe where a degree existed in physical education, for example, was Berlin. In all educational establishments the Nazi propaganda was particularly strong.

In the flat below my parents' lived another couple. The husband had been studying in Germany and now he was not only a member of SDP, but also represented the party in Parliament, although he did not have much influence there. I heard from his wife that she had received financial help from Berlin when he had been out of work and continued to do so whenever they were in need. The differences between the Czechs and Germans grew; the slightest incidents were exaggerated in both the Czech and German newspapers and feelings became easily inflamed.

Only the party members wanted to belong to the Reich: the rest of the German-speaking people in Czechoslovakia wanted things to stay as they were. The threat of Hitler taking over Czechoslovakia was frightening. There were more and more outbreaks of violence. My family was unsure what to believe. I had maintained a dislike of Hitler ever since I had heard him speak, or rather shout, in that Munich street long ago, and had witnessed the Nazis' treatment of the Jews. When it became known that Hitler had shot his friends I turned further from him in disgust, even though I had to admire the economic improvements in Germany. Many others, however, thought him marvellous and could only sing his praises.

Hitler's propaganda campaign in Czechoslovakia, and the way he made new party members in preparation for the future invasion, was devious but clever. At the time I was still going to the sports club twice a week. The instructor there had recently attended the College of Physical Training in Berlin, for a refresher course. When he returned he had suggested we might have a singsong after each session, which we all thoroughly enjoyed. Then he suggested we might arrange some special evenings for folksinging. In order to be able to let us know when the first of these would take place, he asked us to give our names and addresses, so that we could still be informed even if we missed a training session. Harry warned me not to do this. Later it turned out that he had good cause. When Hitler finally marched into Czechoslovakia, everyone who had given their name and address automatically became a party member and was given a membership card, whether they liked it or not.

In the autumn of 1938 the political situation became yet more disturbing. The SDP had by then grown into a big party. Hitler's power loomed threateningly over the frontier. It became increasingly clear that he might invade and that the Czechs would not be strong enough to fight back.

Chamberlain tried to negotiate and visited Hitler in Berchtesgaden. Unfortunately, Chamberlain treated Hitler as a gentleman who would keep his promises and he generously handed the Sudetenland to him, believing that it would really be Hitler's last demand. In fact, Hitler wanted to take all the German-speaking people in Europe into the Reich.

Harry and I were in town in the main square, the *Wenzelsplatz* or *Vaclavske Namesti*, on that fateful evening. When the news came through the loudspeaker that neither France nor Britain would help us and that in fact the Sudetenland would be handed over, there was at first an eerie silence, the shock was so great. Then through the silence came the sound of people crying. I saw grown men with tears running down their cheeks.

The anger and the disappointment of the crowd quickly focused itself on the German-speaking population. Fights broke out, German shops were damaged and it became quite dangerous in the thronged square. I spoke English with Harry so we were left alone, but we could not get out of the square. Many streets led out of it but they were all blocked. The police came with horses; we were pushed along and managed to run. It was a frightening experience being dispersed by the police on horses. We were glad when we finally reached home in safety.

I turned on the radio and translated for Harry. We could hear Hitler shouting his triumph to the world. In disgust I turned the radio off again. It was approaching midnight when there was a knock at the door. It was Papa. 'Mobilisation has just been announced,' he said, 'Everyone has to assemble at the appointed places.' He was breathless with emotion. 'That I should live to see another war!' he gasped.

Papa asked Harry to go and help the couple on the ground floor as they were newly married and the wife was almost hysterical. The young man didn't know what to do. My parents could not help as they were German-speaking. We could hear people shouting outside, cursing the Germans. A group came up the hill towards our house. Luckily we heard the caretaker's voice: 'Go away, there are no Germans in this house, only an Englishman and his wife'. Some shouted back: 'The English are just as bad, they let us down', but eventually they were persuaded to leave. A disturbed night followed.

For the next few days I had to tell Evi not to speak German, especially on the street, as the Czechs were angry with the Germans. We were afraid that Hitler might still bomb us because of the mobilisation. I looked around for safe places for my daughter. There seemed to be none. We decided that we could send Evi with Slava to her home in the country. It was an anxious time. Then the men came home again and there was no war.

When the news had reached us that Britain and France would not help the Czechs in case of an invasion, Harry, together with the French and British Air Attaché, had offered their services as pilots to the Czech Government. There were some articles in the Czech papers stating that not all Englishmen would desert the Czechs in their hour of need, and Harry's name was mentioned.

The great shifting of frontiers now started. Each day it was announced which town and village was to be in Germany. There had also been the question of who was a Sudeten German and who was not. After 1918, when Czechoslovakia came into existence many Czech officials had been moved to places where the population had been 100% German. They, of course, did not want to be in the Reich. It was finally decided that everyone who had lived in the part of the country in question since 1 January 1910 was now a Sudeten German. As it happened my father had moved from Vienna on 31 December 1909. One day made all the difference: he was now a Sudeten German whether he wanted to be one or not!

As Papa was no Jew, the Vacuum Oil Company transferred him to Karlsbad, so that one of the Jewish Directors could come to Prague. If only Chamberlain had foreseen the consequences of his gift to Hitler. There was a great movement of Czech people from the Sudetenland back to Czechoslovakia and of German families from Czechoslovakia to the Sudetenland. Jobs were lost and families torn apart.

Terrible tales of Nazi cruelties were told, but luckily not all were true and many were exaggerated. One morning I heard a story while at the shops. Someone had met someone else who had spoken to a person from the refugee camp outside Prague. The camp was for those who had not yet found accommodation. It was said that a swastika had been burnt into the forehead of every Jew in the camp.

Harry could not believe it: 'Let's go and make sure whether this is true.' On this occasion it was not true, although later even worse atrocities would be committed. Most Jews in the camp were trying to get to Britain or America, but none was hurt, and none had a swastika put on their foreheads. Many of them, when they realised that Harry was from Britain, asked him whether they could give him money to deposit there.

There was no camp in the Sudetenland for those who moved there. It must be admitted that the organisation was excellent. All houses and flats which became empty had to be registered at the town hall. Rents were fixed, as in Germany, and those like my father, who wanted a flat, merely had to go there, state their requirements and were duly allocated one.

Mama missed Evi terribly, so I took her to Karlsbad and let her stay with Mama quite often. It only took one hour by bus and Karlsbad was a place worthwhile visiting. Although the new border was halfway on that journey no special passes were required. Life resumed some kind of normality, until March 1939.

During the second week of March I had taken Evi to my parents and on the Saturday I went to collect her. I arrived in the late afternoon, but my parents and Evi were out. The caretaker informed me that they had gone to a children's matinee. While I waited in the caretaker's flat he asked: 'How are conditions in Prague? Is it very bad?'

'What do you mean?' I enquired. 'It is the same as usual. There have not even been the usual shouts at the queues at German cinemas. Why do you ask?'

'We have been told that there is rioting in Prague,' he explained, 'and we have been on standby since yesterday.'

'Rubbish,' I said, 'they probably want to keep you on your toes.'

He shook his head. 'Troops are assembling from everywhere and our barracks are full; some soldiers are even camping outside the town, and, as I said before, we are on "standby"!'

'Perhaps there are going to be training manoeuvres,' I suggested, trying to convince us both. When my parents and Evi came came back, I forgot his disturbing remarks.

During the Sunday night Evi became feverish and in the morning I called the doctor. Harry went to town early to go to the bank. He was back within a couple of hours. I greeted him with the news that Evi had measles, but he seemed to take no notice. He was terribly excited: 'German troops are marching into town, the banks are closed and the *Vaclavske Namesty* is full of tanks — and the troops are still marching.'

'I can't believe it,' I said.

'Come and see for yourself,' he suggested.

Slava, who had stayed with us when my parents moved, was just as anxious to hear more about what was happening in the city and promised to look after Evi, who was by now fast asleep, so that Harry and I could go into town. It was 15 March.

Sure enough, when we got to the main street, the German troops were still marching and had now been joined by motorcycles and tanks. They marched down the middle of the wide road. Only the stamping of their feet and the noise of the tanks and motorcycles could be heard — no other sound. The Czechs like to show their disapproval by complete silence and ignoring what is happening. The pavements were full of people, but their faces were turned away and nobody looked at the marching troops. The atmosphere was volatile.

Suddenly some commotion erupted in front of us. I saw an arm stretched out in the Nazi salute and a single voice shouted: 'Heil Hitler!' The next minute not only the arm, but also the head, of that person had disappeared and something like a bundle of clothes was thrown into the air. For a brief moment the crowd halted, and then moved slowly forward again. Within a few steps in front of us there lay a bundle of clothes on the pavement. Everybody stepped on or over it, but nobody stopped. When my turn came I saw that the bundle was a dead body, but I dare not stop. I pulled Harry along with me. He too realised the danger. The crowd looked menacing — and we had seen an example of what they might do.

During the next few weeks, goods in the shops were sold out, especially food and shoes. The saying 'guns before butter' seemed to be true. The underlying resentment of the Czechs showed dramatically. Often in the mornings a soldier would be found drowned in the river. Then the ruling was given that no soldier might go out alone, especially not with a girl, nor must they consort alone with a prostitute. The prostitutes were very patriotic!

Hitler himself then arrived in Prague and the SDP made much of his visit. Photographs appeared in the papers showing an enthusiastic crowd welcoming him. He drove through the centre of the city and up through the old town to the *Hradschin*. However, if you looked closely, the same faces could be found in every photograph. That was one time that Harry and I did not go to see the spectacle.

Within a few days we noticed that our flat was being watched, and especially those who came to visit us. A Jewish doctor's flat was then raided after he had spent the previous evening with us. Our comings and goings, too, were noticed. Harry could not understand why. Then we guessed that he might be on the blacklist. It might have had something to do with the newspaper reports in 1938 about him offering

209

his services as a pilot to the Czech Government.

One day when Harry was in our usual cafe in town, he was addressed by a Gestapo official who was an old acquaintance. He had been a former official at Frankfurt Airport, but was also a private pilot and, before Hitler came on the scene, a member of the Aero Club in London. This man told Harry that he ought to leave and go back to Britain. 'There will be a war sooner or later and then you will be the first prisoner, if not before. The slightest thing you do wrong and they will have you. I would sooner meet you in London.'

Harry just laughed: 'There is no war yet, and if there is I will meet you in Berlin.' But the warnings became stronger and stronger. Every time they met Harry was told 'Get out!' Harry thought that his friend would probably have liked to change places with him and would love to get to Britain, but he was hopelessly committed.

Towards the end of June however, although I was still not too keen, we decided it might be sensible to go to Britain now, in case there should be a war. We would have to leave everything behind, and it would not be easy to leave Prague. Since Czechoslovakia had been annexed there had been a five-mile limit round the city. We could only have left freely within the first few days, but then Evi had been ill.

Furthermore, as the daughter of a divorced couple, Evi was a ward of court and as such not allowed to leave the country. Only her father could give such a permission and overrule the court. Although Papa had taken over Evi's guardianship, he did not have the power to permit her to leave the country and I would not go without her, however much I loved Harry. Unfortunately, Karl had gone to Bolivia with the help of his family in 1937. He had been working for the German Embassy there, but when the Germans marched into Prague the family had been informed that he was missing. He had been strongly opposed to the Nazis. The Embassy said that he had left for an expedition into the jungle and not returned.

In order to go beyond the five-mile limit around Prague a special leave pass was required, which was issued at the Gestapo Office. I could not even travel to see my parents without very good reasons. I wrote to Mama about my difficulties and she thought of a way out. She sent me a doctor's certificate, stating that she had been experiencing various angina attacks and needed somebody to be with her all the time. Also Papa was not very well. So would I come and stay with her for a while? I realised that from there I could easily get to Britain via Holland.

I took this letter to the Gestapo Office and asked for a permit to go to Karlsbad. Naturally, I would have to take my child with me.

'Yes', replied the official, 'you can have a permit for the child to go to Karlsbad with you, but you must leave your passport here, as your daughter is on it. You will get permission for a fortnight, then you have to apply again. You can do that in Karlsbad.'

'But I need my passport,' I said. He looked at me intently.

'You cannot have your passport and a permit — one or the other.' 'You want to go to England,' he added sadly under his breath,' 'To England, you lucky one!'

Brusquely he walked over to the filing cabinet and stood with his back to me. I looked at the table. There lay my passport. The official was repeating in a rather loud voice: 'You must understand you cannot have the permit and the passport.' Realising the chance he had given me, I quickly picked up my passport and put it in my handbag. The official turned round and said in the same loud voice. 'There is your permit. You will have your passport back on your return. Good day.'

Hurriedly, I left the room and I have been grateful to that man ever since. We decided that I would pack everything, except what I would take to my parents. After my departure Slava would give notice to the house owners and then have our belongings removed to her home in the country at the end of the month. Later Papa would arrange for everything to be transported to Karlsbad and stored in his home until I returned.

Harry, meanwhile, was driving a car to his friend in Switzerland, who was a Jew. He had already arrived there but had had to leave his own Daimler behind. We would meet in London, or at the home of my Brighton friend, Eva Alexander, providing that I could inform him in time about my arrival at Harwich.

All went according to plan. England had now become the most desirable place in the world. I spent ten days with my parents, then left. It was a sad moment for all of us, as we felt sure that war was now imminent. It was August 1939 when I crossed the border into Holland and felt safe at last. Harry met me at Harwich. I crossed the 'little water' again just as the fortune teller had predicted, but I was not afraid of the other things she had foretold. I was safe in England with my daughter and the man I loved. What more could I want?

19

I WENT FIRST to my friend Eva in Brighton. We had nursed together in the children's hospital and she had also visited me in Prague before my first marriage. Harry stayed in London at the Aero Club to find out what he could do if war broke out. Nobody really believed there would be a war, but preparations and plans were being made for possible evacuation of children. My friend's parents had a small cottage in the country and her mother intended to live there with at least two evacuees, should the need arise. We spent a weekend there and I would have liked to have stayed on with them and helped look after the evacuees, as I dreaded the prospect of being left alone with Evi if Harry had to be away on flying duties.

Eventually we found our own flat in Brighton, consisting of a large living-room, two bedrooms and a tiny kitchen, no bigger than a pantry. We had to share a bathroom. I bought an English cookery book and remembered sadly my own cookery book, which I had left in the kitchen table drawer. Papa had promised to take a bigger flat in Karlsbad and have our furniture transported there with all our other belongings. Meantime, I hoped that Slava had been able to store it in the barn at her home in the country as she had promised. It was the last week in August when I moved into the Brighton flat. Harry was still in London preparing for wartime duty. He had joined the Air Transport Auxiliary.

I remember well the Friday when Hitler was given an ultimatum. It was announced on the radio that this was the last day to send any post to Germany. I walked sadly along the beach with Evi and realised that I would no longer be able to communicate with my parents or with Lilly. Then I remembered my friend from Leipzig, Lore, who had married and was now living in Oslo. I sent her address to my parents and at the same time I informed Lore that my father and I would communicate through her. I hoped she wouldn't mind. On Sunday 3 September, at eleven o'clock in the morning, the ultimatum expired and Britain and Germany were at war. I could not help but feel bitter to think that the only reason for the declaration of war was the fact that Hitler had marched into Poland. Part of Poland had belonged to Germany before the First World War. No part of Czechoslovakia had *ever* belonged to Germany, yet when Hitler marched into Czechoslovakia nobody had raised a finger to help.

At that time we had been told that Britain and France had agreed to help us, but ultimately France had refused, and so Britain decided to let Hitler have his way. Most people in Prague had said that the British were not ready for war, but it seemed that they were ready when Poland was attacked! So on that fatal day I walked again along the beach with Evi, and tried to keep my spirits up by telling her a funny story.

Harry was soon back from London, looking very smart in his navy-blue uniform. He was not quite sure where he would be stationed, or for how long, so I stayed on in the flat.

As the days became cooler, it had one drawback: there was only an open fireplace in the living-room and I had never lit a fire in an open fireplace. Through Eva I had met some of her friends and her sister-in-law, who quite often came to see me. One of them, Janet, came quite often and was very helpful in teaching me to make a fire. 'It is easy to make a fire,' she told me. 'All you need is a bit of paper and a few sticks; pile the coal around it and there you are.' It might have been easy for her, but for me it became a daily torment. I knelt on the hearth rug, like a worshipper, my wide-open arms holding up a newspaper, frantically trying to coax the reluctant flames to blossom forth. More often than not all the paper did was to hide from my eyes the sight of dying flames and greying coal. I spent precious hours from the best years of my life in this occupation, forgetting the war and my worries, but feeling very frustrated.

However, I had at least discovered why the national newspapers in this country are so large — to hold up in front of a fire, of course! But woe betide anyone who is tempted to read something which had been missed when the paper was conveniently placed on the breakfast table. As soon as one started reading, a curious flame would poke through the page and, within seconds, the whole lot would disappear up the chimney.

When I had finally coaxed the fire to burn with a steady flame I would tip-toe out of the room, close the door very carefully, so as not to make an additional draught, and start doing my other chores. How many times did I return to my fire, only to find it dead or dying. Sometimes, if there was still a red glow, I would hurl a shovelful of fresh coal on top, just to see the few miserable flames die completely. I cannot count the times I had to empty the grate and start again. I remember the first weeks of the war most vividly as a time when I had my own private battle with the fire. Such a trivial frustration can over-shadow a great historical event, even though the beginning of the war was very quiet and nothing much seemed to happen.

How I longed to have a tiled stove or central heating, instead of an open grate. I remembered the tall, tiled stoves in the corner of each room at home, before we had central heating. They too, needed only a bit of paper, some sticks and then coal or more wood. But the little door in front could be closed and so you could forget about it for hours. The tiles would quickly warm up and you could sit on a bench and lean against them. I always used to sit with my feet up, my back leaning against the tiles, reading a book; it was sheer bliss.

That was how it always worked: I did some unfamiliar task and then my thoughts would straight away go back, down the years, until I was back home again. Although I had my daughter and husband I still felt a stranger in a foreign land — only here because of the war.

Harry came home every weekend and once brought a jigsaw for Evi, which was a new experience for me as well as her. We did not have them at home, only bricks which had to be turned over to form a new picture. Evi soon became very good at doing the puzzle and so I bought some more. The poor child did not have many toys. In Prague she had enjoyed her own playroom, divided by a curtain from my room. She had a doll's house, and my old writing desk from the office, which we made into a theatre with its own scenery and many wooden puppets of fairy-tale figures. She had become quite proficient at manipulating the puppet strings and always had had an admiring audience — Mama, Slava and me. When we packed for our journey I had put some boxes of wooden toys in a suitcase together with glove puppets and a few games.

Unfortunately, that suitcase had disappeared during the customs inspection on the Dutch frontier.

No sooner had I mastered the fire-making than Harry told me we were moving. He hoped to be flying from an aerodome near Nottingham for quite some time and friends of his would let us stay with them. They were a charming couple, Vera and John, and they had three children; two girls aged twelve and thirteen and a little boy of three. He made me wish that I could have had more children.

Many things remained strange for me, but at least everyone was friendly and kind. Ration books had now started, but Vera proved both a good manager and an excellent cook. She taught me how to make a sponge cake, how to cream the butter and sugar, always in the same direction. I had only ever baked our traditional recipes, like *apfelpitta* and strudel, both of which Grandmother in Moldova had taught me. They either required kneading or throwing the dough again and again onto the baking board and finally stretching it across a table. Grandmother had also given me some good advice. 'One day you will be married,' she said, 'but in every marriage there will be times when you become cross with your husband and some mannerisms of his may have made you irritable. You might have said some angry words just before he left for work. That is the time when strudel-making will help. Make the dough and then throw all your anger away. Each time you throw the dough, you can even say to yourself what you wish or don't wish your husband to do. For instance, "I wish he wouldn't leave all his things lying about"; bang goes the dough — and by the time it is ready for stretching, all your anger is gone. The husband comes home in the evening, perhaps wondering whether there would still be an atmosphere hanging around from the morning, when he finds instead a beautiful apple strudel. You are both happy. Remember — that is one of the secrets of a good marriage, remember!'

Evi had to start school now. Somehow or other she had learned English without any special effort on my part. I had taught her to read German while we were in Brighton. The only German book I had was the fairy tales of Hans Anderson. My method of teaching her was extremely primitive. The German language is phonetic, so I just told her how certain signs were pronounced and then asked her to make a pencil dot under all the same letters in one story. I repeated that with all the letters and dipthongs. Once she knew them all we added them together — and she could read.

When I first took her to school the headmistress of the Infant School was horrified. I did not know that in Britain children went to school soon after their fifth birthday. At home children started school after their sixth birthday, but even then only in September at the beginning of a school year. Evi had been six years old that June. She had attended a Czech kindergarten since she was three but the children there were only playing; once they start school there is no more play except at playtime, out in the yard or playground. Here, it appeared, they played quite a lot in the reception class, only it was called 'activities'. Evi was first placed in the reception class but soon moved up, and by spring she was top of the class in her own age group.

Letters from Oslo arrived regularly. Papa and Mama had moved to Teplitz, not very far from Karlsbad, to a more convenient flat where there was room for some of our furniture and belongings. The couch, kitchen table and chairs had needed to be sold as there was no room for them; Papa had been unable to get a bigger flat in Karlsbad. I was glad that all the other things, especially my books, would be kept for our return, which I hoped would be soon. The war still somehow seemed far away.

We spent Christmas with Vera and her family, and Harry came on Boxing Day. Of course, it was different from all our previous Christmases and Evi was worried that the Christchild could not find her when there were no presents on Christmas Eve. She found a stocking filled with small presents in the morning and when more presents appeared after the Christmas dinner she understood. 'The Christchild had to come a long way to England,' she told me, 'but I am sure Oma gave him our address — and he did find me!' Father Christmas, whom she recognised as St Nicholas, in her opinion, had been helping the Christchild with the English children.

The Air Transport Auxiliary moved to another aerodrome and we moved to Worcester. Harry found lodgings for us. I was sorry to have to leave Vera and her family. She and her husband had been very good to us and I had been able to talk to her about home. She must have realised that I was homesick and worried.

The lady in Worcester who let us share her house had a husband who was on nightshift and slept all day. She was very houseproud and expected me to help her with everything. We paid her £2.10/-, the same amount that we had paid in Brighton for the flat. Apart from the rent, she was also very pleased to have somebody to talk to during the day and tried to flirt with Harry in the most peculiar way. She was small, but quite robust and strong; however, whenever Harry was there she pretended that she was really very helpless. She started all her tales about her difficulties with 'little me' and never said 'I'!

She did all her housework to a strict routine. I still remember Wednesday with horror. That day was 'polishing day'. She pressed a duster and tin of polish into my hands and told me to start at one side of the door and she would start at the other side.

'Fine,' I thought, 'we'll meet in the middle, so there is just half a room to do.' Polishing meant starting at the top and going right down to the skirting board. When we met at the fireplace, I was just about to get up from the floor when she motioned me to go round again, thereby covering and redoing each other's work. I hate housework anyway — and that was too much for me. After several weeks I always developed a blinding headache on Wednesdays, and I was very good at pretending!

Then the bombing started. When Hitler marched into Norway in 1940 I could no longer make contact with my parents. I did not hear anything from Lilly either as she was in Slovakia, which was part of Czechoslovakia but had declared its independence in 1938 when the Sudetenland was given to Hitler. Lilly now had a Slovakian passport and I hoped, as she was living in a small provincial town at the foot of the Tatra mountains, she would be safe from bombs, especially as there were no important factories or airfields in Slovakia. I wished that Papa had stayed in Karlsbad, as I was sure neither the British nor the Americans would bomb that famous spa, which proved to be the case, but they had now moved to Teplitz which, as far as I knew, had important industrial plants. I felt worried and helpless.

Now that Norway was closed to me I tried to write to get news to my parents through Aunt Marie in Moldova. There was no reply. However, in the first letter from Lore, I was given a Red Cross address in Lisbon. The Red Cross was able to exchange letters between allied and enemy countries. We were allowed to write twenty words, including the address, and the letters would be sent on. In this way my parents and I could at least keep in touch, although we could just assure each other that all was well. The Lisbon Red Cross only forwarded the messages, not the addresses. I once put in the message that we had a dog, and I hoped that Papa would understand what I meant: that we were really not starving if we could feed a dog. We were not allowed to write anything about our conditions, the results of bombing or anything else connected with the war.

After several months we moved again. It was a pattern I was to become accustomed to. We moved, settled down and made friends —

and then moved again. This time it was to Bristol, which had been heavily bombed before we went there. Harry took me into the city centre and it was a terrible sight, rubble and broken walls everywhere. Harry, who had been to Bristol before, pointed to and named some of the former streets which now contained only a few ruined buildings.

The BBC building was in Whiteladies Road and we could see it from our flat. One day at lunchtime Evi, who was sitting opposite the window, suddenly exclaimed: 'The whole house is coming down!' It was the BBC building. It had been damaged during the bombing and now had had enough. The walls were slowly crumbling, as though in a slow-motion picture.

One day Harry brought home another of the voluntary pilots; this one came from Australia. A few days later I met his wife, Mary, and small son, Peter. We got on well together and Mary spent whole days with me, especially once Peter started school. All the children loved playing in the bombed areas and we were worried they might be hurt by fallen masonry. It was difficult to keep them away from such places, as they could scarcely avoid them on their way to school.

At Christmas Mary and I decided to celebrate Christmas together and share our rations. We did not have a roast, but a cottage pie made with our combined meat rations. Onions were difficult to obtain, but Mary had been given some by a friend. We had a small Christmas tree and drank to our absent families.

I had news at last from Papa. A message came through the Red Cross, addressed to the Isle of Man. The letter was date-stamped December 1940, yet his letter was written on 2 June 1940. The ways of letters in those days were weird and wonderful! At least I knew he was safe.

I liked living in Bristol. I enjoyed my friendship with Mary. She was about my age, very cheerful, but also very strict with her boy. She might have been Queen Victoria! Peter liked to play jokes but she was usually 'not amused'. Harry came home quite regularly and I was now less worried about him as I could share my fears with Mary, whose husband was in the same danger.

We lived just a short walk away from the zoo and Evi and I visited it often. Sometimes she even went there on her own. I was intending to get her a yearly ticket for the zoo, when Harry announced that we would have to move yet again. The Air Ministry wanted more transport pilots somewhere else.

This time I suggested that we might just as well buy a caravan. I was tired of living with other people's furniture. A caravan would at least be my own home, or rather our home. I wasn't too sorry to leave, as Mary's husband was going back to Australia to do flying duty from there and Mary and Peter were, of course, returning with him.

Harry's aerodrome at White Waltham was not too far from Maidenhead. We went to Slough to look at caravans and bought one which could be made into two separate rooms by opening the wardrobe door. We walked from Maidenhead to look for a suitable field, with Evi riding along on a small bicycle which Vera had lent her, and found one a few miles away which looked promising. We enquired in the nearby village about the owner and then went to his house to ask if we could rent it. Harry's uniform and his rank as captain assured the owner that we were helping the war effort and he let us have the field for nothing. It was separated from the road into the village by a dry ditch and surrounded by hawthorns and elders. There was a tap in one corner, where we could obtain water. We had to share the field with a few cows, but I didn't mind as I liked cows.

As soon as we moved in I told Harry that I must have a dog or I would be frightened when he was away. Harry went to the pub that evening and enquired about a dog. The following morning a cowman brought me a bitch called Flossie. She should have been called 'Heinz', being made of so many varieties! She was slightly bigger than a dachshund, with a head like a small alsatian's and had smooth hair and a bushy tail. However, she was a dog and I loved her from the very first moment. She also took to Evi and me, her tail almost turning a complete circle in her excitement.

I acquired an old bicycle for five shillings, bought a small tin bath, which I pushed under the caravan, a tent and an Elsan — and we were established. I even tried to make a small garden round the caravan by cutting the grass and nettles with a pair of scissors. We had a home now and everything in it belonged to us. Sometimes early in the morning I would walk part of the way with Harry towards White Waltham and collected mushrooms on the way back.

Very soon a young woman with an Irish accent came to see me. She and her husband had moved to Holyport, the next village, from London to escape the bombs, and she was curious to meet 'the people who lived in a caravan but were not gypsies'. We soon became friends and very often when Harry was away in the evenings she and her husband would come to the caravan and we would all have tea together. Her husband still worked in London, but came home each night.

219

She had lovely chestnut hair reaching down to her waist. She usually wore it in a roll round her head, which I tried to imitate but could not do nearly as well. Her name was Eileen. She introduced me to another friend of hers who had also escaped from the London bombing with her husband still working there. They had bought a cottage in the village, but had also aquired two goats. I forget this woman's name, but I remember the goats. One she called Queen Mary, because she looked so dignified. I had never realised that goats have such character and individuality. Their owner milked them and made butter and cheese; I tried to milk one of them once, but she gave me such a disdainful look — and refused to release even one drop of milk. I felt almost embarrassed. Nevertheless, the butter and cheese from the goats tasted good and was an extra to the rations.

In July the fat rations were still quite good: 12oz butter, margarine or fat per person, but extra butter was always a bonus. The landlord of the pub, The Cricketers, let us take our meat ration — one shilling's worth per person per week — ready for cooking in the baking tin, surrounded by potatoes, to be done in his kitchen. So on Sunday mornings, if Harry was at home he would take it to the pub and bring it back ready cooked. Meantime he could have a drink at the pub for his trouble.

One day I had a letter from Moldova from Papa, which he had sent to Oscar, Aunt Marie's son. I was puzzled, as I had previously tried writing to Moldova but never had an answer. After the war I learned that the Gestapo had opened a letter from Lisbon and Papa had to pay a fine for using that address to get in touch with 'the enemy'. However, communications with Moldova eventually stopped and Papa and I used the Lisbon address again.

By now Slovakia had also entered the war and I hoped that all was well with Lilly and Max. Max was exempt from military service, apparently building tiled stoves was necessary, although all his employees had to go and he had to do what work there was by himself. Then we heard that the Russians had moved into Romania and although they were on our side, the German-speaking people from the Banat were forced to leave or they would be interned. Papa wrote that my cousin's wife and some friends of our family in Moldova had arrived at his flat as refugees. They had been travelling for over a week, and were starving and so terribly dirty that my mother did not recognise them at first.

The bombing of London had started in earnest now. The search-lights would compete at night with the full moon; air-raid warnings sounded more often, and, when I was on my own, because Harry was held up somewhere through fog, I did not know what to do. Should I cover Evi with my body, hide her in the ditch or put her under the caravan? Each thought was as ridiculous as the next. I felt terribly exposed in the caravan in the open field.

One night as I walked out for a breath of fresh air, I saw the shadow of a man holding a gun in front of him. The full moon was behind him and I could only see the shadow. He seemed to be walking towards the caravan. I decided to go to him rather than let him come to us.

There had been much talk about parachutists and I was constantly frightened that a German soldier might recognise my accent as being German. Why this should have made it worse for me I don't know, but I just had that feeling. As I walked nearer and nearer the shadow, I was so frightened that I could almost hear my heart beating. Then, suddenly I realised that the 'shadow' was in fact a horse and its head, bent down to nibble the grass, had made the shape of a gun pointing towards me with a little help from my imagination. I was so relieved that I put my arms round its neck which in turn frightened the poor horse.

White Waltham aerodome was bombed. We heard the crash. Harry had just delivered an aeroplane and was walking away, so he was not hurt but the glass of his watch was broken by the blast; one mechanic was killed outright and another was badly wounded. The war had now come very near. Harry brought me a piece of metal from the destroyed plane. Now I was really worried for him, because he was flying to all the aerodomes and many were bombed.

The sky was often red over London and sometimes bombs were dropped in the neighbourhood, but nothing happened to us. I remember once there was a battle going on overhead. The anti-aircraft guns were deafening and the searchlights, with their poking fingers of light, were terrifying. Although Flossie, who now had seven pups with her, was in a kennel the butcher had given me, I was worried that the noise would frighten her.

I let her into the caravan and collected her pups — two at a time and deposited them with her. At first I thought that one must have kept slipping back again when I carried the next two in, but then I realised that there were more than seven. In the searchlights they all looked the same and Flossie welcomed them all, so I thought I must be mistaken.

After a time, when the 'all clear' sounded, I stepped out into the fresh air. Flossie stretched and came out too, followed by thirteen pups! I could not believe my eyes. Six of them disappeared into a bush outside the caravan. Flossie was always sniffing and barking round that bush. I had watched a couple of weasels running along the ditch early in the mornings and it now seemed that they had young ones in the bush. The frightened dogs and weasels had lain together as one family. Throughout all this Evi had slept peacefully.

We had to move again. The Air Ministry changed the aerodromes from where the planes should be delivered. We hired a car, attached the caravan and drove off to a private aerodrome situated between Leicester and Nottingham. It was on a slight hill, the club house was on top and we were allowed to park the caravan at the lower edge of the airfield.

There were several American pilots here who had come over voluntarily to help Britain before America came into the war. One of them had gone out in a bomber over Germany and had been caught in the flak. Somehow, part of the plane had caught fire but he had managed, but only just, to get back to base, although his hands and half an arm were badly burnt. His hands looked as if the bar bones had been covered with only wrinkling skin. It was difficult not to look at them when sitting opposite him when he was eating or drinking.

Most of the Americans came to visit us in the caravan and always brought their own drinks and usually food as well, which they received from home. They brought the beer in wooden boxes which then served us as chairs for sitting outside when visitors came during the day. In the evenings I transferred Evi from her own bed to ours at the end of the caravan, opened the wardrobe door and then there was room on the couches for six people. We tried to speak quietly and we laughed a lot but Evi never woke up, or if she did she must have been very good at pretending to sleep.

Because of the talk about parachutists and spies, all road and village signs had been removed and when Eileen and I cycled around the countryside, sometimes as far as Reading, we never quite knew where we were. Although nobody I spoke to had ever asked where I came from, on those trips I kept my mouth shut and let Eileen ask the way when we became completely lost.

Eileen's husband told us a rather disturbing story about some friends of theirs who had been their neighbours. The wife was a German and had been married to an Englishman since 1953. One day a woman came to her house, introduced herself as a fellow German and said that she was very homesick and wanted to speak her native language with a compatriot. She then came regularly to the house about three times a week and they had tea together, talked about old times at home and became very friendly.

One day, the new German friend brought a gentleman with her. She introduced him as another German who had been living in England for many years. After a while the girl went out to do some shopping before the shops closed. No sooner had she gone than the man became quite formal. He told the woman that he knew where her parents lived. 'All sorts of things can happen to old people in Germany,' he stressed. Then he gave the Nazi salute and said that the Fuehrer wanted every German — wherever they were — to help in the war effort.

'I will come back next week,' he said, 'and you will give me all the information I want. I have put the questions down on this sheet of paper. Your husband is in a position to give the information. Don't forget what I said; some cruel things can happen to old people in Germany,' he repeated as he left.

This friend of Eileen's told her husband about the incident as soon as he came home. He in turn told a colleague, who informed the police. They then arranged to 'arrest' the German woman and her family in such a way that it was obvious to all the neighbours. Of course, she did not go to prison. She was taken to Canada for her own safety.

After Dunkirk quite a number of Germans living in Britain were interned, but it was not really a hardship for them. They were housed in hotels on the Isle of Wight, away from the bombs, and had quite a good time. Eileen's dentist was among the internees and an English dentist took over the practice but had to share the income with him. To our intense annoyance the German dentist not only profited from the practice, but he and his wife were allowed to return home to gather the apple crop in their garden. The British were far too generous; this was more than fair play!

I had not brought many clothes with me when I left Czechoslovakia, but I profited from Harry's bad habits. He would always stand with his back to an open fire and there was one at the Officer's Mess. Under the navy blue trousers he wore his flying boots and did not notice therefore when the fire burnt a hole in his trouser legs. He received, as he said, another present from King George in the form of new trousers. I then cut the burnt part off the old ones, unpicked the trouser legs and restitched them to make a beautiful skirt which, I also pretended, was a present from King George. When I had two of these I presented Eileen with one, but Harry did not like it. He didn't mind me wearing his trousers, but another woman, no, definitely not!

223

One day I was called to the police station to fill in some form. It had come, via the Czechoslovakian Government, from Berlin. I expressed astonishment that private enquiries could get through while there was a war on. This form requested me to state my address and confirm that I was well. Apparently a Mr Stiller — my father — was very anxious to know his daughter's address, and if she and her family were safe and well.

I remembered the story that Eileen had told me and explained to the policeman why I refused to give my address. He was most surprised. It had never occurred to him that this might be a trap. I told him that I had heard from my father through the Red Cross in Lisbon just a few days previously and he knew that I was well.

The war seemed to go on for ever. I wondered when I would see my family again. Then Harry left the Air Transport Auxiliary, as he was offered a job as a test pilot with a firm in Manchester who repaired damaged aircraft. That meant he would be at home more and so we moved to Manchester. Luckily again the worst bombing of Manchester was over. There were only two or three alarms, and the 'all clear' came quite quickly. We sold the caravan and, once again, it was furnished lodgings for us.

I worried constantly about Harry, but he assured me I had no cause, even if he was late. He might have had to deliver a plane and be delayed by fog. Whatever happened, I would be immediately informed if he had an accident. One night, Harry had not come back and so I assumed that he probably had been held up somewhere because of fog. I was woken up by a strange man standing by my bed.

'Don't be alarmed,' he said, 'everything is all right, nothing to worry about.' I got up and followed him downstairs, while he still repeated 'don't worry'. As I entered the kitchen I saw Harry bent over the kitchen sink, which seemed to be full of blood.

'What has happened?' I cried. Harry motioned with his hand that it was nothing. There was another man with him who was trying to put a bandage over his head. The sleeve of Harry's jacket and shirt was ripped and his arm was also bleeding profusely. 'They are only flesh wounds,' Harry managed to say, with a very badly cut lip. The other man explained: 'He crashed somewhere out in the fields and tried to make his way to our farm. Luckily, our dog made such a noise that we went out and met him halfway and then brought him here.'

By now Harry's head was bandaged. He did not want a doctor because he was afraid that he would be grounded. 'I only need a day or two,' he insisted, 'and I will be perfectly all right.' This time King George did not provide a new shirt and jacket, but luckily the flesh wounds soon healed and that was all that mattered to me.

I wished I could have flown with him; flying seemed so safe but testing repaired aircraft was not so easy. Anything could go wrong! I especially disliked the Aero Cobra and Harry didn't like it either. They seemed to be the most vulnerable aircraft. When he was still delivering aircraft, the Air Ministry had an artist on some aerodromes drawing the various planes. I have one of those pictures and it is an Aero Cobra. I have it on the wall going upstairs and everytime I look at it now I am grateful that none of them killed my husband all those years ago.

The headmaster at the school next to us became friendly with us. Harry was allowed to have a phone as it was necessary for his work. The school did not have one and the headmaster used to come to us to borrow ours. One day he turned to me and said: 'I have tried and tried to get a teacher to replace the one who has been called up but I have had no success. They have just told me I could employ anyone who could do the job. Why don't you come and teach; you could do it.' It was a junior school and I realised it would mean taking my daughter's class, as she had told me their teacher had left.

I couldn't believe that he meant it. I could teach them, but what about my English? Was it good enough? However, I was finally convinced that I could do it. 'You have nothing else to do, so why not make it your war effort,' he said. I agreed. Once I had overcome the embarrassment of teaching a class with Evi in it, I began to enjoy my new job.

20

PEACE EVENTUALLY CAUGHT up with us in Manchester. I was still teaching and a colleague had offered to share her home with us. She and her husband owned a large house but had no children. No sooner had we moved in with her than I received a short note from Lisbon from the Red Cross. It simply read: 'Your parents have been evicted and are in danger of transportation. Can you help?' My colleague immediately said that they could move in with us if we only could get them to Britain.

Harry's job had finished with the end of the war and he had been asked by a firm who supplied spares and accessories for aeroplanes to be a representative for them in Europe, where he could use his previous connections. That proved lucky for us now. He immediately applied for a visa for Czechoslovakia and at the same time sent a telegram to the British Embassy in Prague requesting that Mr Stiller and his wife should not be transported, as his son-in-law would come for them, to take them to Britain.

At first, the British Government had agreed that a family could take in one refugee relation. However, there was then a question raised in Parliament, asking whether they would think it likely that an old couple, who had endured the hardships of the war together, would now part and leave one of them to face transportation alone. So an amendment was made allowing both parents to come to Britain. Harry then received his Czechoslovakian visa; it was one of the first issued, but it cost twenty pounds — and was a very expensive visa.

We had no idea what had been happening in Czechoslovakia. There was nothing on the wireless or in the newspapers — except that the Sudetenland had been given back to Czechoslovakia. Many Czechs had come to Britain and fought with the British instead of being conscripted by the Germans, and many others had done their best to become prisoners-of-war rather than fight for the Germans. Benesch, the Czechoslovakian President, who had been in Britain during the war, had returned to Prague. That was all we knew.

When Harry arrived in Prague and went to the British Embassy he was told that the British Government had given Benesch a 'free hand' for one year. The Czechs had never forgiven the loss of the Sudetenland, handed over to Hitler in 1938 by Chamberlain. They blamed the German-speaking population for much of what happened, and when the Sudetenland was handed back to them they were ready to take their revenge.

Harry was told that the Embassy had written to Mr and Mrs Stiller, inviting them to come to Prague, where they would be safe at the Embassy, but they did not come. They did not know at the Embassy that German-speaking people were no longer allowed to use public transport and had to wear armbands printed with the word *Nemec* (German).

Millions of these people were forced to leave the country in the most inhuman fashion. The German-speaking population had been warned that this would happen one day and were told to prepare for it by making rucksacks, slightly smaller than the ready-made ones.

Before even that happened, the Russians marched into the northern part of Bohemia and the Sudetenland. They entered houses and flats, looked quickly round and took what they wanted, mostly watches and clocks. After several Russians had been to my father's flat and taken every clock and watch there, two more soldiers arrived one morning and still demanded watches, My father could speak Serbian and Czech, both similar to Russian, so he explained that all the watches belonging to his wife and himself had been taken and now they had not a single one between them. He showed them their bare wrists and pointed to clockless walls.

One of the Russians looked most upset: 'No watches?' he exclaimed. 'Not a single one?' When my father reaffirmed the sad fact, the Russian pulled up his sleeve and there, all along his arm, were dozens of watches. 'Choose one,' he said to my father. 'You musn't be without a watch.' Then he let my mother choose one also.

When the Russians had gone, the Czechs came. If two Czechs arrived at a house or flat and liked what they saw, they could tell the occupier to leave. My mother was preparing the midday meal when two Czechs arrived at their home. They ordered my parents to leave within half an hour. My mother was not even allowed to finish cooking the meal. They were told to put only two changes of clothes in the rucksacks and go. Papa had to rearrange his rucksack twice as he had no old clothes and the men had insisted that only the old clothes could be taken. Their fur coats had to be left behind; they would not have gone in the rucksacks anyhow. While one of the men supervised the packing, the other man took hold of Papa's two big leather suitcases and filled them with suits, shoes and fur coats. Then my parents had to leave.

Lilly, by this time, also had a flat in Teplitz. I learned later that she had divorced her husband Max and gone to my parents. As she had no children she had to work, at a large industrial firm where she got quite a good job, although she had never worked before. Soon she was able to take a flat of her own, and this was now where my parents went. She had a Slovakian passport and the Czechs had just made an agreement with the Slovakians that they could not be thrown out even if they were Germain-speaking. However, this proved only to be a short respite for my parents: if the letter from the Embassy had not arrived they would have been driven from there also, and would have had to join the thousands of others who had to walk to the German frontier.

Of those who were not so fortunate, many of them died on the wayside from exhaustion, the others were then put into cattle trucks and taken into Germany. The trains would stop somewhere in the country, near some village or small town, and several families were allowed or forced to get out and find their own food and a roof over their head. The majority were taken in by farmers to work on the land, for which they were given a place in an outhouse or stable. (They had no money as their bank accounts had been confiscated.) Only when they had proved that they were good workers, was their situation likely to improve slightly.

Yet more were taken from their home or place of work and put into prison or a concentration camp. Although the camps were not like the German concentration camps, they were certainly not luxurious. They would then have to wait there until it was their turn to be taken by train to Germany. Some situations arose which would have been ludicrous if they had not been so sad. The uncle of mine who owned an iron foundry near Troppau was taken to prison during the night, but taken back to his office each morning to help the new Czech owners settle down in the foundry, which now no longer belonged to him.

Unfortunately all our belongings which were stored in Papa's big flat were taken over by the new owners. Harry went to the Embassy to find out how to get them back. He was told that it would be better if he did not insist on it, as there might be difficulties in getting the old people out. However, he went to the flat and, in his charming way, managed at least to get a big basket and a trunk which had been stored in a spare room. He recognised our furniture but could do nothing about it. Before he left he just grabbed a duvet from one of the beds, smiled at the astonished wife of the new owner and got away with it.

There was a train at that time which travelled right through Europe to the Channel Coast; refugees and anyone else could board it without payment. Harry and my parents took that train. Some other refugees helped them to get the basket and trunk on board and they finally arrived in Dover and then in Manchester.

It was by now December. The night before there had been a warning on the radio that mines were supposed to be somewhere in the Channel. It was bitterly cold and stormy. Mama said she had been seasick, but Papa had been standing on deck, looking like a Viking, anxious to reach land. When I welcomed them at the door, I barely recognised them. They looked like an extremely old couple, completely worn out. Of course, sometimes there had been very little for them to eat — not like here, where we had adequate rations. I was slightly surprised when Mama took out a jar of honey from her rucksack and placed it carefully on the table. Inside was her jewellery and their watches; Mama had insisted that she needed the honey for her health.

Later they told us all that happened and how some of my other relatives in Silesia had been driven out of their homes. Sometimes as early as five o'clock in the morning there would be shouting in the street, 'Get out!' and the occupants had to get out quickly, having put their changes of clothing in the prepared rucksack. My mother's sister-in-law and her family were taken off the train in Bavaria. Some of my friends and some cousins were let off the train with nearly all the neighbours from their street, somewhere near Heidelberg. They all worked hard and a new settlement was later built in Heidelberg, where

229

many streets were named after the Sudeten mountain, *Altvater*, and many other familiar names from their homeland. Many, many years later, when I would travel by car through Western Germany to Austria, I always found that my friends and relations were conveniently situated in Western Germany. I could always rely on an evening meal and bed-and-breakfast stops on my way from Rotterdam!

My parents soon recovered from their ordeal, physically, and Papa was even beginning to get his sense of humour back. He told us about an incident which happened while he was staying with Lilly in Teplitz waiting for Harry to arrive. He met one of the men who had thrown him out of his flat. The man greeted Papa and asked: 'How are you Herr Stiller?' What a question to ask a man who had just lost everything! However, Papa smiled and said that he was well. 'Did you know,' confided the Czech, 'that this town is full of thieves?' Papa looked surprised, although he thought the biggest of them all was standing right in front of him. 'Yes,' the man continued. 'Do you remember the two suitcases I packed in the flat?' As if Papa could ever forget. 'I took them to the station to get a train for Prague. I put them outside a telephone box and while I was on the phone, a thief took them.' Mama said that Papa had laughed heartily for the first time after their ordeal as he told her of that meeting.

While I had been waiting for my parents to arrive, all my friends had been very good and contributed something from their rations so that we could celebrate Christmas as in the old days. In Czechoslovakia they had been told during the war that everyone in Britain was starving. I decided that I would give a party for all my friends who had been so good to us. We made the best of the rations, I made strudel (only flour, a pat of butter or spoonful of oil and water is needed) and I made a *Bowle*, or cold punch. When I bought the wine I thought of the vineyard in Moldova and Grandmother's house; to this day, whenever I buy grapes I think of our vineyards — now gone for ever. Papa had told me that the Banater Germans had also been driven out. Uncle Gustav had died during the war and Aunt Marie soon afterwards. Now a special invitation from a relative is needed to get permission to visit, and there is nobody left who could invite any of us.

Once Papa and Mama were with us, it did not take long for Lilly to follow. Although she had a Slovakian passport, she spoke German and it became more and more difficult for her to remain on her own. She had a very good job but most of her friends had left for Germany and as her Czech was not very good she met with a lot of enmity.

I tried to obtain a work permit for her but the only work allowed was that of a 'help' in a hospital; 'help' meant working as a cleaner in the wards and serving at table. Papa was very upset, but Lilly remained quite cheerful and eventually found herself another job, as assistant in the school for the blind.

We were now all together, but under sad circumstances. Papa's pension, meanwhile, was accumulating in Hamburg at the Esso (which had taken over the Vaccum Oil Company) Headquarters — and we were not too well off. Harry's job was finished because the Marshall Plan for Europe made it impossible to have a European representative for aeroplane parts and accessories, and those countries where Harry had made good business connections were now behind the Iron Curtain, including Romania — and Moldova — of course.

My parents found it difficult to learn another language at their advanced age and, although they were with us, they felt very isolated as Harry and Evi always spoke in English. Mama's brother and family, who had been deposited in Bavaria, had through hard work managed to get a home of their own and he wrote that he could find some furnished lodgings for my parents if they wanted to come. Papa would have no problem obtaining permission to move into that village as he could prove that he had a pension and would not therefore be a burden to the village.

The pension was still accumulating in Hamburg and Papa could not get it transferred to Britain. Harry had a friend in London who knew one of the Esso Directors and, through his intervention, Papa managed to have twenty pounds per month paid into an English bank. It was a small amount but at least it was something and after a few months he was in a position to try and get to Bavaria. The Americans who occupied Bavaria finally gave him permission to join Mama's brother and my parents left for Germany.

The pension in Hamburg was quite considerable and had been lying practically untouched for two years. Unfortunately, however, as soon as Papa arrived in Germany the German currency was devalued, and Papa only received one-tenth of his money. Nevertheless, it was enough to start with. Meantime, Lilly had also been in touch with old friends who were in Western Germany and one was an old colleague of hers who had worked with her in the Sudetenland. She promised Lilly that she could get an equally good job in Duisburg, so Lilly also left us. However, as all were happy I did not mind so much. I could always go and see them in the holidays.

In some ways it was strange that Papa and Mama had finally gone to Bavaria. It was not quite the same region from which Papa's ancestors had emigrated two hundred years previously, but it was near enough. The circle had closed, But they could never go, even on a visit, to Moldova — which we all regarded as the place we really came from.

There is no past we could call back by our longing, there is only an ever renewed now, creating itself from the growing elements of what has been.